# Veteran Narratives
# and the Collective Memory of the Vietnam War

*Hero of the Angry Sky: The World War I Diary and Letters of David S. Ingalls, America's First Naval Ace,* edited by Geoffrey L. Rossano

*Protecting the Empire's Frontier: Officers of the 18th (Royal Irish) Regiment of Foot during Its North American Service, 1767–1776,* by Steven M. Baule

*Citizen-General: Jacob Dolson Cox and the Civil War Era,* by Eugene D. Schmiel

*Veteran Narratives and the Collective Memory of the Vietnam War,* by John A. Wood

# VETERAN NARRATIVES

*and the Collective Memory of the Vietnam War*

**John A. Wood**

OHIO UNIVERSITY PRESS
ATHENS

Ohio University Press, Athens, Ohio 45701

ohioswallow.com

To obtain permission to quote, reprint, or otherwise reproduce or distribute material from Ohio University Press publications, please contact our rights and permissions department at (740) 593-1154 or (740) 593-4536 (fax).

Printed in the United States of America
Ohio University Press books are printed on acid-free paper ⊚ ™

26 25 24 23 22 21 20 19 18 17 16      5 4 3 2 1

*Library of Congress Cataloging-in-Publication Data*

Names: Wood, John A., 1980– author.
Title: Veteran narratives and the collective memory of the Vietnam War / John A. Wood.
Description: Athens, OH : Ohio University Press, [2016] | Series: War and society in North America | Includes bibliographical references and index.
Identifiers: LCCN 2015044413 | ISBN 9780821422229 (hc : alk. paper) | ISBN 9780821422236 (pb : alk. paper) | ISBN 9780821445624 (pdf)
Subjects: LCSH: Vietnam War, 1961–1975—Veterans—United States—Biography, | Vietnam War, 1961–1975—Personal narratives. | Vietnam War, 1961–1975—Literature and the war. | Vietnam War, 1961–1975—Social aspects—United States. | Vietnam War, 1961–1975—United States—Psychological aspects. | Vietnam War, 1961–1975—Influence. | Memory—Social aspects—United States. | Collective memory—United States.
Classification: LCC DS559.73.U6 W67 2016 | DDC 959.704/30922—dc23
LC record available at http://lccn.loc.gov/2015044413

# Contents

# Acknowledgments

Many people have made this book possible. Kenneth L. Kusmer of Temple University provided invaluable guidance from the very beginning. He worked tirelessly as a reviewer and editor of chapter drafts, pushing me to improve my writing and hone my arguments. I also benefited from the considerable knowledge and experience of Gregory J. W. Urwin, James Hilty, and Stanley Katz. More recently, David Ulbrich, Ingo Trauschweizer, members of the Ohio University Press staff, and two anonymous readers helped turn the manuscript into a publishable book. Finally, I am lucky to have friends and family who kept me sane while working on this project. No one, however, has helped me more through this process than my parents, James and Joan Wood. This book is dedicated to you.

# Introduction
## *They Were There*

Robert Mason graduated from US Army Primary He-
licopter School in the spring of 1965, fulfilling a lifelong dream of becoming a pilot. That summer he shipped out for Vietnam.[1] The helicopter
Mason flew during the war was a troop carrier, "the Bell HU-1 Iroquois,
known as the Huey."[2] He often attracted enemy gunfire when he dropped
off or picked up "grunts" (foot soldiers) at landing zones (LZs) throughout
South Vietnam. After numerous forays into such "hot LZs," Mason got
somewhat used to bullets pinging off his Huey, along with "the confusion,
the crackling door guns, the smell of gunpowder, the yells of the grunts,
[and] the radios going crazy."[3] He "learned how to function, even though
[he] was scared shitless, by doing it over and over again."[4] A fellow pilot
eventually dubbed Mason a "chickenhawk." He was a chicken because he
was terrified before every mission, but a hawk because he bravely kept
flying in spite of his fear.

The strain of too many hot LZs, however, started to take their toll
on Mason in the final weeks of his twelve-month Vietnam tour. He had
trouble getting to sleep, and when he managed to doze off, nightmares
about horrible things he had seen over the previous months jolted him
awake. He started blacking out, waking up in a state of utter panic and
dread. He lost weight and even hallucinated.[5] Mason made it back to
the United States in one piece, but his psychological problems persisted.
He left the army and frantically searched for peace of mind, fulfillment,
and a means to support his family. He studied photography, worked as a
car salesman, traveled around Europe, and devised several get-rich-quick
schemes, but nothing panned out. To make matters worse, Mason was
drinking heavily, popping pills, and smoking marijuana in a futile effort to

control his anxiety. One day he confided in an acquaintance who worked as a literary agent that he was thinking about writing a novel based on his Vietnam experiences. The agent was encouraging, but suggested Mason write a memoir instead. He took the advice, and after completing the first seventy pages felt real satisfaction for the first time since returning from Southeast Asia.

Mason finished his memoir in 1980.[6] His agent friend agreed to shop the manuscript around to publishers, but was not optimistic about its chances because "nobody wanted to publish books about the Vietnam War."[7] A few Vietnam memoirs were released in the 1970s, and one of these books, Philip Caputo's *A Rumor of War* (1977), was a great critical and commercial success.[8] Mason discovered that his agent's pessimism was well founded, however, as his manuscript was rejected again and again over the next few years. Publishers "liked the writing . . . but none of them thought people wanted to read about Vietnam."[9] They were wrong. Mason's memoir, *Chickenhawk*, was finally published by Viking Press in 1983. Critics loved it and thousands of copies were eventually sold.[10] And Mason was not the only successful Vietnam book author that year. In December 1983, the *New York Times* announced that titles "about Vietnam [were] rolling off the presses in record numbers."[11] The *Times* reported in 1987 that the "Vietnam-Book Boom" was still in full swing, and it asked several veteran-authors to give their thoughts on this "latest artistic trend."[12] One of the authors, Caputo, dismissed it all as "Vietnam chic." Another, Tim O'Brien, speculated that interest in Vietnam would soon fade, and readers would move on to books about other wars.[13]

Caputo and O'Brien were wrong in thinking that Vietnam War books were only a passing fad. Hundreds of titles about the conflict appeared in the years following the 1987 *Times* article, many of them written by veterans. Some well-known war novels have been produced by ex-soldiers, such as *Paco's Story* by Larry Heinemann, *Fields of Fire* by James Webb, and O'Brien's *The Things They Carried*. Other veteran-writers, such as Bruce Weigl and W. D. Ehrhart, are known for their war-related poetry. Nonetheless, far more nonfiction veteran narratives, namely memoirs and oral histories, have been published since the war ended. And a number of these books, like *A Rumor of War* and *Chickenhawk*, were best sellers, lauded by reviewers, or both. Writing a memoir, moreover, has become a seemingly mandatory milestone for famous Vietnam veterans. Heinemann, Weigl, and other writers who were first recognized for their Vietnam War fiction later penned nonfiction accounts of their tours. Veteran-authors who gained recognition by writing books unrelated to Vietnam, such as Tracy Kidder and Tobias Wolff, later became war memoirists. Colin Powell, John McCain, Bob Kerrey, and other politicians have written about their Vietnam experiences as well.

Owing to their longtime prevalence and popularity, veteran memoirs have undoubtedly influenced America's collective memory of the Vietnam conflict for decades. The same can be said for films, news media reports, political rhetoric, and other cultural products. But war narratives produced by "those who were there" have long held a special authority for people, Americans included.[14] Paul Fussell observes in *The Great War and Modern Memory* that British veterans of the First World War saw recalling their battlefield experiences as a duty or "moral obligation." A war memoirist himself, he adds that all ex-soldiers share this "obsession to some degree."[15] Samuel Hynes, another veteran-scholar, explains that this preoccupation with remembering has long been colored by the assertion that former warriors are the absolute authorities on the conflicts in which they have fought.[16] A veteran maintains that what he says about war "is true *because* he was on the field," and "if you don't know that, you don't know anything."[17] Many Vietnam veterans similarly assert that "the 'Nam" was so surreal and unlike other conflicts that only they can truly comprehend it. Phil Klay, a former marine who served in Iraq, pokes fun at this attitude in *Redeployment*, his award-winning short-story collection. A character in one story tells this old joke: "How many Vietnam vets does it take to screw in a light bulb? You wouldn't know, you weren't there."[18]

Some Vietnam veterans, then, have claimed a special, infallible knowledge of the war. Equally important is the fact that the rest of the country has been primed to believe this assertion. When *A Rumor of War* and other early veteran memoirs were published in the late 1970s, Americans were angry and disillusioned by the recent failure in Vietnam and the Watergate scandal.[19] In this atmosphere of distrust "the veteran was admirably placed to proclaim . . . his knowledge of events and perception of the truth."[20] Feeling that their leaders had lied to them about the war, people turned to the ordinary ex-soldier, someone "who spoke at a worm's-eye level"[21] and "had witnessed the hypocrisy of power first hand."[22] The veteran memoirist consequently came to be seen as an "investigative writer"[23] who was better equipped than anyone else "to solve the mystery surrounding Vietnam."[24]

The late 1970s also saw the emergence of the belief that GIs in Vietnam were denied victory by the actions of antiwar protesters and then

4 literally spat on when they came home. This narrative gained strength in the 1980s, and proponents of America's first war with Iraq used it to silence peace activists in 1991. The populace was warned that if they did not "support the troops" in the Middle East, they would be just as cruel as the radicals who allegedly victimized GIs in the sixties and seventies.[25] The idea that US forces in Vietnam were "stabbed in the back" by malevolent antiwar activists persists in the twenty-first century. This is unsurprising considering that "uncritically hagiographic Support Our Troops rhetoric,"[26] which unquestionably celebrates soldiers, has flourished since the 9/11 terrorist attacks.[27] Tales of abused Vietnam veterans, however, as chapter 5 explains, are of questionable validity. But such stories nevertheless affect public perception and are part of the Vietnam veteran "mystique."[28] Readers, surely wary of repeating the supposed mistakes made by the protesters of yesteryear, are disposed to believe veterans' claims that they alone know what *really* happened in Vietnam.

Despite their importance, Vietnam veteran memoirs have hitherto received inadequate treatment by scholars. Many literary scholars have analyzed veteran narratives, and some thoughtfully postulated on how these works may have influenced how Americans think about the war. Some contended that veteran narratives offered hard-hitting truths about Vietnam that might prevent future military quagmires.[29] Susan Jeffords, conversely, argued that some memoirs, along with movies and novels, actually contributed to Reagan-era jingoism.[30] Other scholars focused more narrowly on how veteran-writers illustrated certain aspects of the war, such as race relations among GIs[31] and the treatment of Vietnamese women.[32] These writers, however, each covered only a small number of memoirs. Plus, they usually made little distinction between nonfiction narratives, veteran-authored novels, films, and other Vietnam-themed pop-culture products.

Many renowned Vietnam War historians have used veteran memoirs in their scholarship, including Christian G. Appy, Marilyn B. Young, and George C. Herring.[33] Unlike scholars working in other fields, however, historians have not seriously explored how these books might have affected collective memory.[34] Most historians take just a few quotations from veteran-authored books to bolster various arguments, but a few others, Peter S. Kindsvatter being a notable example, rely heavily on these sources.[35] Few historians, in any case, scrutinize veteran memoirs any more than they would an unimpeachable primary source retrieved from an archive. This is a problem, since memory, according to historian David

Thelen, "private and individual as much as collective and cultural, is constructed, not reproduced."[36] "This construction," he adds, "is not made in isolation but in conversations with others that occur in the contexts of community, broader politics, and social dynamics."[37] Yes, veteran narratives were written by men and women "who were there," but they are still recollections, not objective historical records. They are, therefore, governed and limited by properties inherent to every form of memory.

This book is a work of history, but it does not treat veteran memoirs as sources that can be straightforwardly mined for information. Instead, it is concerned with what veterans say about the war, but also how and why they say it. Like some pieces of past scholarship, it explores how veteran narratives have affected the collective memory of the war. But this book, unlike past works, presents a comprehensive analysis of the Vietnam narrative genre. It examines fifty-eight of the most prominent memoirs and oral histories published between 1967 and 2005. These books were best sellers, award winners, reviewed in the *New York Times* or another major publication, written by famous people, or referenced in scholarship. Only well-known narratives were included in this primary group because only titles that achieved recognition could have had a significant impact on collective memory.

The analysis of these fifty-eight works addresses the actual fighting experienced by veteran-authors, but it also delves into issues not directly related to combat. These include, as Meredith H. Lair puts it, "[t]he usual factors for consideration in social and cultural history—the troika of gender, class, and race,"[38] but also politics, the war's aftermath, and its commemoration. This approach follows the lead of Lair, Appy, Heather Marie Stur, and other scholars who have clearly demonstrated that there is much more to Vietnam War history than B-52 strikes, firefights, and booby traps. Material gleaned from memoirs is compared to and enhanced by supplemental sources, including newspaper articles, films, US government studies, and historical scholarship. Also employed are narratives that were not included in the primary memoir group because they were not prominent or not written by veterans. These accounts from Vietnamese civilians, African Americans, women veterans, and others are valuable perspectives not often provided by most famous memoirs.

The analysis begins, in chapter 1, by looking at the backgrounds of fifty-one veteran-authors for whom sufficient information is available. Demographic data taken from memoirs and other sources were organized into a variety of categories, including age, amount of time served

6    in Vietnam, education level, and length of military service. These data are important because social, economic, and educational level helped determine both what an author experienced in Vietnam and how he or she interpreted these experiences. Those factors in turn influenced how aspects of the war would be portrayed in the veteran's memoir.

Research into memoirists' backgrounds ascertained that the majority were white, college graduates, and former officers. They served in Vietnam at an average age of twenty-seven. These statistics are potentially troubling because ground combat in the war was primarily fought by men of opposite backgrounds: poor and working-class white and minority enlisted personnel, many of whom went to war before their twentieth birthdays. This demographic disparity suggests that narratives were written by ex-soldiers who did not share the same experiences and viewpoints as the average American combat soldier. Closer examination of the data, however, leads to a more nuanced conclusion. Twenty-six veteran-authors fought as low-ranking, "junior" commissioned officers. Unlike their higher-ranking counterparts, junior officers lived, fought, and sometimes died alongside the men they commanded in Vietnam. The existence, then, of so many former low-ranking officers among the authors ensures that even though most authors were not grunts in background, most were grunts by measure of their wartime experiences.

Chapter 2 explores the interrelated issues of combat conditions and the Vietnamese people. Most veterans describe combat in a graphic, unromantic manner. Their collective depiction of warfare as chaotic, frustrating, and pointless amounts to a searing indictment of the American effort in Vietnam. It is strange, therefore, that these accounts simultaneously depict Vietnamese civilians, perhaps the greatest victims of the war, as two-faced enemy collaborators and greedy exploiters of GIs. Vietnamese rarely appear in narratives as anything more than racist, one-dimensional caricatures. Supplemental sources suggest that Vietnamese actions loathed by many US troops are understandable in the context of Vietnam's tumultuous history. Memoirists frequently say, for instance, that GIs were irritated by the constant presence of beggars, peddlers, pimps, and other Vietnamese in search of American dollars. They do not explain that many South Vietnamese were forced into such activities because the war had wrecked their nation's economy. The omission of this crucial information is understandable, however, since most mid-twentieth-century Americans, soldiers included, were largely ignorant of Vietnam's language, history, and culture.

A great number of African Americans and other nonwhites fought for the United States in Vietnam, and racial tensions were high in the military during the war. Nearly all of the best-known memoirists, however, are white, and many of them do not broach the subjects of race and racism at all. Chapter 3 handles this situation by analyzing nonwhite narratives. Many of these works were not included in the primary memoir group because they are too obscure, but they are used in this chapter to show how ex-soldiers of color developed a race-centric "countermemory" of the Vietnam War. This nonwhite interpretation of the conflict consists of two competing, antagonistic paradigms. The first nonwhite version of the Vietnam experience emphasizes racial cooperation and pride in the combat performance of one's own racial or ethnic group. The second version focuses on incidents of white racism, the self-segregation of GIs, and is influenced by the Black Power movement.

Chapter 4 tackles issues related to women and sexuality. Veterans suggest male soldiers acted generally sexist in their interactions with women in Vietnam. This depiction of male–female relations is confirmed by historical scholarship, wartime newspaper articles, the narratives of American women who went to Vietnam, and other sources. The misogynist behavior of male GIs was rooted in mainstream and military cultures that promoted hostility towards women and the belief that soldiers at war deserved sex. All women were subject to this attitude, but it was intensified in dealings with Asian women because of the racism that pervaded the Vietnam-era US armed forces. Veteran-authors, additionally, often make light of instances in which GIs disrespected and abused women, and both American and foreign females who appear in their narratives are usually depicted as offensive stereotypes.

Chapter 5 examines how memoirists dealt with their homecomings and postwar lives. Many veterans forthrightly admit that they suffered from post-traumatic stress disorder (PTSD) and other readjustment difficulties after returning to the United States. Postwar studies confirm that many Vietnam veterans came home from Southeast Asia with psychological wounds. Not everything memoirs say about postwar topics, however, is supported by other sources, including the contention that Vietnam veterans, unlike soldiers who survived earlier American wars, were harassed or ignored by their fellow citizens. Most veteran-authors, like Americans in general, were evidently unaware that ex-warriors have struggled to readjust to peacetime since the dawn of warfare. Veteran narratives also suggest that the passage of time invariably erased the PTSD and other

8    homecoming troubles of the men and women who went to Vietnam. This is misleading because many veterans never found relief from economic and psychological problems related to their Vietnam service. This was especially the case for ex-soldiers who, unlike most memoirists, came from disadvantaged circumstances.

Political messages conveyed by veteran memoirs are covered in chapter 6. Some narratives feature unambiguous antiwar statements, and most portray the war in an overall unflattering light. Curiously, though, many memoirists also express hatred of antiwar protesters and were obviously proud that they had fought for their country. The chapter concludes by exploring why narratives conveying this ambivalent attitude dominated the memoir genre. One reason is that mainstream literary critics lavished praise and attention only on narratives that portrayed the war in a nuanced but generally negative light. Yet, according to opinion polls, Vietnam veterans as a whole thought the war was a mistake and disliked antiwar protesters, but remained patriotic and proud of their military service at the same time. In this sense, at least, the memoirs accurately reflected the conflicted views held by most men and women who carried out America's mission in Vietnam.

Chapter 7, finally, compares Vietnam narratives to those produced by veterans of pre- and post-Vietnam American wars. Great differences, of course, separate the Vietnam War from World War II, the Gulf War, and post-9/11 conflicts. But this chapter focuses on the amazing similarities that exist between Vietnam memoirs and those that chronicle other wars. Authors who served in the military before, during, and after Vietnam all feature the following themes in their narratives: soldiers loathing civilians, combat-related psychological maladies, battlefield atrocities, and GIs preoccupied with sex. And this is only a partial list. One cause for these similarities is the fact that wartime experiences for the average American foot soldier did not change in many ways from the 1940s to the 2000s. At least some cross-conflict parallels, however, resulted from the supremacy of white, college-educated, former officers in the veteran memoir genre for the last seventy or so years.

# 1

# Who Were the Vietnam Veteran-Memoirists?

Lewis Puller Jr., author of the memoir *Fortunate Son,* always knew he would join the marines someday and, with luck, command troops against America's enemies. This eagerness for combat was a product of his upbringing. Puller's father was Marine Corps legend Lewis "Chesty" Puller Sr., and he raised his son to see fighting for one's country as a duty and an honor. The younger Puller entered marine officer training immediately after college graduation and, a few months later, volunteered to lead an infantry platoon in Vietnam. He had, however, many disillusioning experiences during his combat tour, chief among them the day he realized he was very much unlike the enlisted men under his command. Whereas Puller was a college graduate who grew up in comfortable economic circumstances, half of his men were high school dropouts, and all came from "lower-middle-class backgrounds." He also learned that, at age twenty-three, he was an "old man" compared to the "teenage misfits" who composed the bulk of the platoon.[1]

Puller, as the son of a famous general, grew up in exceptional circumstances, but he was not the only former-officer-turned-memoirist who discovered that his own background differed greatly from those of his men. William Broyles Jr., who had already earned an MA degree from prestigious Oxford University when he joined the marines in 1968,[2] wrote this entry in his journal after meeting his troops in Vietnam for the first time:

> I have fifty-eight men. Only twenty have high school diplomas.
> About ten of them are over twenty-one. Reading through their
> record books almost made me cry. Over and over they read—
> address of father: unknown; education: one or two years of high

school; occupation: laborer, pecan sheller, gas station attendant, Job Corps. Kids with no place to go. No place but here.[3]

Both Puller and Broyles served their combat tours relatively late in the war, a period when many GIs in Vietnam were only there because they lacked the money, connections, and know-how needed to procure a draft deferment. Philip Caputo, however, who led an infantry platoon in the opening stages of the war, was also struck by the generally disadvantaged backgrounds of his troops. Many in his platoon had not finished high school, and most, he writes in *A Rumor of War*, came "from city slums and dirt farms and Appalachian mining towns."[4] Everyone in the platoon was a volunteer, but Caputo speculated that many enlisted to avoid the draft, or because the military offered "a guaranteed annual income, free medical care, [and] free clothing."[5] Caputo was not the son of a war hero or the graduate of a famed European university, but as a college graduate from a middle-class family, his upbringing was nevertheless privileged compared to those of his men.

It is no coincidence that the platoons of all three of these memoirists were composed predominantly of economically and educationally disadvantaged men in their late teens or early twenties. Christian G. Appy argues that most enlisted men who served in Vietnam came from poor or working-class backgrounds; were, on average, nineteen years old when they went to war; and had not gone to college. Most middle- and upper-class young men were able to skip military service in the Vietnam era, primarily through college deferments. Less privileged men generally could not afford higher education in this era, which left them at the mercy of their draft boards. Most disadvantaged men who turned eighteen during the war had only two real choices when it came to the draft: await the arrival of their draft notice, or submit to the inevitable and volunteer for military service.[6]

Over two million American soldiers served in Vietnam, but only a small percentage were consistently involved in combat. As Meredith Lair has shown, most GIs in Vietnam filled a myriad of noncombat roles that a large, modern military force requires to function, from mess-hall cook to intelligence analyst.[7] There is debate over exactly how many American military personnel in Vietnam were combat soldiers, but the ratio of support troops to combat troops was, according to Appy, "at least 5 to 1."[8] It is significant, therefore, that Puller, Broyles, and Caputo were all in charge of infantry platoons. These were the US Army and Marine Corps grunts who carried out the bulk of American ground combat operations during the war.[9] Due to military procedures of the period, recruits with poor educational backgrounds were frequently assigned to the infantry.[10] Since education level was a strong indicator of social-class level in the Vietnam era, these policies ensured that poor and working-class troops filled the infantry's ranks.[11]

The enlisted men commanded by Puller, Caputo, and Broyles represented average combat soldiers. These three authors, like most veteran-authors, were combat veterans too, but they, also like most memoirists, did not resemble ordinary combat troops for several reasons. The majority of memoirists were middle-class college graduates and, on average, twenty-seven years old when they served in Southeast Asia. While most veteran-authors served as officers, nearly 90 percent of the troops in Vietnam were enlisted men.[12] Although underprivileged men of all races and ethnicities were more likely to see combat than their more fortunate counterparts, infantry units were disproportionately staffed by African Americans and other nonwhites.[13] The fact that America's fighting force was heavily populated by the least fortunate segments of its population is a significant facet of Vietnam War history. It is worrisome that people may not have been exposed to this important historical reality if they read books written by veterans who were primarily middle class, college educated, and white.

Despite the importance of the memoirists' socioeconomic characteristics, this topic has garnered little attention from scholars or popular writers. A handful of literary critics and scholars have written about the demographics of Vietnam veteran-authors. C. D. B. Bryan speculated in his 1976 *New York Times* review of Ron Kovic's *Born on the Fourth of July* that few Vietnam veterans had produced memoirs or war novels by that point because those most "capable of writing the Vietnam-era's equivalent to a *Naked and the Dead* . . . were also capable of avoiding the draft."[14] Merritt Clifton, the editor of *Those Who Were There,* a 1984 bibliography of firsthand accounts of the war, theorized that the existence of so many capable Vietnam-era veteran-writers was explained by the relatively high recruiting standards of the Marine Corps, which "drew heavily from those achieving a medium level of education: at least a high school diploma, perhaps a year of college."[15] Philip K. Jason speculated that many Vietnam veterans "had the equipment to turn their experiences into literary documents" because of the post–World War II expansion of educational opportunities in the United States.[16]

Bryan, Clifton, or Jason, however, did not discuss author demographics beyond these few statements. Crucially, these writers also did not speculate on the possible influence of veteran-author backgrounds over readers' conceptions of Vietnam War history. A few other literary scholars, however, touched on this subject. Philip Beidler writes about how the distinctive backgrounds of the veteran-authors affected the portrayal of the war in cheap paperback memoirs and novels.[17] Two other scholars, Herman Beavers and Perry Luckett, speculate about how a lack of African American veteran-writers affected the depiction of racial issues in Vietnam War literature.[18] These literary critics, however, only focus on how a single demographic veteran-author characteristic, such as race or military occupation, influenced readers' conceptions of Vietnam. This limited exploration of memoirist demographics, however, still goes beyond what historians have written about the topic. In keeping with their tendency to only see veteran narratives as unequivocal sources of information, historians have placed little importance on the backgrounds of authors who provided such information.

This chapter takes a different approach by analyzing the available demographic data of fifty-one authors of the fifty-eight memoirs that serve as the basis of this book. The authors' background information, gleaned from the memoirs and other sources, has been organized into eleven categories: year born, race, premilitary education level, method of induction into the armed forces, highest rank achieved while in Vietnam, method of acquiring officer commission, military branch, age upon arrival in Vietnam, number of years served in Vietnam, military occupational specialty (MOS), and total number of years served in the military. In addition to the data organized under these headings, other less quantifiable pieces of information, such as reasons for joining the military and social-class level, are also factored into the analysis.

Examination of the compiled data indicates that the authors fall into three distinct rank-based groups. The first group consists of ten individuals who served in Vietnam as high-ranking officers: nine "field-grade" or "general-grade" commissioned officers, and one senior enlisted noncommissioned officer, or "NCO." These men were white career soldiers who joined the military well before the start of the war, went to Vietnam at the average age of thirty-eight, and served in the military for many years, sometimes decades, after the war. The second group consists of fifteen memoirists who were low-ranking enlisted men and junior NCOs in Vietnam. These authors' backgrounds, in many ways, represent those of ordinary combat soldiers: only one had a college degree, they served in Vietnam at the average age of twenty, and none spent more than a few years in the military. Although nonwhites are underrepresented among memoirists no matter how they are divided up, four of six nonwhite authors fell into this second cohort.

The third and largest group is composed of twenty-six veterans who went to war as low-ranking "junior" commissioned officers. These lieutenants and captains were only slightly older than the enlisted men they oversaw in Vietnam, but most other aspects of their backgrounds set them apart from enlisted grunts. Over half the authors in this group earned college degrees before entering the military, most appear to be from middle-class households, and all but two were white. Though not as career-minded as the senior officers in group one, nearly half of the authors who served as junior officers in Vietnam pursued military careers after their combat tours ended.

Splitting up the memoirists into these groups does nothing to mitigate their overall dissimilarity to regular combat troops. In fact, it demonstrates that only fifteen of the fifty-one authors had backgrounds that closely resembled those of the soldiers who did most of the fighting and dying in Vietnam. Taking this approach, however, indicates that a majority of the veteran-authors were similar to average combat soldiers with regard to one crucial category: type of Vietnam experience. Most senior US officers, like the ten authors in group one, were personally and geographically distant from enlisted men in Vietnam. While American infantrymen searched for the Vietcong in the countryside, the generals and colonels who had ordered such patrols usually stayed out of harm's way. Junior officers, on the other hand, as Ron Milam has shown, worked, fought, and sometimes died alongside the enlisted men under their command.[19] This means that most of the fifty-eight memoirs were written by former low-ranking enlisted personnel and junior officers who, whatever their social or educational backgrounds, experienced the grunts' war.

The possible effects of the memoirists' demographics on how they portray the war are, therefore, both positive and negative. Readers may be misled about what types of Americans actually fought in Vietnam because authors normally have dissimilar backgrounds from average combat soldiers. Memoirists sporadically mention that large numbers of people unlike themselves, poor whites and minorities, fought in Vietnam. But most do not. Consequently, the common story of the poor teenager from the inner-city ghetto or Appalachia who was drafted and became a foot soldier because he could not afford college is rare in these accounts. On the positive side, most of these books were written by combat veterans who were ex-enlisted men or, more likely, authors who fought alongside such men as low-ranking officers.

The government and military leaders who planned and managed America's long conflict in Vietnam were men in or around middle age, most of them members of the generation that grew up during the Great Depression and fought in World War II. In contrast, the great majority of American soldiers who fought in Southeast Asia in the 1960s and 70s belonged to the generation born after World War II, the Baby Boom Generation.[20] The birth year statistics for the memoirists as a group do not reflect this reality. The average birth year for the authors is 1941, and well over half were born before 1945, the final year of World War II. These unrepresentative results mostly reflect the presence of the former senior officers among the fifty-one authors. The average birth year for the senior officers in group one was 1927, with most of their birth dates falling in the 1920s and 30s.[21] Whereas most soldiers who served in Vietnam were born after the United States defeated Germany and Japan, all the former senior officers were alive during that conflict, and three actually *fought* in it. The average birth year for the enlisted men in group two was 1946, and only three were born before 1945, which corresponds to their status as generally average combat veterans. Although only eight of the twenty-six junior officers were true Baby Boomers, most, with an average birth year of 1944, were only slightly older than typical enlisted GIs.

More important than when a veteran was born is at what age he or she served in Vietnam. The average age for an American soldier in this "teenage war" was nineteen, which is young compared to their Second World War predecessors, who marched off to battle at a median age of twenty-six.[22] Almost 44 percent of all US servicemen killed in Southeast Asia were less than twenty-one years old when they died.[23] The average age of veteran-authors during their Vietnam tours, however, was twenty-seven. This outcome was, again, partly the result of the presence of the former senior officers in group one, who served in Vietnam at an average age of thirty-eight.

In contrast to the senior officers, the fifteen ex-enlisted men in group two were sent to Vietnam at around twenty years of age, the former junior officers at twenty-four. This means that the great majority of memoirs were written by two groups of writers who were relatively young when they went to war. The age gap between enlisted men in their teens and officers in their mid-twenties, however, was wider than it seems. Broyles argues in his memoir, *Brothers in Arms*, that "impressionable, immature" teenage soldiers, probably "away from home for the first time," were affected by the war differently than men only a few years older.[24] His assertion is supported by the experiences of memoirist Bruce Weigl, who was forever scarred by the swift, jarring transition from naïve teenager to army foot soldier.[25] There are no real counterparts to Weigl's brutal coming-of-age story in the memoirs of former officers.

The fighting force sent to Vietnam was not just youthful, but also economically disadvantaged. Appy estimates that the "enlisted ranks in Vietnam were comprised of about 25 percent poor, 55 percent working class, and 20 percent middle class, with a statistically negligible number of wealthy."[26] This situation was largely the result of a draft system, dubbed "channeling" by the Selective Service,[27] designed to steer draft-aged men "in directions that served the national interest."[28] The most common and significant manifestation of this system was the draft exemption given to college students, a policy designed to give "the next generation of doctors, scientists, and engineers" the chance to complete their educations.[29] Since most low-income Americans could not afford college during the Vietnam era, middle- and upper-class men were the primary beneficiaries of this policy.[30] Men of more privileged backgrounds were also better equipped to take advantage of other means used to avoid the draft, such as obtaining phony medical exemptions or joining the National Guard.[31]

The benefits of class and education did not disappear when recruits, draftees and volunteers alike, entered the armed forces. After basic training, Pentagon computers assigned recruits to occupational specialties according to their education levels, how they performed on intelligence and aptitude tests, and other relevant criteria.[32] Personnel "with above-average aptitude or ability were . . . assigned special functions, often far from the combat zone."[33] Well-educated recruits, furthermore, were "skimmed out of the manpower pool by officers who wanted reliable clerks, messengers, servants, or other helpers."[34] Soldiers "of lesser talents," conversely, were regularly slated for infantry training, which increased the likelihood of seeing combat.[35] Because low-income recruits had comparatively substandard educations, many fared poorly on the Armed Forces Qualification Test (AFQT), the intelligence test that partly determined a soldier's MOS.[36] Since only a small percentage of Americans from underprivileged backgrounds went to college, fewer GIs from such circumstances were assigned to technical and clerical positions ordinarily staffed by college graduates.

What, then, was the class makeup of the memoirists? Considering the prohibitive expense of higher education in mid-twentieth-century America, education level is a good way to answer this question.[37] Of all the troops who went to Vietnam, 18 percent were high school dropouts, 59 percent high school graduates, 15 percent attended college from one to three years, and 8 percent attended college four or more years.[38] The overall education statistics for the fifty-one memoirists are glaringly unrepresentative of this reality: five were high school dropouts, ten were high school graduates, eleven attended college but did not graduate, and twenty-three—almost half—were college graduates.[39] This overrepresentation of college graduates is a direct result of the preponderance of officers in the study, since a college degree was generally required to obtain a commission.

Over half of the former officers in the study had college degrees before entering the military, indicating that many of them hailed from backgrounds significantly more privileged than those of ordinary combat troops. Only a few of these individuals, however, graduated from elite civilian universities, the US Military Academy ("West Point"), or the US Naval Academy. A closer look at the backgrounds of the college graduates confirms that most were hardly the sons and daughters of the upper class. Caputo points out that his family had "just recently struggled out of the working class," and that his degree came from "a parochial commuter-college."[40] Colin Powell, future Chairman of the Joint Chiefs and Secretary of State, grew up in the working-class neighborhood of Hunts Point in the Bronx, New York, and graduated from City College of New York (CCNY).[41] Everett Alvarez, a former fighter pilot and prisoner of war, paid for college with money his mother earned working in a produce packing plant.[42]

Aside from the few authors who attended military academies, all the former officers who graduated from college before entering the military obtained their commissions through completion of either the Reserve Officer Training Corps (ROTC) program or Officer Candidate School (OCS). ROTC cadets undertook officer training while still in college and received their commissions upon graduation. Those who took the other route enlisted in the military after graduation and were rewarded with commissions upon completion of OCS. There were other ways to become an officer that did not require a college degree, and thirteen of the former officers used one of these methods. OCS was the most common means used by GIs without college degrees to obtain a commission. Although college graduates were preferred, OCS was open to all enlisted men who met the necessary qualifications.[43] Six authors, ranging in education level from less than four years of high school to a few years of college, became officers through this method. The nine other former officers without premilitary college degrees obtained commissions through other less common means, including graduating from an "aviation cadet program," earning a "field commission," or joining the US Army Nurse Corps.

Since West Point produced relatively few officers and participation in ROTC programs plunged as the war progressed, about 50 percent of all the junior army officers who served in Vietnam were OCS graduates.[44] With so many non-college-educated men and women obtaining commissions through OCS or other means, it is likely that the Vietnam-era officer corps was composed of a substantial number of people from poor or working-class backgrounds.[45] Several of the thirteen former officers without college degrees validate this assumption. Tobias Wolff was raised by a single mother, a secretary who worked nights as a waitress. When he joined the army in the mid-1960s, he was a teenage high school dropout. After basic training, however, Wolff went on to complete airborne school, Special Forces training, and finally, OCS.[46] Another memoirist, Frederick Downs, grew up on a farm in Indiana and only completed a couple years of college before he enlisted in the army, but he also made it through OCS and became an officer.[47]

Although the great majority of authors were not from truly wealthy backgrounds, most nevertheless apparently came from the middle class. The disproportionately large number of memoirists with college degrees is one indication of this,[48] but many veterans also provide other clues in descriptions of their pre-Vietnam lives. Authors regularly describe growing up in comfortable surroundings, often in the suburbs, and usually with at least one parent holding a secure, well-paying job. Joseph Callaway's father worked in a "prestigious, major, advertising firm,"[49] and Robert Mason's father sold real estate for a living.[50] Lynda Van Devanter describes her childhood as "middle-class suburban."[51] Even the relatively few memoirists who were raised in unambiguously working-class households sometimes describe their childhoods as stable and carefree. Ron Kovic, for instance, grew up in a working-class suburb, and his father worked in a supermarket. He nevertheless describes his prewar life as an idyllic world of baseball games, John Wayne movies, and parades.[52] The prewar lives of low-income men who ended up in Vietnam, however, were not usually so untroubled.[53] They were instead "full of very adult concerns: money, jobs, and survival."[54]

Class was the most important factor in determining who saw combat in Vietnam, but race also came into play. Like whites in the same economic circumstances, impoverished African Americans were vulnerable to military and draft policies that favored better-educated groups. In the earliest phases of the war, the number of African Americans killed in Vietnam was greatly out of proportion to their overall share of the US population.[55] Less information about other nonwhite groups is available, but it is likely that some, especially Puerto Ricans and Mexican Americans, also shouldered more than their fair share of the fighting. Considering the inordinate sacrifices made by these groups, it is noteworthy that only six of the fifty-one most prominent memoirists were nonwhites: five African Americans and one Mexican American.[56] This dearth of minority authors was probably due to the overrepresentation of officers and college graduates in the pool of eligible candidates. During the war years, only a small percentage of the officer corps was nonwhite and, prior to the 1970s, the number of minorities who graduated from college lagged far behind that of the white population.[57]

The draft struck fear into the hearts of many young men during the war, and the statistics show that their apprehensions were not unfounded. Draftees accounted for about a third of all the troops who served in Vietnam. Between 1965 and 1970, the percentage of American soldiers killed in Southeast Asia who were draftees steadily rose from 16 to 43 percent. In the US Army, the military branch in which most draftees served, the yearly death rates for draftees were even higher, topping out at 62 percent in 1969.[58] But these figures do not tell the whole story. Many young men, preferring to have some degree of control over their fates, or believing that volunteering lessened the chances of going to Vietnam, enlisted rather than waiting to be drafted. Almost half of the respondents to a 1968 Defense Department survey of army volunteers said that the "most important reason" for their enlistments was to avoid the draft.[59] This was true not just for enlisted men, but also for officers: 60 percent of all the officers who volunteered in 1968 signed up because of the draft.[60]

"Draft-motivated" enlistees comprised another third of all the troops who served in Vietnam. The remaining third were "true volunteers,"[61] although this phrase is somewhat misleading, for the great majority of them did not enlist to help the South Vietnamese fight Communist aggression. Only 6 percent of the respondents to the Department of Defense survey said they signed up to "serve [their] country," with the rest (besides the draft-motivated respondents) citing sundry other reasons, including "to become more mature and self-reliant," "to leave some personal problems behind me," and "to learn a trade."[62] John Helmer, as part of his study of Vietnam veterans, *Bringing the War Home,* asked true volunteers for the primary reason they enlisted. The number one response was "nothing else to do."[63]

Veteran-authors differed significantly from average combat GIs when it came to how they joined the military, for only seven out of fifty-one were draftees. As for why the authors joined the military, almost half signed up before the war had even started, so Vietnam played no part in their decision. Those who did join during the war, however, were also dissimilar to regular combat troops because many cited intensely personal reasons for volunteering. A few, such as W. D. Ehrhart, signed up specifically to fight Communism. A true believer who wanted to help South Vietnam in its moment of peril, he forsook college to join the Marine Corps.[64] Many more said they joined out of a general sense of patriotism, to prove their manhood, carry on family traditions, or to fulfill some other noble goal or desire. Michael Norman volunteered for the marines in 1966 because "history was unfolding and [he] had an urge to be a part of it."[65] Charles R. Anderson told his parents he enlisted because he wanted to repay his country for all the freedoms it had given him.[66]

Several memoirists say that the draft factored into their decision to enlist, but most attest that other more profound reasons also propelled them. Rod Kane enlisted because a recruiter convinced him not to wait to be drafted, but he also wanted to emulate his Korean War veteran uncle.[67] Nathaniel Tripp says in his memoir, *Father, Soldier, Son,* that the "draft board was closing in" at the time of his enlistment. But he also "burned for a new adventure" and was inspired to volunteer after a friend was killed in Vietnam.[68]

Now that it is clear what types of Americans fought in Vietnam, what was combat like for these troops? The Vietnam conflict was famously a war without frontlines, so it was possible for any American in South Vietnam to fall victim to an enemy attack. The Vietcong ambushed infantry platoons in the jungle, but they also lobbed mortar shells onto airbases and planted explosives in jeeps parked outside restaurants. During the 1968 Tet Offensive, Vietcong fighters attacked American forces throughout South

Vietnam, including troops stationed in Saigon, the supposedly safe capital city.[69] Van Devanter, who served as a nurse in an army hospital, was told on her first day in Vietnam, to her shock, that the Vietcong considered all Americans legitimate targets, including women.[70]

Even if all US personnel in Vietnam were theoretically at risk of being attacked, most lived and worked in relatively safe areas referred to as "the rear" by GIs. Clerks, truck drivers, and other support troops, labeled "REMFs" ("rear echelon mother fuckers") by resentful infantrymen, were needed to maintain America's massive military machine. Approximately 75 percent of US military personnel in Vietnam served in noncombat positions. Most memoirists, however, saw heavy combat. Veteran narratives, consequently, along with movies and novels, suggest that average Vietnam tours mostly consisted of patrols in Vietcong-infested jungles or days-long battles with the North Vietnamese Army (NVA). Many GIs did live lives of danger and hardship, but most were provided with a level of "comfort unparalleled in military history."[71] Thus, it is the so-called REMFs who experienced the most typical Vietnam tour.[72]

Unlike the majority of GIs in Vietnam, however, most memoirists directly participated in the fighting. That being said, how do their battlefield experiences compare to those of ordinary combat troops? The importance of this information is highlighted by the massive post-1990 output of cheap paperback Vietnam War novels, biographies, and memoirs that focused on the exploits of elite combat outfits. If readers got all of their information about the war from these types of books they might think that practically every soldier in Vietnam belonged to a group like the Army Special Forces ("Green Berets") or the Navy SEALs. Nothing could be further from the truth, however, since such soldiers represented only a miniscule percentage of combat personnel.[73]

A little under half of the fifty-one memoirists belonged to select units like the Green Berets, or were involved in other atypical combat activities, such as the veteran who worked as an advisor to US allies in a remote Vietnamese village.[74] Nine of these atypical veterans were former combat pilots who flew bombing missions over North Vietnam. One of these ex-fliers, Arizona senator John McCain, notes the difference between air combat, which was "fought in short, violent bursts," and the experiences of infantrymen who "slog[ged] through awful conditions and danger for months on end."[75] He and the other ten pilot-memoirists were also members of the tiny minority of American servicemen who were prisoners of war during the conflict.[76] The war POWs lived through was certainly nightmarish, but it bore little resemblance to the ordeals faced by foot soldiers.

About half of the authors, on the other hand, fought as Army or Marine Corps infantrymen, and most served only one tour in Vietnam. Crucially, this group was composed exclusively of either low-ranking enlisted men or junior officers. Field and general-grade officers spent much of their time in the rear, with access to "air conditioned billets with movie theaters, swimming pools, and officer's clubs."[77] Junior officers, conversely, served alongside their men, and had the high casualty rates to prove it.[78] Two authors who fought as junior officers, Downs and Puller Jr., sustained major wounds while on patrol with their platoons. Downs's arm was blown off when he stepped on a "Bouncing Betty" landmine,[79] and Puller lost both legs when he triggered a buried, booby-trapped artillery shell planted by the Vietcong.[80] Richard A. Gabriel and Paul L. Savage contend that officers "must be perceived as willing to share the risks and sacrifices of battle" to be effective leaders.[81] Senior officers in Vietnam, in their opinion, utterly failed to meet this standard, but Puller, Downs, and many others like them demonstrated that the same cannot be said of junior officers.[82]

Just as important as what memoirists did in Vietnam is how long they served in the military, because there are major differences between the points of view of short-term soldiers and professionals. Enlisted men and officers who stay in the armed forces for a short amount of time are "citizen soldiers" who put their normal lives on hold while they serve their country. Despite the training and indoctrination necessary to transform a civilian into a capable soldier, the nonprofessional retains a civilian outlook on life.[83] The career soldier chooses instead to become, as Samuel P. Huntington puts it, a specialist in "the management of violence."[84] In many ways, military men and women are like professionals in other fields, but their focus on warfare sets them apart from the civilian world. Military personnel follow particular codes of honor and traditions, usually live and work only with other soldiers, and often see their career as a "calling" or a "special mission."[85]

Someone who enlisted in the armed forces during the Vietnam era generally signed up for a two- to four-year commitment; draftees had to serve at least two years. Most enlisted men did not choose to stay in the military beyond their first enlistment, which is no surprise since the ranks were filled with draftees and draft-motivated volunteers at that time.[86] Officers were nearly as unwilling to pursue military careers as enlisted men.

From 1966 to 1970, the number of army OCS officers who stayed on beyond their initial years of obligated service fell from 56 to 22 percent. In 1970, only 11 percent of ROTC officers signed up for additional years. At the beginning of the war, almost 100 percent of West Point graduates remained in the army after fulfilling their mandatory term of service. This figure dropped to 72 percent by war's end.[87]

As usual, the fifteen enlisted memoirists resemble ordinary GIs, for none of them served any longer than four years in the military. The former senior officers joined the armed forces well before the war started and, in most cases, continued their military careers after coming home from Southeast Asia. Eleven (43 percent) of the junior officer memoirists stayed in the military after completing their combat tours. Taken as a whole, then, the authors consist of thirty veterans who were short-term soldiers and twenty-one who were career officers. This proportion of career soldiers is high since most GIs returned to civilian life shortly after finishing their Vietnam tours. Half of the veterans, nevertheless, no matter how long their military careers lasted, were low-ranking officers in Vietnam and shared the hardships of the enlisted men they commanded.

A publishing company executive quoted in a *Washington Post* review of Kane's 1990 memoir, *Veteran's Day*, asserted that the book was important because it "filled a void that was societal as much as literary":

> It's a curious thing that many of the Vietnam books have been written by [veterans] who had lots of education and came from relatively sophisticated backgrounds, guys who had been to college and were officers. Rod Kane really represents the disenfranchised, the people who came out of the high schools, the drifters, the kids who had no one to speak for them. They were the ones who paid the price, they were blown to pieces.[88]

The executive's assessment is accurate. The fifty-one most prominent Vietnam veteran-memoirists had, as a whole, strikingly dissimilar backgrounds from the average American combat soldier. Whereas the typical infantryman was a teenage enlisted man with a high school education, veteran-authors were generally former officers who served in Vietnam after graduating from college. Most GIs in Vietnam came from low-income families and were primarily draftees or draft-motivated volunteers, but most memoirists were middle class and often volunteered for idealistic reasons. Finally, although combat infantry units in Vietnam were disproportionately composed of African Americans and other minorities, all but six memoirists were white.

The unsettling fact that the nation's poorest citizens bore the heaviest burden in Vietnam is one of the most important aspects of the war. It is subsequently unfortunate that this facet of the conflict's history is largely absent from the most popular veterans' memoirs. The authors of these narratives had uncommonly privileged backgrounds, and most did not mention that their pre-Vietnam lives were any different than those of average combat soldiers. This hole in the depiction of the war is partially compensated for by the existence of several popular oral histories that feature numerous interviews with apparently ordinary combat veterans, but because these titles are small in number compared to veteran memoirs, their influence has been limited.[89]

Although the backgrounds of the memoirists were different from average combat troops in many respects, the two groups were similar in one crucial aspect: wartime experiences. Most memoirists were either junior officers or enlisted men who spent a year in Vietnam and then returned to civilian life. About half were former infantrymen who took part in conventional combat operations, and most were actively involved in combat due to low rank. The publishing executive was correct in stating that most memoirists came from exceptional backgrounds. But the majority of authors, former junior officers and enlisted men alike, still "paid the price" and risked getting "blown to pieces."

# 2 Combat Conditions and the Vietnamese People

Of the hundreds of memoirs written by American veterans of the Vietnam War, *And a Hard Rain Fell: A GI's True Story of the War in Vietnam* is perhaps the most bitter, unromantic, and depressing. Its author, John Ketwig, developed an apolitical, instinctual abhorrence of the growing war in Southeast Asia as he approached draft age. It was only because of a lack of options that he enlisted in the army in late 1966. A recruiter assured Ketwig that volunteering would keep him out of Vietnam, but he was shipped off to Southeast Asia not long after basic training anyway. He worked mostly as a mechanic on an army base in Vietnam, but had several combat experiences that left deep psychological scars. While driving a truck that was part of a convoy tasked with resupplying combat troops, Ketwig was nearly killed when the vehicle in front of him was destroyed by a landmine.[1] When his convoy finally reached the battlefield, he was met with the nightmarish scene of dispirited GIs "kneeling in the mud, peering into the shadows and awaiting death."[2] The soldiers were under constant enemy harassment and, owing to sniper fire, the only way they could retrieve their slain comrades was to chain their corpses to the back of an armored vehicle and drag them out of the line of fire.[3]

For days after his stint with the convoy, Ketwig "shook," went into rages, and "shivered," haunted by the memory of the "string" of American bodies being dragged through the mud.[4] The most damaging experience of his tour, however, did not come on the battlefield, but at an encampment of US Army Special Forces soldiers, the famous "Green Berets." Ketwig went to the camp hoping to barter for black market goods, but when he got there the Green Berets and their Vietnamese allies were torturing a woman they suspected had played some part in the death of a comrade.

He describes the torture and the woman's eventual murder in sickening detail, and recalls the crushing guilt he felt afterward at not having done something to stop it.[5] Ketwig even questioned at the time whether he would "ever be able to return to everyday life in" the United States after witnessing such a horrible episode.[6]

Ketwig openly denounces the war in *And a Hard Rain Fell*. Additionally, the despairing tone of the book and its graphic descriptions of combat and atrocities amount to an implicit indictment of the war. It therefore seems odd that another reoccurring theme in the book is his contempt for the war's greatest victims: Vietnamese civilians. Ketwig perceived the Vietnamese to be greedy, untrustworthy, and ungrateful. He disdainfully describes Vietnamese cities as dangerous, trash-strewn centers of vice,[7] and South Vietnam in general as "a society of murderers, thieves, [and] carnival hucksters."[8] Ketwig was shocked that civilians, such as children who pelted US Army buses with garbage, were openly contemptuous of Americans.[9] During his last day "in country" his wallet was stolen and he saw an old woman brazenly selling a US military rifle in the marketplace.[10] After these events it suddenly became clear to him that "the Vietnamese people didn't care about our noble mission, and until they cared it was hopeless."[11]

The portrayal of the Vietnam experience in *And a Hard Rain Fell* may seem peculiar, but it is actually typical. Most memoirists, like Ketwig, describe combat as terrifying and exhausting rather than glorious, and they render battlefield wounds and deaths in graphic detail. Veteran-authors also accurately depict the great difficulty American forces experienced in their attempts to counter the Vietcong's unconventional tactics. Veterans make it clear that the war was fought among civilians who were indistinguishable from the enemy, a situation that led to death and injury for countless innocent bystanders, including women and children. Memoirs also show that a profound anti-Vietnamese racism existed among American troops; the use of racial slurs such as "gook," "dink," and "slope" was commonplace. Such racial hatred was obviously the driving force behind some of the most heinous atrocities chronicled by veterans, including the practice of keeping enemy body parts, chiefly ears and skulls, as souvenirs.

Most authors, also like Ketwig, portray the Vietnamese as covetous of American dollars, yet unappreciative of American sacrifices. Such depictions lead to the formation of an unlikely theme in veteran narratives: Vietnamese civilians as the victimizers of US troops. Sharing the role of victimizer with civilians in narratives are Army of the Republic of Vietnam (ARVN) soldiers, America's chief military allies in Vietnam.[12] These

"ARVNs" are portrayed as lazy cowards who were inexplicably disdainful of the GIs who fought to defend South Vietnam's freedom. All Vietnamese—friends and enemies, civilians and combatants—usually appear in narratives as racist caricatures.

If most veteran-memoirists explicitly or implicitly condemn the war, why do most also depict Vietnamese civilians in unsympathetic ways? The reason for the coexistence of these two seemingly incompatible themes is directly related to the fundamental weakness of personal narratives: limited and biased perspective. Veteran narratives provide valuable information about how American troops experienced combat in Vietnam. But since veteran memoirs represent the experiences of only one specific group of people, they are inherently limited in their outlook on the war. American soldiers generally arrived in Vietnam with little knowledge of the country's language, culture, or history. They likewise lacked a nuanced understanding of the conflict in which they fought, knowing only the US government's oversimplified conception of the war as a battle between Communist aggression and the forces of democracy. Most American soldiers, moreover, largely due to communications problems, had no meaningful contact with local people during their tours. No wonder few veterans knew the real reasons for Vietnamese actions that they despised.

This chapter compares memoirist representations of warfare and the Vietnamese to what other sources, chiefly historical scholarship and non-veteran narratives, say about these topics. Using this approach shows that veterans' representations of combat often correspond to how historians and other writers depict Vietnam War combat. Outside sources also provide information, missing from veterans' memoirs, that explains the cultural, social, economic, and historical reasons for the attitudes and behaviors of South Vietnamese living during what they called the "American War."

———

Memoirists regularly explain that their conception of combat before Vietnam was largely based on the staged battles they saw played out in war movies, especially those about World War II. Such films often inspired future soldiers to mimic the exploits of John Wayne and other celluloid warriors in the woods, backyards, and vacant lots of their hometowns. Ron Kovic, who cheered on Wayne in the *The Sands of Iwo Jima*,[13] and W.D. Ehrhart, who killed imaginary "Krauts and Japs"[14] as a boy, realized early in their tours that their boyhoods had ill prepared them for actual warfare. GIs should have learned during training that mimicking the flashy maneuvers they saw in movies usually led to death or injury, not glory. But some soldiers apparently did not get the message. A young, inexperienced marine in Lewis Puller's platoon, for instance, was immediately hit by Vietcong gunfire when he "suddenly stood up and began firing his rifle John Wayne fashion from the hip" during a firefight.[15] Larry Heinemann explains that the term "John Wayne" was a "flat-out insult" in Vietnam, used to refer to "hot-dog, hero wannabes" not smart enough to realize the foolishness of performing cinematic-style stunts in real-life combat.[16]

Many GIs also discovered that movies and training had not prepared them for the most gruesome and unavoidable aspects of warfare: wounds and corpses. Real battlefield deaths and injuries were far removed from movie scenes of soldiers who grimaced and fought on with bloodstained shirts after getting shot, or doomed men who let out a final yell or an inspiring slogan before they slumped to the ground and died. Philip Caputo observes that the devastating gunshot wounds suffered by a Vietcong soldier killed by US troops were nothing like "the tidy holes as in the movies."[17] Charles R. Anderson soberly relates that "what happens to human beings in mechanized warfare has absolutely no poetic or theatrical possibilities."[18]

After commenting on the falseness of movie war wounds, Caputo goes on to describe the dead Vietcong's injuries, noting that his body lay in "a crimson puddle in which floated bits of skin and white cartilage."[19] Two pages earlier he writes of another dead Vietcong with "brains spilling out of the huge hole in its head like grey pudding from a cracked bowl."[20] Such hideously realistic descriptions are one of the defining elements of Vietnam veteran memoirs. In stark contrast to the war movies veterans watched as children, their narratives are full of descriptions of battlefield gore that are graphic, disgusting, and difficult to read. The purpose of this technique is clearly not exploitative, but a symptom of memoirists' desire to "tell like it was" in their narratives; to do so necessitates authentic descriptions of even the most horrible aspects of warfare.

Using World War II (either in its film or real-life incarnations) as a basis for understanding warfare led GIs to hold other preconceptions about combat that did not apply to the war in Vietnam. The Second World War featured, for the most part, battles waged by conventional armies for control of territory, but America's Vietnamese adversaries, in contrast, frequently employed guerrilla tactics. The Americans tried to draw their elusive enemies into fighting traditional battles that the US military, with its vastly superior firepower, was sure to win. This approach was taken by

General William Westmoreland, the commander of US forces during the opening phases of major American military operations in Vietnam.[21] He devised a strategy in which US patrols conducting "search and destroy" operations in the countryside "would . . . locate the enemy and then call in artillery and airpower to eliminate him."[22] In theory, such operations would eventually drive "large enemy units . . . from populated areas," giving US troops the opportunity to secure and "pacify" these locales by rooting out remaining "local guerillas" and Vietcong political leaders.[23] These tactics were also part of a "war of attrition" strategy that entailed using the massive resources of the American military to kill as many enemy troops as possible.[24]

Westmoreland's tactics, however, often failed to produce the desired results, and many memoirs feature stories that confirm this. Former infantrymen who took part in search and destroy patrols often describe these operations as bewildering, exasperating affairs. Some recall long stretches with no enemy activity, and when contact was finally made it was usually in the form of a Vietcong ambush. These accounts represent the experience of most US infantrymen. Studies show that US small-unit patrols infrequently made contact with the enemy,[25] and that when they did it was usually initiated by the Vietcong.[26] A common theme in the description of these actions is the idea that Americans in Vietnam, from privates to generals, did not really know what they were doing. Anderson consistently uses words like "blunder," "idiocy," and "chaos" in his memoir, *The Grunts*, to portray the infantry operations in which he participated.[27] Rod Kane describes his own unit's patrols as follows: "we wander around, bumping into things. Things bump into us."[28]

Another symbol of the futility of US tactics was the fact that GIs, no matter how many enemy soldiers they killed, did not permanently take control of territory. Nathaniel Tripp says that because US forces did not "hold" the land they struggled over, it "didn't take long to figure out that [the Vietnam conflict] was a hopeless war."[29] The ostensible irrationality of this strategy was compounded by the fact that regions deemed officially "pacified" did not always live up to that designation. This phenomenon infamously occurred following Operation Cedar Falls, a 1967 US attempt to clear out a Vietcong enclave near Saigon dubbed the "Iron Triangle." American troops evacuated all the civilians in the area, destroyed all the villages contained within it, and supposedly cleared it of enemy fighters. Six months later the Vietcong was again operating there.[30]

The best depiction of the hopelessness of American tactics is found in a chapter of *A Rumor of War* called "Officer in Charge of the Dead." For part of Caputo's tour in Vietnam he was put in charge of tallying casualties.[31] This task put him right in the middle of the war of attrition, a war in which the performance of an American unit was evaluated "by the number of enemy soldiers it had killed (the body count) and the proportion between that number and the number of its own dead (the kill ratio)."[32] Caputo kept track of these statistics on a "scoreboard" that the commander of his battalion consulted in order to determine which companies needed to increase their body counts.[33] GIs, under pressure to perform, were not scrupulous in the identification of enemy remains, going by the maxim: "If it's dead and Vietnamese, it's VC."[34]

GIs were infuriated by many Vietcong tactics, but the use of booby traps, especially landmines, was perhaps the most maddening enemy tactic of all. It was bad enough to fight an enemy who attacked and then fled before any revenge could be exacted, but it was even worse when casualties were inflicted by inanimate objects. The most vivid account of the demoralizing effect that booby traps could have on US soldiers is found in Puller's *Fortunate Son*. Puller, maimed by a booby trap himself, describes the weeks before his wounding as a "living hell" in which his men were constantly being taken out by landmines. The platoon felt that every step they took might be their last, and their morale was sapped by not being able to retaliate for such attacks.[35] Puller and his men struggled to answer a question posed by a veteran in another narrative: "How do you fight back against a booby trap?"[36]

Though a cynical attitude predominates in memoirists' depictions of combat, a number of authors express pride in their service. Such veterans do not suggest that their tours were a waste of time, or that American efforts in Vietnam were ridiculously futile. Virtually no memoirs, however, even those that present a generally positive view of the war, depict their authors' tours as having achieved much of anything. The majority of veterans portray the months they spent in Vietnam as one long series of firefights interrupted by brief periods of rest and inactivity. Almost never is the impression given that the actions of the authors and their comrades, including killing scores of "VC" and NVA, somehow contributed to an ultimate victory. At the end of most memoirs, the author leaves Vietnam and the war continues on without him, as if nothing changed at all since he arrived a year earlier.

Added to this sense of low achievement is the admission of some veterans that they eventually gave up caring about who won or lost the war. Tripp purposely kept his platoon out of an area with a strong Vietcong presence in order to avoid enemy contact.[37] Such examples of "combat avoidance" reportedly occurred throughout the war, but were especially common in the final years of US involvement.[38] Memoirist Matthew Brennan served three tours in Vietnam between 1965 and 1969. The war seemed so hopeless by his last tour that he decided his only mission would be to make sure he and his men made it home alive.[39] Most American troops, unlike Brennan, did not serve in Vietnam longer than the required yearlong tour, but like him, many decided at some point that their sole duty was not to defeat the enemy, but to stay alive long enough to make it back to the United States.[40]

A hallmark of guerrilla warfare is that it is fought amongst the people, and for this reason, civilians are inevitably caught in the crossfire and become unintentional casualties. The exact number of civilians killed in Vietnam is disputed and probably unknowable, but in 1975, the US Senate "subcommittee on refugees" estimated that approximately "430,000 South Vietnamese civilians were killed between 1965 and 1974 and more than 1 million were wounded."[41] The Senate's estimate is probably too low because it does not account for the thousands of slain civilians erroneously added to the enemy body count.[42] Mostly because of their "heavy reliance on firepower in and near populated areas," as much as 80 percent of the civilian casualties in South Vietnam were caused by US and allied forces, rather than their foes.[43] Though the bombing of North Vietnam has received more attention, US aircraft also dropped millions of tons of explosives on South Vietnam. It is likely that a high percentage of Southern civilians killed in the conflict were caught in these air raids.[44]

Accounts of civilian casualties are common in veterans' narratives, but not in the form of deaths caused by American air or artillery bombardments. Instead, the most common civilian casualties recounted by veterans are those that were inflicted by American ground troops, even individual soldiers. In such cases the memoirist knew who was directly responsible for the accidental killing of a civilian, often saw it take place and, in a few instances, is among those responsible. Such episodes are invariably described as moments of horror for the soldiers at fault, especially when women and children were the victims. Brennan writes of a GI in his platoon who wept after shooting an unarmed man he mistook for a Vietcong fighter.[45] Puller tells the story of a marine who was no doubt inflicted with "psychic wounds" when he accidentally shot a young girl during a skirmish in a village.[46] Perhaps the most memorable episode of this kind was recounted by Kovic in his famous memoir, *Born on the Fourth of July*. Kovic's platoon opened fire on a village it believed housed enemy troops, but when the shooting stopped the marines discovered that they had "shot up a bunch of kids." After Kovic and his comrades made the harrowing discovery, they cried, fell to the ground, and prayed for God's forgiveness as they desperately tried to help the children they had wounded.[47]

American troops in Vietnam, as Marilyn B. Young explains, "fought different wars depending on when they arrived and where . . . they were in combat."[48] South Vietnamese insurgents opposed to the US-backed regime in Saigon announced the establishment of the National Liberation Front (NLF) in late 1960. The NLF was dominated by Communists, but it was "an umbrella organization that included non-Communist individuals and organizations."[49] The military forces of the NLF were "formally organized into the People's Liberation Armed Force (PLAF)" in early 1961.[50] The PLAF was made up of "main force" units "which operated like a regular army throughout" South Vietnam, and local militia groups that operated in their home regions or villages. The NLF was composed almost wholly of native Southerners, but its "overall strategy" was determined by the Communist leadership of North Vietnam, officially known as the Democratic Republic of Vietnam (DRV). The DRV, in response to escalated US military involvement, started sending its own troops south to aid the PLAF in 1965.[51]

GIs stationed in the thinly populated northern regions of South Vietnam often squared off against the DRV's troops, officially known as the People's Army of Vietnam (PAVN). Referred to as the NVA by Americans, these were conventional, uniformed troops.[52] US troops in South Vietnam's lower latitudes, however, fought PLAF guerrillas, or as they were called by Americans, the Vietcong. VC fighters usually wore "traditional peasant garb" instead of uniforms, which generally made them indistinguishable from civilians.[53] GIs became justifiably paranoid because of this situation, learning not to trust any Vietnamese. Several veterans recount instances in which outwardly friendly civilians turn out to be Vietcong. William Broyles Jr., for instance, knew a twelve-year-old boy who joked with Americans one day and helped to kill them the next.[54] Memoirists focused a lot of attention on stories of women and children fighting for the Vietcong. Accounts of toddler suicide bombers and enemy assassins disguised as prostitutes that circulated amongst GIs were undoubtedly rumors. But a significant minority of Vietcong fighters were indeed women,[55] and children were used by the guerrillas to relay messages, act as lookouts, and plant booby traps.[56] Tim O'Brien's assertion that there was no way "to distinguish a pretty Vietnamese girl from a deadly enemy" because "often they were one and the same person," is not hyperbole.[57]

War crimes or atrocities occur during every war, and the Vietnam conflict was no different. It is impossible to determine the exact number of atrocities committed in Vietnam, but it is safe to say that they were widespread and committed by all sides in the conflict. Atrocities committed by American troops in Vietnam first became an issue of nationwide concern in the United States with the 1969 revelations concerning the My Lai Massacre, an event in which US Army soldiers murdered over two hundred Vietnamese civilians, most of them women and children.[58] The horrors of My Lai are important to the history of the war in many ways, but one of its most important, if little known, consequences is that it sparked a secret five-year study conducted by the US Army into American atrocities. Only declassified in 1990 through the Freedom of Information Act,[59] the study compiled about eight hundred cases of possible "rapes, torture, murders . . . and other illegal acts" committed by army personnel, three hundred of which were substantiated by further investigation.[60] There is no way of knowing how many other war crimes never made it into the investigation because perpetrators, witnesses, and victims stayed silent.

The army based most of its investigation on "sworn statements from soldiers and veterans who committed or witnessed" atrocities.[61] Not long after the public first heard about My Lai, over one hundred veterans publicly testified about American war crimes during the Winter Soldier Investigation, an event sponsored by Vietnam Veterans Against the War (VVAW).[62] A few months later, VVAW member and future US senator John Kerry, famously summarized the testimonials of the Winter Soldier participants before the Senate Foreign Relations Committee:

> They told stories that at times they had personally raped, cut
> off ears, cut off heads, taped wires from portable telephones to
> human genitals and turned up the power, cut off limbs, blown
> up bodies, randomly shot at civilians, razed villages in fashion
> reminiscent of Genghis Khan, shot cattle and dogs for fun,
> poisoned food stocks, and generally ravaged the countryside of
> South Vietnam in addition to the normal ravage of war and the

normal and very particular ravaging which is done by the ap-
plied bombing power of this country.[63]

Several Winter Soldier veterans alleged that the atrocities they had
witnessed were not isolated incidents, but integral aspects of US operations.[64] Such allegations are supported by the experiences of journalists who covered the war. Journalist Philip Knightly writes in his book,
*The First Casualty: The War Correspondent as Hero and Myth-Maker from the
Crimea to Iraq,* that after news of the My Lai Massacre broke in late 1969,
"nearly every war correspondent who had been in Vietnam had an atrocity story to tell."[65] These stories were not reported earlier "because the
killing of civilians was not unusual either on a small or on a large scale."[66]
One journalist, for instance, saw US Army troops attack a group of women
and children. He did not publicize the incident because he assumed news
agencies in Saigon would reject "a story about Americans killing Vietnamese civilians" as unexceptional.[67]

There is an apologist attitude towards American atrocities expressed
in some prominent memoirs that runs counter to how the Winter Soldier speakers dealt with the subject. Broyles Jr. suggests that the victims
of My Lai were partly responsible for their own deaths because they had
"watched impassively" when their killers "had been cut to pieces by booby
traps all around [their] hamlet."[68] David Donovan was revolted by My Lai,
but asserts that the atrocity issue was overblown because civilian deaths are
an unavoidable consequence of war.[69] Caputo admits that two of his men
executed a captured Vietcong on his implicit orders. He argues, though,
that neither he nor his men were to blame for the prisoner's death because
the madness of war drove them to commit the act.[70]

Even though a few memoirists minimized or made excuses for American atrocities, these sentiments are overshadowed by the huge number
and wide variety of war crimes that are documented in veterans' narratives.
Perhaps the most commonly related atrocities are those committed against
enemy soldiers. Numerous authors say prisoners were beaten, tortured,
or executed by GIs and their Vietnamese allies. Such acts were sometimes
retribution for enemy atrocities. Mason saw an American sergeant shoot a
group of bound NVA prisoners because his comrades had recently been
tortured and mutilated after being captured.[71] In other cases, US soldiers
committed atrocities against their enemies out of frustration. Two of Frederick Downs's platoon mates slashed a corpse with knives because of the
rage they felt at all their efforts resulting in only the death of "one lousy

dink."[72] In still other cases, there is no obvious reason for such behavior. Anderson's unit, for instance, executed a group of wounded NVA soldiers simply because there were "no witnesses in the bush."[73]

The most disturbing, and probably most frequent, atrocity against enemy combatants that appears in veteran narratives is the taking of body parts as souvenirs. Memoirists write about GIs who wore necklaces strung with human ears,[74] drank whiskey out of skulls, joked about tossing severed ears into mess hall soup,[75] and rigged a skull to open and close its jaw so that it appeared to sing along to music.[76] Several veterans even claim that they knew of soldiers who brought their macabre trophies back to the United States, or at least hoped to.[77] Others say that GIs did not just hack up enemy bodies for souvenirs; they also set them in lifelike poses to get a laugh out of their comrades. Bodies were propped up, cigarettes put between their fingers,[78] beer cans in their hands,[79] and *Playboy* magazines placed on their laps.[80] Johnnie M. Clark's platoon mate retrieved a "spare leg" from a pile of NVA corpses, "shoved it into the crotch" of an enemy body to create the illusion that the dead man had three legs, and then laughed at his gruesome handiwork "until tears filled his eyes."[81]

Twentieth-century GIs, Peter S. Kindsvatter explains, learned during training "that killing America's enemies was not only legally sanctioned but also [their] duty."[82] But "this license to kill did not automatically instill willingness; soldiers also wanted to believe that the enemy deserved to die."[83] Soldiers were thus told that their foes were "godless, evil, barbaric, greedy for conquest, even bestial."[84] This propagandizing caused enemies to be dehumanized. Adversaries of various races and ethnicities received this treatment, but Asian enemies, who were "not ethnically and culturally akin to white America," were especially dehumanized.[85] This happened when US forces fought Japanese, Korean, and Chinese troops, and it happened again when they squared off against Vietnamese fighters. Vietnam-era GIs were taught from basic training onward that the VC were inhuman "gooks" and "dinks" that had to be exterminated.[86] In light of this indoctrination, it is not surprising that US soldiers sometimes treated Vietnamese corpses more like playthings or slain animals than dead human beings.

Americans were not the only perpetrators of war crimes in Vietnam. Many veterans say that the Vietcong tortured captured GIs to death and mutilated their bodies. Mason, for example, writes about the horrific fate of two fellow helicopter pilots who were shot down during his tour. The pilots' corpses were found skinned and dismembered, proof that they had been "caught on the ground" by the Vietcong after they crashed.[87] Veteran memoirs, however, contain few references to enemy atrocities committed against civilians. This is appropriate because although "the Vietcong and North Vietnamese killed thousands of civilians . . . most of their atrocities were calculated assassinations of specific individuals."[88] In 1958, two years before the NLF was even officially established, "an estimated 700 government officials" were victims of such murders.[89] In October 1966, Neil Sheehan of the *New York Times* reported that "over the past decade, about 20,000 persons have been assassinated by Communist terrorists."[90] Sheehan added, though, that "the gun and the knife of the Vietcong assassin are . . . far more selective" than US bombing raids that indiscriminately killed dozens of people at a time.[91]

The Vietcong had to be selective in their killing because they could not afford to alienate "the people." The guerrillas relied on South Vietnamese villagers for food and shelter and needed civilian complicity to evade their adversaries, mount ambushes, and plant booby traps.[92] The Vietcong infamously strayed from this pattern of behavior after taking control of the city of Hue during the Tet Offensive. During their brief rule the Communists attempted to "not only destroy the government administration of the city, but to establish, in its place, a 'revolutionary administration.' "[93] Hundreds of Hue residents connected to the South Vietnamese government or the US "imperialists" were executed during this attempted political transformation.[94] The victims were thrown into mass graves;[95] some were buried alive.[96] But the "Hue Massacre," as despicable as it was, did not represent typical Vietcong or NVA conduct.

American troops, on the other hand, were not desperate to cultivate the goodwill of villagers. On top of this, civilians looked like the enemy, often aided the enemy, and were generally of a different race than GIs. Veterans document a wide range of war crimes involving civilians in their narratives, including beatings, rape, and murder. Caputo says that on two occasions his platoon went "nuts," turning into "unrestrained savages" who burned down villages in fits of rage.[97] Lee Childress, a veteran who contributed to *Everything We Had,* an oral history, says a fellow GI shot an old Vietnamese woman because she stole his pack of chewing gum.[98] One of the first veteran narratives published was the ghostwritten memoir of Lieutenant William Calley, the only American soldier convicted for the My Lai murders. Calley is shockingly frank about his participation in the massacre, but he asserts that killing unarmed women and children was justified because they aided the Vietcong.[99]

36    Few narratives can be categorized as definitively antiwar. But many facets of these works put the American venture in Vietnam in a poor light, from the seemingly senseless and ineffective tactics employed by the US military, to the horrendous atrocities attributed to American troops. It seems odd, then, that another reoccurring theme in these accounts is the idea that American soldiers were victimized by Vietnamese civilians, the people who suffered the most in the war. Some reasons for this hatred of civilians are obvious. GIs became enraged when peasants did not warn them about booby traps planted in and around their villages. Many non-combatants actively aided the Vietcong and NVA, and many more were unwilling for various reasons to help American troops find their elusive enemies.

The idea of civilians as victimizers, however, goes beyond the role they played in hindering American combat operations. This concept also involves the feeling that while US soldiers were dying for South Vietnam's freedom, the majority of its citizens were ungrateful and scornful of these sacrifices. One common manifestation of this attitude in memoirs is the portrayal of Vietnamese civilians as motivated by a single-minded desire for American dollars. The great majority of Vietnamese who appear in veterans' accounts are people who tried to part GIs from their money: beggars, prostitutes and their pimps, sellers of shoddy souvenirs, thieves, and hustlers. The people portrayed as the greediest members of South Vietnamese society are the children who constantly swarmed US soldiers wherever they went, pleading for handouts of money, candy, and cigarettes.[100] During James R. McDonough's first day in Vietnam he was initially delighted to see groups of "smiling children . . . with grinning teeth and sparkling eyes" waving at him as he passed by in a jeep.[101] But his delight turned to shock when he leaned out of the jeep to wave back at a group of boys and they instantly grabbed onto his arm and stole his watch.[102]

ARVN soldiers, according to memoirists, also ruthlessly took advantage of American soldiers. These US–allied Vietnamese troops, called ARVNs by GIs (pronounced "arvins"), were allegedly so incompetent that Americans were forced to do all the fighting. The scorn heaped upon ARVN troops in veteran narratives cannot be exaggerated. They are called "pathetic" and "chickenshit sons-of-bitches,"[103] "fucking cowards" and "babies,"[104] and are shown either running away from danger, avoiding the enemy, or acting like happy-go-lucky clowns who would rather lounge around than fight. Puller saw an ARVN unit whose members smoked cigarettes, chatted, and listened to transistor radios while on patrol.[105] Malevolent ARVNs laughed at Downs and his platoon one day as they marched off in search of Vietcong. The Vietnamese soldiers evidently thought it was funny that the Americans were risking their lives in "the bush" while they stayed behind and relaxed in hammocks.[106]

Veterans express the most anger towards Vietnamese who initially hid their greed or contempt by treating GIs with, as Broyles puts it, "exaggerated kindness."[107] Caputo writes of street children who praised Americans when they passed out money and treats, but hurled curses and insults at them when they did not.[108] A formerly friendly beggar child threw rocks at Broyles when he did not offer up his usual handout.[109] Puller was heartened when a village chief invited his platoon to sit down for a lavish meal, but was furious when the chief presented him with a bill after they finished eating.[110] Tobias Wolff worked closely with ARVN troops, and they treated him to a farewell dinner shortly before his tour ended. When his Vietnamese hosts broke into hysterical laughter during the meal he realized that they were not honoring him. Wolff had instead been set up for a cruel practical joke; they had fed him his dog.[111]

Besides being portrayed as pitiless exploiters, most of the Vietnamese who appear in veteran narratives basically serve as scenery or props. These nameless figures are the "villagers," "people," or "gooks" with whom GIs briefly interact as they pass through rural hamlets or urban neighborhoods. The occasional Vietnamese who rise above this status invariably speak in snippets of broken English and GI slang. Caputo, for instance, records begging children saying "Gimme cig'rette gimme candy you buy one Coka. One Coka twenty P you buy," and a teenager who says, "Hokay, hokay. Kill buku VC."[112] Readers are only rarely presented with Vietnamese who seem like real human beings with thoughts, feelings, and complex motivations for their actions.

The Vietnamese, of course, *were* real people, and many had good reasons for acting in ways that American soldiers found annoying or despicable. So many South Vietnamese seemed greedy because prying dollars away from comparatively wealthy American servicemen was their best option for survival.[113] Before the war, the great majority of South Vietnamese lived in rural areas and relied on agriculture, principally rice production, for their livelihoods. But the countryside became increasingly dangerous as the war escalated, and US forces, as part of their "pacification" efforts, laid waste to farmland with bombs and chemical defoliants. These developments led to an exodus of people to cities,[114] causing "the urban population of South Vietnam [to increase] from 15 to 40 percent of the total population" by 1968.[115] The South was "normally a rice-exporting area," but with much of its rice crop destroyed and farmers fleeing their paddies, it was forced to import rice by 1967.[116]

Deprived of their livelihoods, refugees who settled in slums or the shantytowns that surrounded US bases were forced by necessity to get what they could from the Americans. For some this meant working as laborers or maids for the Americans, but for others it meant pursuing more illicit occupations.[117] An example of how this process played out for one South Vietnamese citizen is found in the memoir of Le Ly Hayslip, *When Heaven and Earth Changed Places.* Hayslip spent the first years of her life in a small village, but fled her home after local Vietcong cadre sentenced her to death because they mistakenly believed she was a government informant. She ended up in Saigon and became pregnant while still a young girl. Hayslip first made money peddling black market goods to US soldiers. She later lived with a series of American boyfriends who paid her expenses, a route taken by her sister and many other South Vietnamese women. On one occasion, after being offered what to her was a fabulous amount of cash, Hayslip reluctantly had sex with a GI for money.[118]

In addition to disruptions caused by the random destructiveness of war, the lives of millions of South Vietnamese were upset by their government's "strategic hamlet" program. Initiated in 1962 by South Vietnam's first president, Ngo Dinh Diem, this plan was designed to separate the Vietcong from civilians by forcibly removing peasants from their villages and relocating them to fortified government-run camps.[119] Citizens conscripted into the program had to build their own new housing and were charged for building materials, including the barbed wire strung around the encampments. No matter that the construction supplies were "provided free by the United States" to the Saigon government.[120] People were "motivated as never before to support the Viet Cong" after they suffered such indignities.[121]

The great economic and social upheavals caused by the war also gave many South Vietnamese good reasons to treat American troops with hostility. Prior to the American War, many South Vietnamese followed a way of life that had changed little in thousands of years. Existence for such people revolved around rice agriculture and family, and to move away from one's home village and ancestors' graves was anathema.[122] It is no shock that people whose villages and crops may have been wiped out by American bombs and chemicals were unfriendly towards Americans. Vietnamese were even more likely to dislike GIs if family members or friends had been killed or maimed in the fighting, as was the case for millions of people. In the early 1990s, journalist Martha Hess traveled throughout Vietnam and interviewed people about their memories of American air raids and atrocities. One man posed a question to her that was echoed by other interviewees: "With all the American soldiers did to the Vietnamese people, how can we not hate them?"[123]

Besides their own alienating actions, American troops were tainted in the eyes of many Vietnamese because their stated mission was to protect a government that was inept, oppressive, and thoroughly undemocratic. The corrupt South Vietnamese officials propped up by American power really represented only a small class of urban elites. A majority of the population was Buddhist, but many high-level Saigon politicians and bureaucrats, including President Diem, were Roman Catholics. American troops were also a foreign army, and Vietnam had a long, proud history of resistance to invaders. Such a history led many Vietnamese, rightly or wrongly, to regard GIs as the successors to the French colonialists who were driven out of Southeast Asia in the 1950s.

All of these reasons for hating Americans also served as compelling motivations to join the Vietcong insurgency. Whereas the South Vietnamese government frequently acted imperiously, the Vietcong generally adhered to policies designed to win villagers to its side. The Vietcong also produced propaganda that successfully appealed to ordinary Vietnamese, whereas the Saigon officials were never willing or able to convince many people of their worthiness to rule.[124] One prisoner told his American interrogators that he had joined the Vietcong because he was a poor farmer. The message of Vietcong "propaganda cadres," that he had been exploited by the government and the rich landlords it represented, appealed to him.[125] It is unlikely that many South Vietnamese fully comprehended or believed in the ideology of the Communists who predominated in the Vietcong.[126] Large numbers of Vietnamese nevertheless joined the insurgency because they, like the prisoner, saw it as the only alternative to a distasteful government seemingly controlled by the "puppets" of foreign imperialists.[127]

Another significant reason why many rural South Vietnamese hated their national government was because it drafted thousands of their sons into the ARVN. Rice agriculture in South Vietnam was labor intensive, and when the young men who performed much of that labor marched off to war, peasants suffered greatly. Maintaining a force of rice workers was so important that village leaders frequently helped local men avoid military service. In 1964, farmers in the Mekong Delta blocked roads in protest against conscription policies that emptied their fields of workers. Ever eager to exploit antigovernment sentiment, the Vietcong provided peasants with workers who aided in planting and harvesting.[128]

The major unrest caused by the draft is an indication that there was more to ARVN troops than the scathing portrayals included in American narratives. There is some truth in the memoirists' depictions, as the ARVN's twenty-year existence was marred by failure and defeat. The ARVN was born in 1955 after the United States decided to build an army for its newly formed ally, the Republic of Vietnam (South Vietnam).[129] By the end of 1962, after nearly a decade of American training, advisement, and funding, the ARVN counted 219,000 soldiers in its ranks and seemed to be making some headway against the Vietcong insurgency.[130] It was a shock to many Americans, then, when 1963 began with an embarrassing ARVN defeat. On 2 January, an ARVN "battalion of regulars . . . and a company of M113 armored personnel carriers complete with air and artillery support" attacked a contingent of Vietcong near the village of Ap Bac.[131] The outnumbered guerrillas held off the assault "until nightfall, when they slipped away undetected." The Vietcong, who possessed no armored vehicles or aircraft, shot down five helicopters and killed or wounded almost 200 ARVN soldiers before they retreated.[132]

Andrew Wiest maintains that the ARVN, despite the debacle at Ap Bac, made significant gains against the Vietcong during most of 1963.[133] This progress, however, was wiped out virtually overnight when a November "military coup led to the downfall and assassination" of President Diem.[134] The chaos resulting from the political turmoil in Saigon allowed the Vietcong to build strength and go on the offensive throughout South Vietnam. US President Lyndon B. Johnson finally decided in 1965 that this dire state of affairs could only be rectified with the deployment of American combat troops.[135] The US military subsequently sidelined the ARVN and, in Wiest's words, "simply decided to win the war for them."[136]

America's next president, Richard Nixon, promised the American people that he would bring their boys home from Southeast Asia while fulfilling the nation's promise to protect its Vietnamese allies from Communist aggression. He would achieve this feat through "Vietnamization," a gradual withdrawal of US troops accompanied by the strengthening of South Vietnam's military. Suddenly, fostering ARVN victories became a US priority again. Between 1968 and 1975, the US provided South Vietnam with billions of dollars in military equipment, including top-of-the-line

infantry weapons, tanks, and helicopters.[137] By the end of 1972, South
Vietnam's armed forces (the ARVN plus other branches) "had grown to
over one million men and women,"[138] and its air force was the fourth largest in the world.[139]

Despite America's attempt to prepare South Vietnam to fight on alone,
the post-1968 ARVN was, for the most part, just as disappointing as its
earlier incarnations. The Saigon government withstood the Tet Offensive
in 1968, and the US was encouraged by the ARVN's performance in the
1970 US-led invasion of Cambodia. But Operation Lam Son 719, the
1971 ARVN invasion of Laos, which quickly ended in a frantic, igno-
minious retreat back to South Vietnam, proved that such optimism was
unfounded. News media images of terrified ARVN soldiers hanging off
the skids of evacuation helicopters were broadcasted around the world.
Nixon asserted that Lam Son 719 was a success,[140] but the demoralized
"South Vietnamese forces who retreated from Laos knew they had been
defeated."[141]

In March 1972, Soviet-made tanks and thousands of NVA soldiers
charged across the DRV's border with South Vietnam and sent the ARVN
reeling. South Vietnam eventually turned back the invaders, but only with
the help of massive US air strikes conducted against Communist forces in
both North and South Vietnam. Numerous ARVN troops broke and ran
during the NVA assault,[142] and many others "refused to fight and often
gave up with only token or no resistance."[143] Some deserters took advantage of the anarchy caused by the invasion to loot and prey on civilians. In
early March 1975, with all US troops withdrawn from Vietnam, the North
launched another invasion. As in 1972, thousands of ARVN soldiers fled
before the advancing enemy or quickly surrendered. This time, however,
no American B-52s came to the rescue. By early May, the ARVN had dis-
integrated, the Vietcong flag flew over Saigon's Independence Palace, and
the Republic of Vietnam ceased to exist.[144]

The ARVN's long record of failure and its ultimate total defeat, however, is not the whole story. The reality that over two hundred thousand
members of the South Vietnamese military were killed during the war is
just one indication that not all ARVNs resembled the craven fools found
in veteran memoirs.[145] South Vietnamese troops, in fact, displayed courage and fighting prowess on countless occasions throughout the conflict.
ARVN units were instrumental in the bloody struggle to retake the city of
Hue from Communist forces during Tet. A photograph of ARVN troops
raising their nation's flag over Hue instantly became a symbol of pride for

South Vietnamese patriots.[146] During the retreat from Laos in 1971, the ARVN "4th Battalion, 1st regiment, acting as a rear guard . . . fought a running four-day battle against two entire NVA regiments."[147] The regiment's valiant actions enabled other units to escape to safety.[148] Many South Vietnamese soldiers fought similarly well in other instances during Lam Son 719 and the 1972 invasion. There are even stories of ARVN heroism from the otherwise humiliating last days of its existence.[149] At Xuan Loc, site of the last major battle of the war, the 18th ARVN division held out against the North Vietnamese "for three weeks against overwhelming odds, destroying thirty-seven NVA tanks and killing over 5,000 attackers."[150]

If "the rest of the South Vietnamese had fought as hard and courageously as the 18th ARVN division" at Xuan Loc, James H. Willbanks postulates, "the outcome of the war might have been drastically different."[151] But, in the end, far too few ARVN soldiers fought with the tenacity and skill of the defenders of Xuan Loc. What accounts for this mixed record of inspiring victories and crushing defeats? The ARVN's biggest flaw throughout its existence was poor leadership.[152] Senior positions in the ARVN were dominated by "a cadre of Francophile officers"[153] who ascended through the ranks with the aid of family and political connections. Many of these generals cared more about scheming and securing creature comforts than beating the Communists.[154] A close aide to Nguyen Van Thieu, South Vietnam's president from 1965 to 1975, concluded in 1974 "that more than two-thirds of sixty ARVN generals and full colonels were involved in some form of illegal activity."[155] These revelations probably did not surprise the president, however, since "ample evidence exists that Thieu either tolerated or directly profited" from such corruption.[156]

ARVN's leadership issues consistently affected its performance on the battlefield. When ARVN troops were led ably they usually fought well, but many ARVN officers fled at the first sign of the enemy. South Vietnamese troops who ran from the NVA in 1972 and 1975 were often just following the example of their commanders.[157] The incompetence of one general, Hoang Xuan Lam, helped "wreck both the invasion of Laos and the ARVN's defensive efforts against" the 1972 NVA offensive."[158] Thieu, a former ARVN general himself, made several strategic military blunders during his presidency that likely hastened the demise of the nation he led.[159] Not all ARVN commanders were inept. General Ngo Quang Truong, for instance, was admired by American contemporaries and is described as an eminently capable leader by historians. Men like Truong, however, were not the norm in the ARVN officer corps, especially in its upper echelons.[160]

Bad leadership, however, was far from the ARVN's only problem. Many South Vietnamese men simply did not want to serve in the armed forces of their autocratic government. As a result, "drafted soldiers represented about 65 percent of [the ARVN's] total troop levels, making it one of the most heavily conscripted armies in history."[161] ARVN recruits were generally given inadequate training,[162] leaving many troops with "the sinking feeling that they were no match for the Communists."[163] In the last years of the war, "ARVN officers and men could feed neither themselves nor their families on their dwindling pay."[164] Hungry, cash-strapped soldiers deserted in droves during this period. Others stayed on but sold their weapons and equipment to the enemy for money to buy food.[165]

Neither the occasional triumphs of the ARVN nor the many factors contributing to its failures, however, are included in the memoirs of American veterans. The ARVNs in these narratives win no battles and avoid fighting simply because they are inherently horrible soldiers. Besides occasionally mentioning the extent of poverty in wartime South Vietnam, most veterans do not speak of the real reasons for civilian actions that they witnessed either. Without this contextual information, the few things readers learn about the Vietnamese people are often inaccurate.

The lack of accurate information about the Vietnamese in veteran memoirs is understandable considering how little the average GI really knew about the people they were supposed to save from Communism. Most troops arrived in South Vietnam with a knowledge of the country that did not extend beyond the information imparted to them from "a few brief lectures and a film."[166] Combat soldiers frequently trained in mock Vietnamese villages, but these often preposterous attempts to replicate Southeast Asian rural life on US military bases did little to prepare anyone for the real thing.[167] But if few GIs began their tours with a real understanding of Vietnamese history and culture, fewer still understood the Vietnamese language. Even many advisors, US servicemen whose mission was to work closely with the ARVN, had an inadequate comprehension of Vietnamese by the time they shipped out.[168] A study of advisors who served in South Vietnam in 1969 and 1970 found that "over 57 percent . . . said that their lack of language training detracted 'seriously' or 'moderately' from their duty performance."[169]

Most Americans in the 1960s and 1970s, from ordinary citizens to people in the highest levels of academia and government, knew little about Vietnam.[170] Robert S. McNamara, US Secretary of Defense from 1961 to 1968, admitted years after the war ended that the Vietnamese were "a people whose language and culture we did not understand and whose history, values, and political traditions differed profoundly from our own."[171] This overall American ignorance helps explain why a majority of GIs started their tours knowing so little about Vietnam. What it does not explain is why or how many Americans troops only barely added to their knowledge of the country during their tours. This feat was made possible by the extraordinary efforts of the US military to create an "Americanized world" in South Vietnam.[172] The majority of GIs, by at least 1970, spent their entire Vietnam tours eating American food, listening to American music, watching American television programs, and living in American-style housing.[173] And there was no incentive to venture outside this cultural bubble because GIs were only required to serve in Vietnam for a year. Even many advisors did not bother to familiarize themselves with the difficult language and alien culture of their advisees because they knew another American would show up in six to twelve months to take their place.[174]

———

Although Ketwig hated military life from day one and regarded his assignment to Vietnam as akin to a death sentence, he initially saw his tour in Southeast Asia as a potentially illuminating "adventure" in an "exotic, ancient land."[175] He thought, at first, that his strange new surroundings resembled the "curious cultures" he had read about in *National Geographic* magazine. But, as time passed, Ketwig became disgusted by South Vietnam and its people. He sought an "exotic, inscrutable Asian culture,"[176] but found instead piles of garbage, gift shops selling "cheap gaudy souvenirs," and people interested in killing GIs or cheating them out of their money.[177]

Because of Ketwig's experiences, he offered readers a mostly unfavorable depiction of the Vietnamese. He was not unique, however, for veteran narratives in general branded the local population as money hungry and treacherous. What Ketwig and most other veterans did not include in their narratives were explanations for the Vietnamese behaviors and attitudes they witnessed. If they had, readers would have learned that the South Vietnamese only seemed avaricious because the war had upended their nation's economy. They would have also discovered that many South Vietnamese joined the Vietcong because they wanted to get rid of an

oppressive government; and that ARVN soldiers often avoided battle or
fought poorly not because they were imbeciles, but because they suffered
from terrible training, morale, and leadership.

Veterans are not to blame for the lack of appropriate context in their
memoirs, for most of them, like most Americans, were not privy to the
reasons behind South Vietnamese actions. This highlights the danger of
only using US veteran narratives to understand the war, for these accounts
are fundamentally limited in scope. On the other hand, such accounts are
indispensable sources for those who want to better comprehend what
combat was actually like. The architects and managers of the Vietnam War,
the generals and statesmen, can give us insight into grand strategies, but
ordinary veterans can tell us how those plans played out on the battlefield.
From the accounts of former infantrymen, readers learn what happened
when demands for higher body counts trickled down to platoon level, or
what pacification looked like from the perspective of the GIs who did the
pacifying. And veterans usually depict combat in a realistic fashion; readers
are confronted with a view of warfare that is as authentic as it is terrifying.

# 3

## Race and Racism

Richard Ogden learned how to handle himself in combat soon after arriving in Vietnam. He became an expert with the M-79 grenade launcher and his lieutenant recommended that he be awarded a Bronze Star for battlefield heroics. But for all of Ogden's combat skills, he was still a teenager who had not finished high school and knew very little about the world outside of the isolated, "tiny ranch" where he grew up. Ogden is white, but his childhood playmates were mostly "Indian kids, Mexican kids and Negro kids." His grandmother, the woman who raised him, treated all the neighborhood kids equally, no matter their color, and eventually married an African American man. Racism surely existed in their rural Pacific Northwest community, but Ogden's family shielded him from such attitudes. Consequently, he was "naïve" about America's "racial problems" when he joined the Marine Corps in 1965.[1]

Ogden first realized his ignorance when he met Elgin Johnson, a worldly black marine who had graduated from high school and was headed to college after Vietnam. Johnson taught Ogden about Watts, his Los Angeles neighborhood, and the 1965 riot that occurred there. He also planned to help Ogden, who nicknamed him "Professor," prepare for "the GED test to get [a] high school diploma." Ogden and Johnson became close comrades, and their friendship did not go unnoticed by "Simms," a white member of their platoon. One day, Simms called Ogden a "nigger lover" and warned him that "back home," in Alabama, "people who fraternize with niggers" are lynched. Ogden reacted to this racist onslaught by severely beating Simms. Later in his tour, Ogden's platoon was ambushed by the Vietcong. He was only slightly wounded, but Johnson, who was hit multiple times, died in his arms.[2]

The racism Ogden encountered in the Marine Corps and his cross-racial friendship with Johnson are central issues in his memoir, *Green Knight, Red Mourning*. This makes him unique, however, among white Vietnam veteran-memoirists. A few other white authors make brief statements about racial matters. Tim O'Brien, for instance, mentions in *If I Die in a Combat Zone* that black GIs in Vietnam were resentful because they were assigned to rear-area noncombat positions less often than whites.[3] Most white memoirists, however, make no mention of race or racism at all. As a result, white narratives convey the impression that racial issues were, at most, a marginal problem in Vietnam. In reality, the opposite was true. The war coincided with the most significant African American civil rights movement since Reconstruction, and it was the first conflict fought by fully integrated troops since the United States was founded. African Americans, Latinos, Native Americans, and other minorities served in Southeast Asia in large numbers. Vietcong propaganda highlighted American racism, lionized the Black Panthers, and beseeched black GIs to lay down their arms. In the final years of the war, racial violence was commonplace on US military bases throughout the world.

The lack of attention to racial issues among white veterans would not be a problem if a sufficient number of minority veterans' memoirs were available to provide counterbalancing viewpoints. Unfortunately, this is far from the case. The number of published minority narratives is tiny compared to those written by whites, and the number that achieved any critical or popular success is even smaller. Still, despite their relative rarity and lack of recognition, these accounts are the best available representations of nonwhite soldiers' experiences. Few films[4] and novels focus on minority soldiers, and though several white veterans have written successful novels about the war, they have virtually no minority counterparts.[5]

There were also few historical studies of the African American experience in Vietnam for many years after the war. In recent years, however, historians such as James Westheider, Herman Graham III, and Kimberly L. Philips have fortunately written books about the topic.[6] There is still a dearth of historical scholarship, however, that deals with the Vietnam experiences of other nonwhite groups, such as Latinos and Native Americans.[7] The narratives of black veterans have been used as primary sources by historians who have written about the war, but none have considered these documents worthy of analysis in their own right. In fact, the only existing piece of scholarship that focuses wholly on black veteran narratives is a single journal article written by a literary scholar.[8] Scholars have

48    paid even less attention to Vietnam memoirs written by Latinos and other
non–African American people of color

This chapter addresses these gaps in the scholarship by extensively analyzing the narratives by nonwhite veterans, including memoirs, oral histories, and magazine-article-length narratives. African Americans, Native
Americans, Latinos, and Asian Americans are the primary groups represented in these works. As a whole, these narratives constitute a "countermemory" of the war. Countermemories document past events in ways
that challenge how they are remembered in mainstream culture. African
American countermemory typically does this by "recounting known history in a way that points out racism" and highlights black accomplish-
ments.[9] Minority veteran narratives precisely fit the definition because
their collective portrayal of the war is race-centric. Many nonwhite authors, in fact, viewed nearly every aspect of their Vietnam experiences
through the lens of race.

This is not to say, however, that the countermemory represented in
nonwhite memoirs is exclusively concerned with racial issues, for these
documents offer a complex depiction of the war beyond the question of
race per se. The overall portrayal of the war by minority veterans is best
described as two competing, antagonistic versions: one positive, the other
negative. The first version is not "pro-war" or "hawkish" in its assessment
of Vietnam, as very few minority narratives evince support for US war
aims. Instead, this version offers a portrayal of the war that is reminiscent
of the confirmatory attitude that African Americans and other nonwhites
have traditionally held toward wartime military service. This attitude emphasizes racial cooperation and friendship and expression of pride in the
battlefield performance of one's own racial or ethnic group.

The second version of the war is, in many ways, the opposite of the
first, as it focuses on white racism and self-segregation. It is obviously
influenced by the Black Power movement, which emerged in the late
1960s when young activists broke away from their Civil Rights elders to
pursue more militant approaches to achieving social justice.[10] From the
late 1960s until American troops withdrew from South Vietnam in 1973,
Black Power had a great presence among African American GIs.[11] Nonwhite memoirists often approved of certain aspects of Black Power ideology, including racial separatism, cultural nationalism, and solidarity among
the world's nonwhite peoples.

This competition between the two perspectives on the war occurs
between different narratives. But it also occurs *within* narratives, since

veterans sometimes voice sentiments which support one view then a few pages later make statements that support another, often contradicting the first statements in the process. The complicated nature of nonwhite veteran portrayals of the war reflects overall minority attitudes on the subject. All nonwhites, civilians and soldiers alike, were confronted with conflicting viewpoints on Vietnam, some traditional and others newer and radical. It was difficult for anyone in such a situation to make sense of the war, but even more so for the soldiers who had to fight it.

———

Military commanders, convinced that black men were unfit to fight, relegated African American troops to noncombat duty during the early stages of most American wars before Vietnam. In response, civil rights leaders, convinced that combat duty would be indisputable proof that African Americans deserved the full benefits of citizenship, waged "right to fight" campaigns. Although such campaigns were successful, and black men invariably proved their mettle when given the chance to fight, these advances were usually forgotten or ignored by whites not long after a conflict concluded.[12] Some African Americans initially viewed the Vietnam War in the same way, but attached even more importance to this latest conflict because it was the first fought by a truly integrated military in the nation's history. President Harry Truman desegregated the military in 1948, and some integrated units saw action in the Korean War. But Vietnam was the first real test for the colorblind military.

Early on, many African Americans were encouraged by the fact that blacks and whites were serving jointly in Southeast Asia. African American magazines and newspapers of the period closely followed these developments.[13] A November 1965 *Ebony* article, for instance, featured a large photograph of two young army troopers, one white, the other black, sharing a foxhole near Bien Hoa, South Vietnam. The piece was titled "Negroes in Vietnam: 'We Are Americans Too.'"[14] The mainstream media also highlighted the integrated nature of American forces in Vietnam during this period. In January 1966, the *New York Times* published an article titled "Negro and White Fight Side by Side."[15] As late as May 1967, a *Time* article, "Armed Forces: Democracy in the Foxhole," proclaimed that "Black-white relations in . . . [Vietnam] are years ahead of Denver and Darien, decades ahead of Birmingham and Biloxi."[16] A documentary, *Same Mud, Same Blood,* which focused on the interracial amity that supposedly reigned in Vietnam, appeared on national television later that year.[17]

By 1968, the mainstream media no longer praised the integrated military, and most African Americans—leaders, media figures, and ordinary people alike—had turned against the war even earlier. Testimony to the beneficial effects of integration in Vietnam, however, did live on in nonwhite veteran narratives. Black memoirist Samuel Vance, for instance, states "that in war a man is a man . . . someone you can rely on, and you don't worry about the color of [his] face."[18] Robert Rawls wistfully recalls in *Everything We Had* that he was so close to one white soldier that "he should've been [his] brother."[19] Robert Sanders, coauthor of *Brothers: Black Soldiers in the Nam,* says that the personal relationships he formed with whites were the only positive aspects of his combat tour.[20] Stanley Goff, Sanders's *Brothers* coauthor, laments that the interracial unity he experienced in Vietnam was absent from his life back in the United States.[21]

The Vietnam experience, however, was not all about racial cooperation. Racial segregation was especially prevalent when GIs pursued leisure activities, many of which revolved around alcohol and prostitution. White servicemen in search of a good time in Saigon headed to Tu Do Street, while African Americans went to Khanh Hoi Street, dubbed "Soul Alley." The savvy entrepreneurs of Soul Alley offered black troops "soul food" on restaurant menus and "soul music" on saloon juke boxes.[22] Khanh Hoi Street, *Time* reported in 1970, even had a semipermanent population of "between 300 and 500 black AWOLS and deserters" who lived there as fugitives from military justice.[23] Soul Alleys grew up in other South Vietnamese cities as well, and establishments in other locales around the globe catered exclusively to either black or white American servicemen.[24]

Throughout much of the twentieth century, African American GIs stationed overseas were often banned from bars and brothels frequented by white troops.[25] By the 1960s, segregation of such locales was most often instituted by business owners who acceded to the racist attitudes of their white customers.[26] White racism, however, was not always the only reason behind the segregation of nightlife in the Vietnam era. The "white" saloons and nightclubs of Tu Do Street and other locales were certainly off-limits to nonwhites, at least unofficially. But at the same time, African American servicemen themselves embraced the type of segregation represented by Soul Alley. A 1969 survey found that a majority of black troops in Vietnam *preferred* to eat, live, and socialize only with other African Americans.[27] Soul bars and restaurants are portrayed by black memoirists as wonderful oases where African Americans socialized in familiar, comforting surroundings. Former marine Terry Whitmore describes a soul bar in Japan, a

place which featured "funky music," "huge plates full of chitlins," and lots
of friendly "brothers," as "heaven" for black GIs far from home.[28]

The self-segregation practiced by many black soldiers was strongly
influenced by the Black Power Movement, which rejected earlier Civil
Rights campaigns that focused on integration. Given the violent reac-
tions of whites towards desegregation demands, Black Power advocates
saw the goal of engendering a future society in which "dissimilar peoples
would . . . accept and love one another" as a fantasy.[29] These militants,
echoing Malcolm X and other ideological predecessors,[30] believed that
separation from whites would lead to self-reliance, self-determination, and
true freedom for African Americans. Complementary to racial separation
in the minds of many Black Power activists was the celebration of African
American history and culture, and a general pride in being black.[31] One
can easily see the confluence of these elements of Black Power theory,
separatism and cultural nationalism, in the stories of black soldiers reveling
in the sights, sounds, and smells of Soul Alley.

Self-segregation was the rule not just in bars, brothels, and the like, but
throughout the rear. Some memoirists, however, suggest that the inclination towards racial separatism was so strong that it manifested whenever
and wherever interracial cooperation was not absolutely necessary, including during combat operations. It was in everyone's best interest to work
together during a firefight. But during "quiet times," notes veteran Manny
Garcia, GIs "gravitated towards their own kind," "whites . . . with whites,
blacks with blacks, Chicanos with Chicanos."[32] As this quote suggests,
self-segregation was not a strictly black–white phenomenon. Apparently,
any time two or more soldiers of the same race or ethnicity were present
in a unit, they formed an exclusive social group. And there was apparently
scant intermingling between the various nonwhite peoples represented in
the US military. Even the two biggest Latino groups in Vietnam, Mexican
Americans and Puerto Ricans, clashed with each other.[33]

Self-segregation, however, seems benign when compared to blatant
racism and violence. In the late 1960s and early 1970s, fights between
white and black servicemen broke out on or near US military installations
throughout the globe. A July 1969 fight involving forty-four marines at
Camp Lejeune, North Carolina, resulted in numerous injuries and a cor-
poral's death. Between 1972 and 1973, race riots erupted aboard at least
six navy vessels, the worst being a melee on the aircraft carrier *Kitty Hawk*
that ended with twenty-six black seamen under arrest. Most incidents
of racial violence in the Vietnam era, however, were small-scale events.

Such episodes were especially prevalent in and around establishments that served alcohol.[34] An African American memoirist, Ed Emanuel, for instance, got into a bar brawl that started when a "glassy-eyed drunken" white GI called him a "nigger."[35] Not all unrest took place in bars or even between strangers, however, as some veterans say their own units were smoldering powder kegs of racial enmity. The main reason the tense atmosphere in Garcia's platoon did not degenerate into bloodshed was that each side in a potential racial conflict was "heavily armed."[36] Whitmore threatened to shoot a white platoon mate who made racist remarks,[37] and James A. Daly says that racial discord even plagued Vietcong jungle camps that held American POWs.[38]

African Americans and whites were the main participants in the racial battles that raged within the US military in the latter years of the war. Most Native Americans, Latinos, and Asian Americans were not affiliated with either white or black GI factions. "Ernest," a contributor to Soldados, an oral history of Mexican American veterans, told the warring racial groups in his unit that he wanted to "stay out of it."[39] Another Mexican American, Juan Ramirez, maintained neutrality in black–white conflicts due to his ambiguous racial identity; he was not black and, in his words, "not really white" either. One of Ramirez's white friends could not understand why he was offended by the word "nigger." The Caucasian GI was puzzled because he saw Ramirez as just another white man.[40] Most nonblack minorities did not take sides in fights between blacks and whites, but they nevertheless fought their own battles. Several Mexican Americans say they fought with equal frequency against whites, blacks, and Puerto Ricans.[41]

Also in contrast to accounts that stressed racial harmony are those that suggest nonwhites had more in common with the Vietnamese than their white comrades. Some nonwhites realized that their physical features made them superficially similar to the Vietnamese. Howard Kim, an Asian American, became "overwhelmed" while burying enemy bodies because it occurred to him that the rest of the burial detail was Caucasian, but the corpses all "looked like [him]."[42] A Vietnamese child told "Antonio," a contributor to *Vietnam Veteranos,* another oral history of Mexican American veterans, that the two of them looked the "same."[43] Some minority soldiers discovered, whether they agreed or not, that their fellow Americans thought they looked like the Vietnamese. Asian Americans were routinely called "gooks" by other GIs,[44] and both Latinos and soldiers of Asian heritage were occasionally almost gunned down when they were briefly mistaken for Vietcong. After getting wounded so badly he appeared dead, Roy Benavidez, a Latino, was nearly thrown onto a pile of Vietnamese bodies. In his incapacitated state he heard someone finally exclaim, "That's no damn Gook. That's Sergeant Benavidez."[45]

It was not necessary, however, for a minority soldier to resemble the Vietnamese to identify with them. A 1978 Veteran's Administration study found that almost 50 percent of surveyed black veterans held positive views of the Vietnamese, while a mere 9 percent held negative views. In contrast, over 30 percent of white veterans answered negatively, 27 percent positively.[46] African American memoirs echo these findings. Ed Emmanuel, a black army veteran, for example, "acquired a secret admiration for the Vietnamese people" because, like African Americans, they "were victims of social and economic inequality."[47] "Charley," a *Vietnam Veteranos* interviewee, similarly related to Vietnamese peasants because he was a poor agricultural laborer before becoming a soldier.[48]

One of Charley's platoon mates once nearly killed an old Vietnamese woman "for nothing." He was too afraid to say anything when the GI pointed his firearm at her, but he silently decided: "If he shoots her, I'm going to shoot him."[49] Charley, a Mexican American, thought the woman reminded him of "one of those little *chenchas* in the barrio."[50] Accounts of atrocities against civilians are not unique to minority narratives, but the story above highlights a difference between how whites and nonwhites depict these acts. Some minorities claim that nonwhites, because of their sensitivity to racism and frequent identification with the Vietnamese, never perpetrated war crimes. Native American author Dwight W. Birdwell, for instance, says that mistreatment of civilians was anathema to him because of the "old cruelties inflicted upon American Indians at the hands of the US Army."[51] White GIs, on the other hand, according to some minority memoirists, committed heinous acts against the Vietnamese because of racism. David Parks, an African American who saw white soldiers amuse themselves by luring Vietnamese children onto a busy highway, asserts that "you never [saw] a soul [brother] doing anything like that."[52]

Claims that only whites were responsible for war crimes in Vietnam, however, are not credible. The actions of "Charlie Company," the US Army unit responsible for the My Lai Massacre, are proof of this. Nearly half of the company's soldiers were African Americans and several were Mexican Americans, including their captain, Ernest L. Medina. The captain was open about his hatred of the Vietnamese and personally beat up and terrorized prisoners in the weeks leading up to My Lai.[53] It was

Medina, according to some members of the company, who ordered them to kill any man, woman, or child they saw in the hamlet the US military had named My Lai 4. In the waning moments of the massacre, several witnesses later testified, Medina walked up to a wounded, prostrate woman and shot her in the head.

A few minorities in Charlie Company showed compassion for My Lai's inhabitants. Harry Stanley, a black GI who was labeled a "gook lover" because he taught himself Vietnamese, hid a young boy from his rampaging comrades. A group of Vietnamese survivors later testified that they escaped the carnage with the help of an African American soldier. Leonard Gonzalez, a Latino GI, refused to take part in the killings and tried to comfort a dying Vietnamese girl wounded during the attack. But other survivors said that both black and white soldiers acted as mass executioners. Esequiel Torres, a Latino from Texas, took part in the massacre and, according to his fellow soldiers, tortured "VC suspects" during previous operations.[54] Varnado Simpson, an African American veteran, told interviewers in 1989 that he was "personally responsible for killing about 25 people" at My Lai.[55] The only American who exhibited any real moral courage during the massacre was Hugh Thompson Jr., a white helicopter pilot. He spearheaded the evacuation of a group of villagers out of the ravaged hamlet and threatened to "blow away" GIs who intended to kill them.[56]

Nonwhites may have participated in war crimes, but a number of minority memoirists sympathized with the Vietnamese nonetheless. This attitude is reminiscent of the antiwar arguments espoused by Black Power figures who openly supported the Vietcong and the North Vietnamese, seeing them as allies in a worldwide struggle against white imperialism.[57] Stokely Carmichael, the outspoken Black Power leader, told the crowd at a 1967 antiwar rally that he saw "no reason for black men, who are daily murdered physically and mentally in this country, to go and kill yellow people abroad, who . . . are, in fact, victims of the same oppression."[58] Eager to exploit America's racial problems for propaganda purposes, the North declared its support for the Black Panther Party and Carmichael met with Ho Chi Minh, the president of the DRV, during a 1969 visit to Hanoi.[59] Revolutionary forces in Vietnam also produced radio broadcasts and leaflets that beseeched black GIs to lay down their arms.[60]

Black Power ideology shaped the thinking of many African American troops, as more than half of black GIs surveyed in 1969 saw Vietnam as a "race war" between "whites and nonwhites."[61] Few nonwhite memoirs, however, even those produced by veterans who say they identified with

the Vietnamese, contain direct statements of support for the enemy.[62] In
fact, the idea that America's foes were the natural allies of nonwhite GIs
is passionately denounced in the narratives of several black former POWs,
who were subject to countless hours of racial propaganda. Norman Mc-
Daniel, for instance, a black Air Force pilot captured by the North Vietnamese in 1966, told his captors that the United States was not "waging
a war of genocide . . . against dark-skinned people," but was "in Vietnam
trying to help the South Vietnamese."[63]

Some narratives, however, suggest that many nonwhite troops were attracted to some aspects of enemy propaganda. Perhaps the most commonly
believed piece of propaganda was the Vietcong claim that they would try
to avoid killing black troops.[64] Whitmore surmises that a guerrilla shot
his lieutenant but did not harm him because of this supposed Vietcong
vow. "The lieutenant," he explains, "was white. Charlie [the Vietcong] was
yellow. I'm black."[65] Even a steadfastly patriotic former POW, James E.
Jackson Jr., admits that Hanoi radio broadcasts about the "race situation"
in the United States "made [him] and some of the other Negro prisoners think."[66] The propaganda was ultimately unsuccessful, however, as no
veteran-authors or their friends defected or refused to fight. But revelations that these ideas had widespread currency among nonwhite troops
contribute to a negative portrayal of the war.

Another aspect of the positive version of the war is an emphasis on
personal choice. One manifestation of this concept is the assertion by
nonwhites that they, like their forebears who fought in earlier conflicts,
wanted to go to war. Luther C. Benton, a contributor to *Bloods,* an oral
history of African American GIs, volunteered for combat duty because
he "wanted to see what the war was all about."[67] Two *Vietnam Veteranos*
interviewees, Charley and "Joe," welcomed their Vietnam tours because
they, like other young Mexican American men, wanted to prove their
"machismo."[68] Leroy TeCube, a Jicarilla Apache, was not worried when
a draft notice arrived in his mailbox because it felt natural to follow "the
warrior tradition" of his people.[69] A majority of Native American veterans
surveyed by the Veterans Administration felt the same way, as they said they
joined the military to continue "tribal and/or family traditions." This answer indicates, in the words of Tom Holm, that many respondents "actually
wanted to participate in combat."[70]

Some memoirists also maintain that nonwhites consistently volunteered for the most dangerous combat roles in Vietnam, such as "point
man" (the head of a combat patrol) or "radio man." A few authors

proudly note that they held such roles during their tour, such as Goff, who loved to carry the M-60 machine gun.[71] The effectiveness and distinctive sound of this weapon made it a prime target for enemy gunners. It is impossible to know exactly how many of these risky positions were filled by nonwhites, but there is evidence that many minorities signed up for crack fighting outfits early in the war. Magazines and newspapers noted in the mid-1960s that the army's all-volunteer airborne divisions contained large numbers of black troops.[72] Other studies found that significant numbers of Native Americans and Mexican Americans fought in first-rate combat units.[73] Examples of participation in such groups are found in a number of minority narratives, such as the Special Forces veteran who "volunteer[ed] for the toughest combat training they had" after basic training.[74]

In contrast to an emphasis on individual choice, the negative version of the war asserts that minorities ended up in Vietnam because of white racism. Most minority memoirists apparently came from poor or working-class households, backgrounds that, as chapter 1 demonstrates, made them "draft bait." Minority narratives are full of stories of young men who were drafted after high school because they could not afford college or volunteered because they figured they were going to be drafted anyway. Black veteran Harold Bryant, for instance, became a prime candidate for the draft after financial problems forced him out of college. Afraid that if drafted he, like two of his friends, would be sent to the marines, he enlisted in the army.[75]

Half of black enlisted men polled in 1969 believed that "blacks [were] assigned more hazardous duty than whites."[76] Many memoirists wholeheartedly agreed with this charge. More minorities than whites, they claim, were ordered to "walk point," carry the M-60, or act as "forward observers," soldiers who directed artillery fire and airstrikes onto enemy targets. Forward observers often ventured deep into hostile areas to fulfill their missions, which is why a racist white sergeant evidently took great pleasure in making Parks an "FO."[77] Another feature of the negative version was the claim that minorities were overrepresented in Vietnam. Garcia alleges that whites were the minority in infantry units,[78] and Emmanuel asserts that "black soldiers became a majority . . . of the fighting force" in Vietnam.[79] Fenton A. Williams, an African American army doctor, noticed that infantry units were comprised of an inordinate number of black soldiers. While still in Vietnam he obtained casualty statistics that confirmed his suspicions.[80] Luis Martinez claims in *Everything We Had* that

"25 to 35 percent of those Puerto Ricans who had served in Vietnam had 57 either been killed or wounded."[81]

Even if some of these allegations are exaggerated, they nonetheless reflect an important reality: African Americans and other nonwhites saw combat in numbers out of proportion to their respective percentages of the US population. The disproportionate sacrifice of African American troops is evident in their casualty rates. Almost a quarter of Americans killed in Vietnam in 1965, the first year of major ground combat for US troops, were black. The African American casualty rate fell to acceptable levels after the Pentagon enacted measures to remedy the problem, but this was not achieved until 1968.[82]

US military personnel in the Vietnam era were placed in one of five racial categories: Caucasian, Negro, American Indian, Mongolian, or Malayan.[83] This outdated and imprecise classification system makes it possible to accurately determine the casualty rate for only one other minority group besides African Americans: Native Americans. In an inverse of the situation for blacks, Native American soldiers did not suffer a disproportionate overall casualty rate, [84] but they *were* overrepresented in Vietnam.[85] Mexican Americans and Puerto Ricans also probably fought in disproportionate numbers, but this is not definite because Latinos were not counted separately. The author of a 1971 study, however, concluded that "Mexican American military personnel have a higher death rate in Vietnam than all other servicemen" because a high percentage of casualties from southwestern states had Spanish surnames.[86]

The reality that nonwhites served in much greater numbers than their percentage of the population in itself presents a negative image of the war. But the negative impression is even more pronounced in some memoirists' explanations of why overrepresentation occurred. African American leaders criticized the high casualty rate for black troops early in the war, but Black Power activists offered a new critique of this phenomenon in the late 1960s. These militant voices alleged that the overrepresentation of blacks in Vietnam was evidence of a genocidal "federally sponsored" plot to wipe out the "cream of black youth."[87] This charge, of course, was false. The disproportionate presence of nonwhites in combat was primarily an unintended consequence of military manpower allocation policies. Soldiers in the Vietnam era were assigned to military occupations based on how well they did on the Armed Forces Quotient Test (AFQT), an evaluation similar to civilian "IQ" tests. Mostly because of educational disadvantages, nonwhites generally performed worse than whites on the

AFQT. And since low scorers were usually channeled into combat training, an inordinate number of minorities ended up on the frontlines.[88]

The Black Power explanation for high African American troop levels may have been incorrect, but memoirists suggest that many black GIs believed it nonetheless. Goff learned in basic training that his fellow African American recruits thought "blacks were being drafted for genocidal purposes."[89] Emmanuel believed in this conspiracy theory himself, as he calls the presence of large numbers of black soldiers in combat an example of "institutionalized genocide."[90] His support of this dubious concept is ironic since he was the member of an all-volunteer reconnaissance unit. Emmanuel's platoon, moreover, was nicknamed the "soul patrol" because it was composed entirely of African Americans.[91] These were top-notch soldiers who obviously wanted to fight, not pawns of a racist government. The contradiction between Emmanuel's genocide claims and the nature of his service is an excellent example of positive and negative versions of the war appearing within the same nonwhite narrative.

Another feature of the more traditional depiction of the war is satisfaction in the fighting abilities of one's own race. Vance states that the focus of his memoir, published during the war, is "the Negro in Vietnam and his ability to wage war and lead men in battle."[92] Emmanuel says African American troops "were inherently superior warriors" who possessed unmatched "raw physical agility."[93] Mexican Americans declare that the men of La Raza were the best and bravest soldiers in Vietnam, always eager to fight and willing to take on any challenge. Miguel Gastelo proudly asserts that Mexican Americans always volunteered for the most hazardous duties on the battlefield.[94] Some Native American veterans allege that they were frequently put in harm's way because their superiors assumed that "Indians" were natural warriors. Many did not appreciate this stereotype,[95] but memoirist Delano Cummings happily insists that his Native American heritage made him innately skilled in the ways of war.[96]

Nonwhite portrayals of the war, however, are always complicated, so even expressions of racial pride often feature negative elements. Some African Americans who attest to the battlefield prowess of black soldiers also denigrate the fighting skills of whites. Bryant says he discovered in Vietnam that whites were less "tough" and "more cowardly than [he] expected."[97] Even Vance, who promotes the power of an integrated military to break down racial barriers, contends that while black GIs never shirked combat duty, "white boys" faked illnesses to avoid the frontlines.[98] This combination of black pride and antiwhite sentiment was common among

African Americans during the Black Power era. A majority of blacks polled by *Newsweek* in 1969 "saw the war as evidence that Negroes make better combat soldiers than whites."[99] Nor was this attitude confined to African Americans. Several memoirists claim that their fellow Mexican Americans were universally courageous in Vietnam, but many whites *and* blacks, conversely, were poor soldiers.[100]

Susan Jeffords argues that "a prominent motif of Vietnam films, personal narratives, [and] novels" is that the shared experience of combat led to "the eradication of social, class, ethnic, and racial boundaries" in American military units.[101] Another scholar contends that Vietnam War novels employ this theme so extensively that the soldier characters in these books are "de-racialized."[102] A few white veterans stress racial togetherness in their memoirs as well. Frederick Downs asserts in the *Killing Zone,* for instance, that racial strife was unknown in his platoon of "whites, blacks, Puerto Ricans, Mexican-Americans, an Indian, and a Japanese-American."[103] The problem with white narratives, however, is not *how* they portray racial issues, but that most do not talk about race at all. Readers learn from white memoirs something worse than the idea that racial harmony was the rule in Vietnam: the false notion that race played almost no role in the history of the war at all.

The near absence of race in white narratives is likely unintentional. Most whites, presumably, either did not recall any racial issues that arose during their tours, or did not consider them worthy of inclusion in their narratives. A memoir is not an objective or comprehensive history of the war, but an account of one veteran's experiences. Such a limited outlook guarantees that some issues will not receive proper attention. The problem is that prominent white perspectives on Vietnam are not counterbalanced with a satisfactory number of nonwhite counterparts. Analysis of minority memoirs confirms their value, as it shows they represent a counter-memory of the war that puts race in the forefront. Depictions of the war offered by nonwhite veterans reflect the complexity of nonwhite thinking on Vietnam. Two primary attitudes vied for control in minority communities: a positive, traditional version and a negative version that adhered to certain facets of Black Power ideology. The latter overtook the former in the minds of most nonwhites by war's end, but memoirs show that a competition between these two conceptions, at least for veterans, continued into the post-Vietnam era.

# 4

## Men, Women, and Vietnam

Michael Lee Lanning, a onetime army officer, assiduously recorded his daily activities in a journal while in Vietnam. Years later, he converted his journals into two memoirs, *The Only War We Had: A Platoon Leader's Journal* of Vietnam,[1] and *Vietnam, 1969–1970: A Company Commander's Journal*.[2] Lanning's books are about the lives of infantry grunts in the Nam, men who inhabited a world in which they mostly interacted with other men. But women, too, played a part in his Vietnam experience. Married only a few months before deploying to Southeast Asia, Lanning thought constantly about his wife, Linda, especially after she became pregnant. Linda is a periodic presence in his books, but so too are Vietnamese prostitutes and bar girls.[3] Although Lanning did not participate himself, he cheerfully abetted the sexual exploits of his men. He allowed them to construct a temporary brothel,[4] and laughed along when one "grabbed a mini-skirted waitress and threw her on top of the table" during a drunken night on the town.[5] Lanning and his men also ridiculed female Red Cross workers, whose supposed lack of sexual attractiveness was said to "improve" after extended months in Vietnam.[6] Not all of Lanning's encounters with women, however, were lighthearted. He once ordered the body of a female Vietcong leader to be displayed "half-naked" in a public square.[7]

Lanning's memoirs are not unique. Women appear throughout veteran narratives as wives, girlfriends, prostitutes, enemy soldiers, and in other capacities. And, as Karen Dixon Vuic puts it, "sexuality permeated the war zone's military culture."[8] Several scholars have written about these subjects. Susan Jefford's *The Remasculinization of America: Gender and the Vietnam War,* published in 1989, tackled, among other issues, the relationship between masculinity and popular culture treatments of the war.[9] In more recent years, historians such as Vuic and Heather Marie Stur have explored the wartime experiences of American and Asian women. These authors also explore how American military men, from grunts to generals, viewed and interacted with women in Vietnam.[10]

No scholar, however, has yet done a comprehensive study of how veteran narratives deal with the interrelated themes of women, sex, and masculinity. This chapter does just that by elucidating what happened, why it happened, and how it was portrayed. What veterans say happened is that a generally misogynist attitude animated US troops in their interactions with women. Why did this happen? Memoirs and supplemental materials show that the sexist behaviors of GIs were rooted in military and mainstream cultures that were hostile to women and promoted the belief that sex was a just reward for men at war. Racial stereotypes common among GIs heightened the intensity of these feelings when they dealt with Asians. How do memoirists depict male–female interactions? Most make light of or romanticize episodes in which GIs mistreated women, demonstrating that they still approved of such conduct years after their Vietnam tours ended.

The perspectives of veteran-memoirists are limited because all but a few of the most successful memoirists are men. It is for this reason that this chapter uses the narratives of American and Vietnamese women to provide different viewpoints, just as minority narratives in chapter 3 offer a countermemory of racial issues. These women experienced many of the same events as male authors, and their recollections often support male accounts. Specifically, the same sexist conduct recalled by men was reported by women as well. Female observers, however, were the chief victims of this debauchery. Their accounts, subsequently, stand in sharp contrast to laudatory male representations of sex and gender issues.

In recalling their first impressions of South Vietnam, memoirists invariably list the same few items: sweltering heat and noxious smells, the poverty of local people, the urban squalor, and the visibility of the sex trade. Saigon and other South Vietnamese cities teemed with bars, massage parlors, and brothels that catered to GIs. Shantytowns made of cardboard and flattened beer cans that sprung up on the outskirts of American bases featured makeshift bordellos known as "boom-boom houses."[11] If a soldier could not make it to a brothel, the prostitutes might come to him. Some veterans insist that women selling their bodies had the uncanny ability to appear wherever US troops were present. Former officer Robert Hemphill, for instance, caught one of his men having sex with a prostitute only minutes after his company established a perimeter around a hostile village.[12]

Memoirist portrayals of wartime South Vietnam as a nation plagued by prostitution is accurate. The sex trade was already booming in 1962 when President Ngo Dinh Diem's sister-in-law, Tran Le Xuan, better known as Madame Nhu, accused US servicemen of leading Vietnamese girls down "decadent paths."[13] By the time Diem was ousted from power in 1963, there were only about sixteen thousand American military advisors in South Vietnam. But thousands of US combat troops arrived in 1965, and Saigon's formerly fashionable Tu Do Street was transformed into a thriving red-light district by the end of the year.[14] In 1966, US Senator J. W. Fulbright was criticized by the White House for his description of the South's capital as "literally . . . an American brothel."[15] Other cities were affected as well. Pleiku saw an influx of eight thousand to ten thousand "bar girls" (essentially a euphemism for prostitute) when US troops were first allowed within its limits in 1968.[16]

Many South Vietnamese were enraged by the prostitution explosion. Elites railed against miniskirt-wearing "harlots," women's groups protested in the streets,[17] and ordinary people complained about the problem in newspaper letters to the editor.[18] The South Vietnamese government, in response to this clamor for societal reform, battled prostitution throughout its existence. Diem, South Vietnam's first president, outlawed the sex trade in the early 1960s, but the ban was repealed soon after his assassination. The South's last president, Nguyen Van Thieu, also issued antiprostitution edicts during his tenure. But all of these measures, including a 1971 attempt to shutter bars and nightclubs, were ineffectual. In 1977, two years after the Communist takeover, a Catholic nun who oversaw the rehabilitation of prostitutes estimated that there were three hundred thousand former sex workers living in South Vietnam, sixty thousand in Saigon alone.[19]

It is no mystery why prostitution flourished in South Vietnam during the war. Sex workers have followed armies since the beginning of warfare. Women are often forced to sell themselves to survive in wartime, especially when a nation's economy is ravaged by conflict. Thousands of women fled violence and economic disaster in the countryside for Saigon and other urban centers during the 1960s and 1970s. A few thousand women directly aided the war effort by joining the Women's Armed Forces Corps or the National Police. Many others worked in civilian jobs vacated by men engaged in military service. Still thousands more found employment related to the US military presence. Some of these women worked for the Americans as maids or typists, but countless others catered to GI needs by becoming "taxi dancers," bar girls, "hostesses," or outright prostitutes.[20]

Many of the reasons why American soldiers patronized prostitutes in Vietnam are also as old as war itself. Young men are more inclined to pay for sex when they are far away from home, removed from the social constraints of their communities for perhaps the first time. Living in an all-male society, such as the military, that encourages members to prove their masculinity by abusing alcohol and being sexually promiscuous is another factor. And moral and legal restrictions against prostitution may seem pointless for men who face death and injury every day. One need only look to the habits of American troops during World War II to understand that the actions of GIs in Vietnam were far from extraordinary. The bordellos of North Africa, Italy, France, and numerous other locales around the globe were full of US troops during the 1940s.[21]

Many veterans suggest, however, that there was another reason for the widespread use of prostitutes in Vietnam: the tendency of officers at all levels to tolerate, even promote such habits. A number of memoirs include stories of low-level officers who accepted prostitution, and several former officers say they condoned and engaged in such behavior themselves. The best example of this comes from *About Face,* the memoir of David Hackworth, a former army officer who became famous for excoriating the military's Vietnam strategy during a 1971 television interview.[22] Hackworth periodically organized trips to a bordello called "Madame Nhu's House of Pleasure" when his men needed to "let off some steam."[23] He sympathized with the sexual needs of his troops because he remembered that as a young soldier during the Korean War "you were always horny and never discriminating; you weren't looking for love, you were looking for pussy."[24]

Several veterans go a step further by alleging that the US military operated its own brothels in Vietnam. Harold Bryant says in *Bloods,* for example, that the army operated a collection of "whorehouses" near An Khe that were "built . . . for soldiers to go relieve themselves."[25] Such claims may seem farfetched, but they are nevertheless based in fact. Although it was officially illegal for servicemen to pay for sex, the military nonetheless oversaw at least two "semiofficial bordellos" near Pleiku and An Khe.[26] A 1966 *Time* article explained that the An Khe brothel, a twenty-five-acre complex nicknamed "Disneyland," was Vietnamese-owned, but US military police "patrol[ed] the compound and check[ed] the pass of each GI entering."[27] In order to control the spread of venereal disease, its workers were required to make a weekly visit to a clinic "for a medical examination . . . and a U.S.-provided shot of a long-lasting penicillin-type drug."[28]

Most narrated sexual encounters took place in Vietnam, but many memoirists also write about paying for sex during Rest and Recuperation ("R&R") trips to other countries. In an effort to boost morale, every GI in Vietnam was granted a weeklong excursion to one of ten destinations (most of them in East Asia) during his or her one-year tour.[29] Some soldiers spent R&R with wives, girlfriends, or relatives in Honolulu,[30] but the other cities on the list were swarmed with American soldiers only interested in, as Robert Mason puts it, "drinking and fucking."[31] According to most narratives, buying sex was the primary activity of GIs during their week away from Vietnam, and numerous memoirists unabashedly say they slept with prostitutes during R&R. Many soldiers chose a city solely for the rumored attributes of its sex trade, and they swapped information about how to find the cheapest brothels and the most attractive women. Tim O'Brien's army pals, for instance, discussed where to find the girls who "performed the best tricks."[32]

Several veterans recall that military authorities approached R&R in the same tolerant way it dealt with prostitution in Vietnam. Tracy Kidder and his fellow R&R travelers were briefed at the beginning of their trip by an officer who offered tips on how not "to catch something" from "ladies of the night."[33] Similar stories appear in other narratives, and the *New York Times* reported in 1968 that the "R and R center" in Taipei took "a realistic attitude" by handing out brochures that warned about disease and instructed GIs how to avoid paying too much for sex.[34] As in Vietnam, the military did not just tolerate the illegal R&R activities of soldiers, but it also facilitated their search for sex. The tourist agency contracted by the US military to handle Bangkok travel plans booked soldiers in hotels that provided female companions for "$25 a night or the flat rate of $125 for a seven-day week."[35] Mason and Charles R. Anderson both chose "girl-friends" from lineups of women during R&R.[36]

The ostensible reason for the military's lenient attitude towards prostitution was that it was part of a practical approach towards controlling the spread of venereal disease. Commanders decided that if they could not stop soldiers from paying for sex they could at least control their access to prostitutes. This situation was wholly in keeping with how the US armed forces dealt with the sex trade throughout much of the twentieth

century. During both world wars, the US government, determined to secure the moral purity of the nation's fighting men, passed tough laws that
effectively shut down the sex trade in America for the duration of those
conflicts. Military commanders overseas, however, often found it nearly
impossible to enforce bans on prostitution, especially when stationed in
countries that featured legal brothels. Military leaders reacted to this state
of affairs by quietly regulating prostitution, believing this to be the most
efficient way to prevent "VD" outbreaks. Semiofficial brothels, which were
staffed by US military policemen who kept order and made sure GIs used
"prophylactic stations," sprung up all over Europe and Asia during World
War II.[37] In Japan, Thailand, and other nations occupied by American
troops after the war, unofficial regulation of prostitution continued unabated into the Vietnam era and beyond.[38]

The desire to prevent the spread of disease was definitely a primary
motive behind the military's toleration of prostitution, but a less acknowl-
edged reason for this attitude was the belief that "men at war required the
sexual use of women's bodies."[39] This attitude can be seen in Hackworth's
outings to the local bordello and in other accounts of officers who allowed or encouraged their men to pay for sex. American women who
went to Vietnam offer numerous accounts of such actions as seen from an
outsider's perspective. Women recall "obscene" USO shows that featured
scantily clad entertainers,[40] rows of pornographic magazines for sale in the
PX, and strip shows held at officers' clubs.[41] Former army nurse Winnie
Smith witnessed, to her great embarrassment, the standard lecture about
VD, condoms, and "clean" women given to troops at the beginning of
R&R.[42]

Media coverage of R&R and Vietnam's bar girls shows that these
ideas were not restricted to the military, but widely accepted in American society. Mainstream periodicals "blithely quoted the going rates for
prostitutes" in Vietnam[43] and published photographs of grinning GIs on
R&R cavorting with foreign women.[44] Articles were often written in a
wry tone, employing phrases like "perfumed professionals"[45] and "leggy
blonde."[46] This writing style conveyed the feeling that buying sex, at least
for soldiers, was a perfectly understandable practice. Further evidence of
the currency of this attitude was Fulbright's subsequent apology for his
controversial brothel comment. The senator clarified that he was not "ma-
ligning the brave young Americans in Vietnam," but warning of the impact
GIs "behaving in the way that is to be expected of men at war" might have
on a "fragile Asian society."[47]

Sexism was also evident in veteran portrayals of prostitution. Memoirs often contain extended anecdotes about prostitution that serve as humorous breaks in books otherwise dominated by death and destruction. Mason writes about a clueless commanding officer who gave his men "permission" to substitute masturbation for trips to the local brothel.[48] And Richard E. Ogden tells the story of a hapless GI who "contracted something" from a prostitute in Okinawa.[49] Memoirs, which often feature reconstructed dialogue, frequently contain exchanges in which soldiers joke and brag about encounters with prostitutes and other sexual exploits. The humorous tone of these stories sometimes makes it seem as if an author is encouraging readers to participate vicariously in these moments of soldierly camaraderie.

The jocularity of veterans' sex stories indicate that they still believed, years after the war ended, that visiting prostitutes was a normal activity for fighting men. Save a few exceptions, the closest veterans come to criticizing prostitution is expressing dissatisfaction with their personal experiences. Such memoirists were disgusted by the foulness of brothels or disliked the physical appearance of prostitutes. Anderson was disappointed when a woman he paid for sex was an unenthusiastic "dud" who did not feign romantic interest in him.[50] Almost no one condemns prostitution because of its deleterious effects on society and the lives of sex workers.[51] Often there is a tinge of nostalgia in veterans' accounts of their youthful sexual exploits. Some memoirists, like a veteran who felt "like a king" during R&R in Hong Kong because his paid companion was "a beautiful broad," candidly proclaim their fondness for "the good old days."[52]

Memoirists often describe visits to prostitutes in graphic, near-pornographic detail. This is partly a manifestation of the trend among Vietnam veterans to eschew self-censorship. Another factor is the willingness of post-Vietnam publishers to print material once considered unfit for distribution.[53] It is obvious, though, that veterans also describe sex in such explicit detail to entertain and titillate readers. This motive is most evident in memoirs that describe R&R as a voyage to a sort of sexual fantasyland. Perhaps veterans or their publishers felt compelled to include explicit sexual content in memoirs out of the assumption that films and novels had led consumers to expect Vietnam War stories to feature sex. Just as likely, though, this is another example of the memoirists' inclination to romanticize illicit sex and frame it as a natural pursuit of men at war.

Though most of the sexual encounters in personal narratives are brief and businesslike, some veterans say they established (or at least tried to

establish) legitimate romantic relationships with Asian women. A few fell
for "regular girls," such as Anderson and Tobias Wolff, who both pursued
women who worked on American bases,[54] and William Broyles Jr., who
dated a student in the English language class he taught.[55] Some deride
lonely GIs who naively fell in love with prostitutes,[56] but others claim
that they found real love inside brothels. John Ketwig became engaged to
a prostitute during his R&R trip to Malaysia, and even signed on for an
extra year of service in Thailand because it kept him relatively close to his
fiancée.[57] Stanley Goff almost deserted from the army to stay in Taiwan
with a woman he "rented" during his R&R trip to Singapore.[58]

Such unions were beset by a host of obstacles, but over eight thousand Americans nevertheless returned to the United States with Vietnamese "war brides." US servicemen also married women from Thailand and
other Asian nations during the Vietnam era.[59] It is likely that some of these
couples met during R&R excursions. The great majority of these affairs,
however, ended when soldiers left Vietnam at the end of their tours, if
not before. The more than seventy thousand children of American fathers
living in South Vietnam at war's end is one indicator of a great number
of failed wartime relationships. Some were undoubtedly the unplanned
children of prostitutes, but others were the products of seemingly loving
unions that ended when their fathers returned to America.[60] No memoirist says he fathered a child in Vietnam, but all those who say they fell in
love during their tours left their girlfriends behind when they returned
to the United States. Broyles vowed he would find a way to stay with his
girlfriend, but in the end he took the "freedom bird" back to America
without even telling her goodbye.[61]

These doomed love affairs show that even women who were part of
ostensibly loving unions were often treated by GIs in much the same way
they treated prostitutes, as sexual objects that could be thrown away when
convenient. One probable reason for this behavior was the sexual mores
of mid-twentieth-century America. Although the Vietnam War took place
while the Sexual Revolution was underway in the United States, a traditional double standard in sexual matters was still firmly in place. Premarital
sex became progressively more common in America after the 1920s, but
a majority of men in the post–World War II era still wanted to marry
virgins.[62] Men solved this paradox in earlier times by visiting prostitutes.[63]
In the twentieth century, however, most single men satisfied their sexual
desires by dividing women into "bad girls" and "good girls." Bad girls had
sex, and for this reason were acceptable "to play with," but men looked

for a chaste good girl when it came time for marriage. A bad girl was someone a man saw as beneath him, sometimes because she was of a lower social class, but often just because her willingness to have sex supposedly indicated immorality.[64] Coming from this cultural background, it is no wonder that GIs showed little respect for the women, prostitutes or not, with whom they had sex during their tours.

Racial attitudes played a significant role in shaping these attitudes toward Asian women. Veteran narratives suggest that most GIs regarded "love-making with a Vietnamese," in the words of former Green Beret Donald Duncan, "as a higher form of masturbation."[65] Anderson explains that the most common way for an American soldier to satisfy his sexual urges was to "stare at an underfed, prematurely aged, Vietnamese woman and fantasize her into Raquel Welch."[66] Statements such as "good-looking for a Vietnamese,"[67] or "She's a pretty woman . . . for a gook," are common.[68] When GIs encountered an attractive Asian woman, Vietnamese or otherwise, they usually assumed she had some Caucasian heritage. Members of Johnny M. Clark's marine platoon, for instance, assumed a Vietnamese girl was "half French" because she was "too fine to be all gook."[69]

The depiction of individual Asian women in veteran narratives is also marked by racism. In most memoirs, Asians of any sex or age are rendered essentially as scenery, or maybe props with which American soldiers interacted. They are hardly ever afforded more than peripheral roles in a narrative. This kind of portrayal particularly applies to prostitutes, the largely voiceless, faceless nonentities referred to as "the whore" or "the girl." The only Vietnamese prostitutes referred to by name are those with demeaning monikers, such as "Madame Fred," "Slash,"[70] or "Butch."[71] In the rare instances in which prostitutes are quoted, their dialogue solely consists of broken English, GI slang, and obscene propositions.

Both veteran memoirs and Vietnam War novels sometimes contain stories of love affairs between Asian women and American soldiers. Female love interests in most novels are portrayed as western stereotypes of Asian women: meek, submissive, and only interested in serving the needs of their men.[72] This manner of depiction also basically applies to Asian paramours in memoirs, except that the personalities of the real-life women are even more muted. Readers never learn the names of most of these women. One veteran calls his wartime paramour "this woman,"[73] and Goff knew his Taiwanese R&R girlfriend only as "Suzanne," surely a pseudonym she used with GI customers.[74] Like female novel characters, a typical Asian woman in a memoir had "no real life before" she met her American lover, "and none that is pursued after" the love affair ends.[75] It is telling that one of the few females described by a male memoirist as strong, independent, or intelligent, is a white European woman W. D. Ehrhart met in Hong Kong.[76]

A different perspective on American–Asian couplings is clearly needed, and Le Ly Hayslip's memoir luckily provides one. Hayslip eventually decided that immigration to the United States was her son's best chance at a good life, but she needed an American husband to make this possible. She eventually married a civilian contractor, a kind, decent man who brought her to the United States in 1970. But Hayslip first endured three other liaisons with American men, all of them disastrous. The first man tried to convince her to work as a topless dancer to impress his friends; the second was deported after he almost strangled her to death in a drunken rage; and the third, though he promised to never abandon her, left one day for the United States without warning.[77]

Not all the sexual encounters between Vietnamese women and American men were consensual. US military records show that more than fifty servicemen were convicted of rape, "rape and assault," attempted rape, and related crimes in Vietnam. The actual number is certainly higher since it is highly probable that the great majority of such crimes were never reported.[78] A precise accounting of such atrocities may not be possible, but veteran memoirs suggest that they were not uncommon occurrences. These accounts, in fact, "are replete with . . . acts of rape, gang rape, assaults on women, torture, mutilation, and murder."[79] Ketwig saw those Green Berets torture a woman to death.[80] Arthur Woodley Jr. says in *Bloods* that he saw GIs rape, torture, and murder Vietnamese women on several occasions.[81] Even narratives that do not feature such crimes sometimes include stories of thwarted rapes and assaults. Clark, for instance, prevented a Vietnamese woman from being gang-raped by members of his own platoon.[82]

The rape of Vietnamese women by American soldiers is also a common element in films and print fiction about the war. Some scholars argue that rape is often glorified or trivialized in these mediums,[83] but this is never the case with nonfiction narratives. The lighthearted tone memoirists use to describe nearly every other type of sex act is entirely absent from accounts of rape. Some record these acts without comment, while others express horror and outrage. The few individuals who forestalled rapes are obviously proud that they took stands against immoral acts. It would appear that rape, unlike patronizing prostitutes or harassing women, did not fall within the limits of acceptable conduct for American fighting men.

Rapes may have been common in Vietnam during the war, but not all Vietnamese women were victims. Many women fought in the struggle against the United States, and the Vietcong propagandized the existence of these "long-haired warriors."[84] It is significant, then, that women who were held up as examples of feminine strength only appear in veteran memoirs as wounded and abused, or dead and defiled. Such is the case with the female sniper whose corpse was stripped naked and thrown into a fire,[85] or the captured guerrillas who were nearly gang-raped.[86] Though they represented some of the bravest women in Vietnamese society, these soldiers invariably appear in veterans' memoirs as stereotypically weak and helpless. It is not veterans' fault that the only times they came into contact with these women they were in such degraded situations, but the fact remains that narrative readers see female fighters only in this context.

American women in Vietnam, most of them nurses, Red Cross workers, and USO entertainers, were referred to as "round eyes" or "round-eyed women" by GIs. Any American female could theoretically be called a round eye, but in practice the term was essentially a synonym for Caucasian. The great majority of memoirists are white, and they give no indications that the women they called round eyes were not white. Only a tiny percentage of American women who went to Vietnam, in fact, were women of color. The US Army Nurse Corps was "an overwhelmingly white organization" during the war,[87] and the total number of black Red Cross volunteers sent to Vietnam was in the single digits.[88] African American women were such a rarity in the Nam that "the attention [they received] from black GIs could be overwhelming."[89] Gloria O. Smith, "Miss Black America," who toured South Vietnam in 1970, said that her visit was much appreciated by black soldiers because so few of the female entertainers who performed for the troops were African American.[90]

Whereas Asian women were described as generally unattractive by memoirists, American women were held up as the epitome of beauty. Many narratives make it seem as if every GI in Vietnam was obsessed with round eyes and practically driven mad by their scarcity. On the rare occasions that soldiers were able to see such women in person, such as USO shows featuring "ripe American beauties,"[91] it was a cause for celebration. Sydney, Australia was a popular R&R destination for GIs principally because most of its female inhabitants were Caucasian.[92] The veteran who so enjoyed the Hong Kong R&R he spent with a "beautiful broad" originally wanted to go to Australia. In East Asian cities, he explains, "you're dealing with slant eyes. I wanted to see something with round eyes."[93] This outlook was shared by an army helicopter pilot who told *Time* in 1967 that he enjoyed his visit "down under" because it "was great just to see white girls with round eyes again."[94]

Referring to women as round eyes is the height of objectification, and narratives show that most GIs judged the worth of American women in Vietnam solely on their physical characteristics. Women considered attractive were ogled and lusted over, but those who did not live up to the ideal of round-eyed beauty were ridiculed and dismissed as unworthy of attention. The two types of American women that appear most frequently in memoirs, military nurses and Red Cross volunteers dubbed "Donut Dollies," were frequent targets of this kind of behavior. Ehrhart muses that Dollies were "invariably homely" and overweight.[95] Some soldiers called Dollies "Biscuit Bitches"[96] or, in reference to the color of their uniforms,[97] "Blue Blimps."[98] Mason and his drinking buddies purposefully offended a group of disgusted nurses to drive them out of a Vietnamese bar. The men disapproved of the nurses because they were all "elderly" or "very plump."[99] On top of the abuse Donut Dollies received for their alleged lack of physical beauty, both Clark and another memoirist, Alfred Bradford, ironically claim that at least some of these women were part-time prostitutes.[100]

Most veterans portray the GI obsession with round-eyed women as an amusing quirk, and episodes in which soldiers harassed and ridiculed nurses and Donut Dollies as moments of harmless fun. These depictions show the need for a different viewpoint, and luckily there are narratives that tell what it was like to be a round eye in Vietnam. Many of these women felt great affection for the men they entertained or cared for,[101] and were glad "that their feminine appearance and gentle demeanor reassured wounded and frightened soldiers."[102] Some enjoyed all the attention they received as women in a predominately male environment. Former army nurses quoted by Vuic, for instance, say they felt "in charge" because they "had their pick" when it came to choosing boyfriends.[103] Such women experienced a "sexual freedom" in Vietnam that was not easily realized in Cold War America.[104]

But many other women hated being a constant center of attention and treated, as former army nurse Mary Reynolds Powell put it, as an "object of curiosity."[105] Smith was always barraged with the stares, whistles, and catcalls of GIs when she walked down the street in Vietnam.[106] She eventually became "fed up" with being "treated like a piece of meat at the market."[107] Lynn Hampton, another former nurse, was propositioned for sex innumerable times by servicemen, often complete strangers, during her tour in Vietnam.[108] GIs sometimes taunted Donut Dollies with crude jokes or offers to trade cash for sexual favors.[109] Former Dolly Cherie Rankin was groped by a group of soldiers who believed the rumor that Red Cross workers were "loose" women.[110]

Nurses, Donut Dollies, and other American women in Vietnam are almost never more than marginal figures in veterans' memoirs, but another group of American women, wives and girlfriends left behind in the United States, play an even smaller role. These women send letters and figure in lonely soldiers' reminiscences of their prewar lives, but that is usually all. GIs saw Vietnam as such a faraway, alien, almost surreal place that they called the United States the "World," as if it were another planet.[111] Combat troops felt especially alienated from the comparatively cushy existence of American civilians. Therefore, it is perhaps accurate for these documents to portray people back in the World, men and women alike, as remote and inconsequential to the experiences of troops in Southeast Asia.

Numerous narratives include memories of basic training, virtually all of which centered on the verbal abuse spewed at recruits by drill instructors. A favorite "DI" tactic was to tell recruits that their "sweethearts" were "whores" who were sleeping with other men. O'Brien and his fellow army trainees were taught in "basic" that "Women are villains. They are creatures akin to Communists and yellow-skinned people and hippies."[112] In light of such indoctrination, it is fitting that the few instances in which women back home became the center of attention in narratives is when they committed acts of betrayal. Several veterans write of heartless wives or girlfriends who broke up with soldiers through "Dear John" letters. Broyles explains that the arrival of such a letter was regarded as the worst thing that could befall a GI in Vietnam.[113] Ehrhart called his girlfriend a "bitch" and a "whore" after reading the Dear John letter she sent him. He also vowed to kill her if he made it home alive.[114]

———

Broyles writes the following in his memoir about the strange effects war has on human sexuality:

> Most men who have been to war, and most women who have
> been around it remember that never in their lives was their
> sexuality so palpable. War cloaks men in a costume that con-

ceals the limit and inadequacies of their separate natures. It gives them an aura, a collective power, an almost animal force.

War heightens all appetites. I cannot describe the ache for candy, for taste; I wanted a Mars bar more than I wanted anything in my life. And that hunger paled beside the force that pushed us toward women, any woman. Even the homeliest women floated into our fantasies and lodged there. Too often, we made our fantasies real, always to be disappointed, our hunger only greater.[115]

In many ways, veteran narratives portray Vietnam as a very masculine experience: groups of men mostly fighting other men, proving their manhood, and forming deep bonds with each other. But women are never really absent from memoirs because of the "hunger" that Broyles writes about, along with the never-ending quest to satiate that hunger. The women GIs most often used to fulfill sexual appetites, Asian prostitutes and girlfriends, frequently appear in memoirs. American nurses and Donut Dollies do not often appear in narratives as sexual partners, but they are included anyway because their sexual attractiveness was constantly evaluated by male GIs.

Veteran narratives are valuable sources for learning about how American soldiers viewed and interacted with women in Vietnam. Analysis of these documents shows that, overall, GI attitudes towards women were sexist and, in regards to Asian women, racist. Memoirs, along with secondary sources, demonstrate that these attitudes were found not only in the armed forces, but in the media and other segments of American society in the Vietnam era. Just as important as what happened and why is how these issues were portrayed, and for the most part, veterans' depictions, no matter when they were recorded, indicate an adherence to the sexist and racist attitudes of the Vietnam era. Because published Vietnam War narratives are dominated by male American veterans, it is their perspective that reaches the widest audience. This viewpoint is undoubtedly worthwhile, but the narratives of Vietnamese and American women highlight the pitfalls of relying on just one side of the story when trying to understand the past.

# 5

## The Return Home and Life after Vietnam

During the year that memoirist Lynda Van Devanter spent working as a nurse at an army hospital in Pleiku, South Vietnam, she witnessed scenes of unspeakable carnage almost every day. Tending to a constant stream of hideously wounded Americans and Vietnamese gradually destroyed her former self, an idealistic young woman eager to serve her country. This old self was replaced with a cynical, bitter, and emotionally exhausted veteran. Thoroughly disillusioned with the war, her country's leaders, and the values that led her to join the military, Van Devanter was overjoyed when her Vietnam tour ended in June, 1970.[1] When the plane taking her and other military personnel back to the United States finally took off, she and other passengers exuberantly shouted "Vietnam sucks!!" and then "there was laughter and hugging and tears."[2] They "were the lucky ones," as Van Devanter saw it, who "had made it out alive."[3]

Not long after this outburst of joy, however, "a vague uneasiness" fell over Van Devanter and the other veterans as they started to wonder "what [they] would face back in the real world."[4] She realized soon after her plane landed in California that this uneasiness was justified. Van Devanter needed to get to San Francisco International Airport to catch a flight to her hometown, but the army bus would only take her as far as the Oakland Army Terminal. Finding no public transportation available, she decided to hitchhike the twenty or so miles to San Francisco. Because she had hitchhiked numerous times in Vietnam, she saw no problem in trying to "thumb a ride" on an American highway. Van Devanter, however, claims that numerous passing motorists, instead of picking her up, shouted obscenities, made vulgar gestures, and threw trash at her. The drivers, she assumed, were enraged at the sight of her uniform. Eventually someone pulled over: two men in a Volkswagen bus, the driver sporting long hair, wire-rimmed glasses, and a "peace sign" T-shirt.[5] The unkempt man behind the wheel offered Van Devanter a ride, but when she approached the bus she discovered the real reason he had stopped:

> But the guy slammed the door shut. "We're going past the airport, sucker, but we don't take Army pigs." He spit on me. I was stunned.
>
> "Fuck you, Nazi bitch," the driver yelled. He floored the accelerator and they both laughed uncontrollably as the VW spun its wheels for a few seconds, throwing stones back at me before it roared away. The drivers of other passing cars also laughed.
>
> I looked down on my chest. On top of my nametag sat a big gob of brownish-colored saliva. I couldn't touch it, but I didn't have the energy to wipe it away. Instead, I watched as it ran down my name tag and over a button before it was absorbed into the green material of my uniform.[6]

Van Devanter eventually made it back home, but due to emotional problems related to the trauma of her war experiences, her homecoming troubles continued. Plagued by nightmares and depression, and feeling alienated from family and friends, she spiraled out of control into a life of alcoholism and "one-night stands."[7] During those years of despair she "thought a lot about suicide," but "always chickened out" when it was time to follow through on her "perfectly organized" plans to kill herself.[8] Van Devanter eventually married, her depression and the frequency of her nightmares subsided, but an "emptiness" still "lurked in a dark corner of [her] soul."[9]

In the final pages of Van Devanter's memoir, *Home Before Morning*, she finally gets on the path to really healing her psychological wounds after becoming involved with the Vietnam Veterans of America (VVA). Talking with other veterans at VVA meetings made her feel better, and soon after joining the group she founded the VVA's Women Veterans Project, an initiative to raise public awareness of female veterans. Van Devanter is enrolled in college at the book's end, on her way to a psychology degree, and her work with the VVA has led the Veterans Administration to recognize women veterans for the first time. These successes, coupled with an eye-opening return trip to Vietnam, caused her to proclaim that even though the war left a permanent scar on her psyche, "the emptiness is gone now."[10]

Although *Home Before Morning* is primarily concerned with Van Devanter's Vietnam experiences, a large portion of the book is devoted to her postwar life. Her narrative is far from atypical in this respect. Many veteran memoirists included much information about their post-Vietnam experiences in their books, and in some of these works, the author's life after returning home is more important than his or her war stories. A few veteran-writers covered Vietnam in a first memoir, then released one or two subsequent books that covered their postwar experiences. Veterans who added their stories to oral histories also often spoke of their lives after Vietnam. The final two chapters of the 1981 oral history compilation, *Nam: The Vietnam War in the Words of the Men and Women Who Fought There,* are devoted to accounts of reentry into civilian life.[11]

The focus of veterans on their postwar lives typifies how the war has been remembered in the United States. From the late 1960s onward, journalists, academics, politicians, filmmakers, and other opinion makers have paid much attention to what happened to Vietnam veterans after they came home. As the war receded further into history, the actual conflict veterans fought in became almost secondary in importance. In 1978, Hollywood ended its longtime avoidance of the war by releasing two high-profile "Vietnam movies," *Coming Home* and *The Deer Hunter,* both of which intensely focused on the readjustment troubles of returning soldiers.[12] By the time the Vietnam Veterans' Memorial was dedicated on the National Mall in 1982, many Americans were probably more familiar with stories of spat-on soldiers and mentally disturbed veterans than the My Lai Massacre or the Tet Offensive.

*Home Before Morning* is not only typical of veterans' memoirs because it includes much information on Van Devanter's post-Vietnam experiences, but also because many of these experiences are commonly found in other narratives. Many memoirists say that they were disrespected and insulted by the American public when they returned home. Numerous others admit to suffering from nightmares and "flashbacks," using alcohol and drugs to dull their pain, and having difficulties interacting with loved ones. Finally, a number of veterans say they eventually overcame their readjustment difficulties and made successful lives for themselves, often doing so with the help of fellow veterans. These experiences can be organized into three stages: painful homecoming, struggles with psychological problems and readjustment to civilian life, and eventual healing and hope for the future. In many narratives, as in *Home Before Morning,* these stages unfold in the chronological order outlined above. In some cases, they play out over the course of multiple memoirs written by a single veteran.

The depictions of postwar lives offered in *Home Before Morning* and so many other memoirs, however, are, in several ways, inaccurate and misleading. These accounts, first of all, incorrectly assert that antiwar activists and everyday Americans frequently abused returning military personnel. Stories of spat-upon soldiers have been around since the 1970s. In recent years, however, scholars have put these claims in doubt. Another problem with veteran memoirs is that they do not provide the accurate historical context needed to compare Vietnam veterans' experiences with those of veterans of earlier wars. Authors who fought in Vietnam suggest that their postwar troubles were unique because previous generations of soldiers supposedly had few readjustment troubles and were welcomed home as heroes. Historical scholarship and other sources reveal, however, that veterans of pre-Vietnam conflicts did not always have wonderful, trouble-free homecomings. Many of the most popular authors, finally, became famous or wealthy before or after their books were published, and an inordinate number earned postgraduate degrees after the war. The successes of these authors belie the fact that many Vietnam veterans struggled to readjust to the civilian world for years after the war's end.

The perception that Vietnam veterans were denied the warm reception accorded to soldiers of America's past wars pervades their narratives. Van Devanter states in *Home Before Morning* that "when the soldiers of World War II came home, they were met by brass bands, [and] ticker-tape parades, and people . . . thankful for their service."[13] Her own homecoming, of course, did not at all resemble these iconic images. Philip Caputo somberly notes in *A Rumor of War* that he and other soldiers who fought in Vietnam did not "return to cheering crowds, parades, and the pealing of great cathedral bells."[14] W. D. Ehrhart's return to the United States in no way corresponded to the "brass bands, victory parades . . . and starry-eyed girls clinging to his neck" that he had once envisioned.[15] Army veteran Frederick Downs fully expected to be met with "a band and welcoming committee" when his plane landed in the United States, "just like movies and books had always portrayed." But, to his immense disappointment, nothing of the sort happened.[16]

The theme that veterans were unappreciated is also present in other types of homecoming stories. Winnie Smith and her father, for instance, went shoe shopping soon after she returned from Vietnam. Her father proudly announced to a clerk that his daughter had just returned from the war, but the man was wholly uninterested.[17] Even when civilians were interested in hearing about newly returned soldiers' experiences, however, their comments and questions often sounded stupid or insensitive to veterans' ears. A family friend offhandedly asked Brian Delate, for instance, who was a helicopter door gunner in Vietnam, "Well, did you kill anybody?"[18]

Van Devanter, however, was not simply denied a parade when she came home, but was ridiculed by soldier-hating civilians. Similar claims are made in other veterans' narratives. Johnnie M. Clark's plane was met by "war protestors" who "threw tomatoes and waved Baby Killer signs,"[19] and Robert Mason was called a "murderer" by a girl working at a gift shop in an American airport.[20] Another veteran was insulted and spat on when he tried to walk down a Berkeley, California street in his uniform. When he ducked into a bar to escape this torrent of abuse, people inside threw peanuts at him.[21]

Such episodes are reminiscent of accounts published in Bob Greene's 1989 book, *Homecoming: When the Soldiers Returned Home from Vietnam*. In the mid-1980s, Greene, a syndicated newspaper columnist, posed this question to his readers: "Were you spit on when you returned from Vietnam?" He received "well over a thousand" responses to his query, and 132 of them were eventually published verbatim in *Homecoming*. About half were written by veterans who said they were spat on, and they are downright shocking.[22] Page after page, letter writers tell of landing in US airports and being assaulted by "hippies" who threw eggs, spit in their faces, and called them "baby killers" or "army pigs."[23] While antiwar protestors are blamed for most of these incidents, ordinary citizens, including "a middle-aged lady"[24] and three "nicely dressed" teenagers,[25] are identified as attackers as well. One letter writer asserts that "verbal and physical abuse of returning Vietnam veterans" was not just meted out by "hippies," but by people "in all levels of American society."[26]

In part because of Greene's book, stories about reviled soldiers became an integral part of America's collective memory of the Vietnam War. Several scholars have nevertheless posited convincing arguments that question the validity of such accounts. A 1995 study published in *Social Problems* analyzed 380 articles about demonstrations against the Vietnam War published in the *New York Times*, the *Los Angeles Times*, and several other newspapers. The sociologists who conducted the study found no reports in any of the publications "of behavior as crude as spitting on . . . or directly taunting" returning soldiers.[27] Only 6 percent of protests covered by the newspapers "could, using a liberal interpretation, classify as anti-troop activity initiated by activists themselves."[28] In most cases, these "anti-troop" protests involved National Guardsmen, military police, and other "uniformed personnel in a domestic policing role," not regular GIs.[29] Moreover, 15 percent of the surveyed newspaper articles were "clear and explicit . . . accounts of movement members speaking or acting favorably toward ordinary enlisted men."[30]

Jerry Lembke, a sociologist and Vietnam veteran, provides additional arguments against the legitimacy of spat-upon soldier stories in his 1998 book, *The Spitting Image: Myth, Memory, and the Legacy of Vietnam*. He contends that not only are there no Vietnam-era newspaper accounts of protestors harassing GIs, there is no contemporary documentation for such stories whatsoever—no photographs, court transcripts, police records, or FBI files.[31] Protestors, Lembke points out, "undoubtedly would have been arrested" if they were regularly accosting soldiers at the nation's airports.[32] A newspaper photographer or "some enterprising GI" with a camera, he adds, would have taken a picture of such an incident at some point.

Because GIs returned from Vietnam to a country deeply divided by the war, it is possible that there were isolated incidents in which veterans were insulted, maybe even spat on. It is unlikely that such episodes were widespread, however, because the antiwar movement generally supported veterans and active-duty military personnel throughout the war.[33] A prevailing theme at peace protests was that American soldiers should be brought home before any more were killed in a senseless conflict. In late 1969, for example, forty thousand civilians gathered in Washington, D.C., to participate in the "March against Death." Every participant in this two-day event carried a candle and a placard inscribed with the name of an American soldier killed in Vietnam.[34] GIs participated in the movement from the beginning, but antiwar activism among the troops, including those stationed in South Vietnam, was rampant after Tet. Thousands of soldiers participated in peace demonstrations, signed petitions against the war, and met to discuss their opposition to the conflict in "GI coffeehouses" operated by civilian activists.[35] Antiwar organizations in the United States lauded the actions of such soldiers and declared 1968 "the 'Summer of Support' for the GI antiwar movement."[36]

Many memoirs, however, feature attacks on veterans that are perpetrated by ordinary citizens, not "radicals" or hippies. Other sources, however, do not support the suggestion that most Americans despised Vietnam veterans during and immediately after the war. Harris polls taken in 1971 found that 80 percent of Americans "strongly agreed" that Vietnam veterans deserved respect, and only 3 percent of veterans described their reception from people their own age who did not serve as "not at all friendly." The results were essentially the same when veterans and nonveterans were asked these same questions eight years later.[37] A 1980 US Senate study based on these polls, *Myths and Realities: A Study of Attitudes toward Vietnam Era Veterans*, concluded that even though the American public thought the war was a mistake, it did "not hold the warrior responsible for the war."[38]

There are other less quantifiable reasons why spat-upon soldier tales are not credible. Greene was convinced that such stories were true, but admits that certain aspects of them do not "make sense." He questions whether hippies would have "the nerve" to spit on soldiers "fresh from facing enemy troops in the jungles of Vietnam," or if GIs, as *Homecoming* accounts claim, would have done nothing in response.[39] Additionally, most of these anecdotes, notes Christian G. Appy, follow the same basic formula: "A returning veteran . . . walks through the [airport] terminal, a hippie, often a girl, approaches, calls him a baby-killer, and spits at him."[40] Even harassed-veteran stories that do not closely follow this narrative almost always contain one or more of its essential elements, such as someone using the epithet "baby-killer." The "sameness" of these accounts, Appy argues, calls into question their "literal truthfulness."[41]

Veterans' accounts of being spat upon may be exaggerated, but it is unlikely that they consciously lied about their homecomings. The inaccuracy of these accounts is instead probably due to the inherent malleability of memory. The letters published in *Homecoming* were written in the late 1980s, and no memoirs or oral histories featuring harassed-veteran stories were published before 1981.[42] The years separating memoirists' homecoming experiences and when they recorded these episodes are crucial. As time passes, memories are inevitably distorted by external influences, and after the war ended veterans were bombarded with the notion that they were figuratively and literally spat upon when they came home.

*No Victory Parades: The Return of the Vietnam Veteran*, a book based on interviews with two hundred veterans, came out in 1971, while the war was still in progress. The book's author, Murray Polner, states in the introduction that the people he talked to were "unlike the returning servicemen of earlier wars, they have not been celebrated in film or song; there are no more victory parades."[43] Around the same time that *No Victory Parades* was published, the news media and mental health professionals were starting to disseminate the claim that large numbers of Vietnam veterans were suffering from readjustment problems because they did not have proper homecomings. In 1973, the image of the "forgotten" veteran was contrasted in the media to the attention and praise directed at the American POWs who were released as part of the agreement that ended the war.[44] In the 1980s, thousands of Americans tried to make up for the supposedly poor treatment of Vietnam veterans in years past by cheering them on as they marched in "welcome home" parades.[45]

The exact origin of the idea that Vietnam veterans were spat upon is unclear, but a similar event is portrayed in *Coming Home* (1978). At the beginning of the film, chanting antiwar demonstrators accost one of the main characters soon after he disembarks from the plane that has brought him home from Southeast Asia. The first major manifestation of the spat-upon soldier motif was in the 1982 film *First Blood*, starring Sylvester Stallone. *First Blood* is about John Rambo, a disturbed Vietnam veteran who goes on a rampage in a small American town after being hassled by a local sheriff.[46] Near the conclusion of the movie, Rambo, who is cornered by the police and experiencing an emotional breakdown, identifies the source of his troubles:

> And I did what I had to do to win. But somebody wouldn't
> let us win. Then I come back to the world and I see all those
> maggots at the airport. Protesting me. Spitting. Calling me baby
> killer, and all kinds of vile crap. Who are they to protest me?
> Huh?[47]

Subsequent Vietnam War films perpetuated the concept of the abused veteran. A character in 1987's *Hamburger Hill* says that "hippies" at the airport threw bags of "dog shit" at him when he returned to America after his first combat tour.[48] In *Rambo: First Blood Part II* (1985), Rambo tells another character that when he came home from Vietnam he "found another war going on. . . . A war against the soldiers returning."[49] By the end of the 1980s, the concept of the spat-upon veteran was so ingrained in the minds of Americans that it affected how they viewed the Persian Gulf War of 1991, America's first major military conflict since Vietnam. In the lead up to the war, the Bush administration and proponents of its Mideast policies urged Americans to support the troops poised on the border of Saddam Hussein's Iraq. Supporting the soldiers in the Gulf, according to this point of view, meant doing the opposite of what most Americans had supposedly done a generation earlier: undercut and abuse the soldiers who fought in Vietnam. During this prewar period, the news media reported that GIs were worried about being spit on, and antiwar groups struggled to distance themselves from the cruel acts allegedly committed by their Vietnam-era predecessors.[50]

Stories of spat-upon veterans were part of a larger shift in the collective memory of the Vietnam War that occurred in the years following its conclusion. There was widespread "antimilitarist" sentiment in the United States in the immediate postwar period, with many Americans regarding Vietnam as a lesson against military interventionism. One sign of this shift in societal attitudes was the removal of war from childhood pursuits. The war games, films, and toys that many post–World War II boys grew up with were discredited in post-Vietnam America. The presidency of Ronald Reagan indicated, however, that the war had not fully extinguished what Tom Engelhardt calls American "victory culture." Reagan was the chief advocate for the rehabilitation of Vietnam into a "noble cause" that was thwarted by protestors and weak-willed politicians. According to this new conception of the war, Vietnam veterans were the war's chief victims because, as Rambo laments, their leaders and fellow citizens would not let them win. This revisionist interpretation of the war suffused American culture in the 1980s and has gone mostly unchallenged in the years since.[51]

For veterans with post-traumatic stress, hostile or indifferent civilians were the least of their worries. In the final years of the war, medical authorities and journalists were already finding that some soldiers who fought in Southeast Asia had psychological issues linked to their service. Early on, before they were completely understood, these problems were grouped under the unofficial heading of "post-Vietnam syndrome," or PVS. Most Vietnam veterans afflicted by war-related psychological maladies, however, were eventually diagnosed with post-traumatic stress disorder, or PTSD, a condition officially recognized by the American Psychiatric Association (APA) in 1980.[52]

PTSD, according to the APA's *Diagnostic and Statistical Manual of Mental Disorders,* is not restricted to Vietnam veterans, or even to war veterans in general. It can potentially strike anyone who has "been exposed to one or more traumatic events—events that are psychologically distressing and

outside the range of usual human experience."[53] People who suffer from       83
PTSD exhibit "three classes of symptoms":

> Re-experiencing of the traumatic event, avoidance of stimuli
> associated with the event or numbing of general responsiveness,
> and increased arousal. Examples of re-experiencing phenomena
> include recurrent, intrusive, and distressing memories or dreams
> of the event(s). Avoidance and numbing symptoms include
> deliberate efforts to avoid or escape thoughts or feelings associ-
> ated with the event(s) and feelings of detachment or estrange-
> ment from others that develop after the trauma. Symptoms
> of increased arousal include difficulty falling or staying asleep,
> hyper-vigilance, exaggerated startle response, and physiologic
> reactivity in the face of events that symbolize or resemble an
> aspect of the traumatic event.[54]

In 1983, after years of speculation about the mental health of Vietnam
veterans, the US Congress launched an investigation into the issue dubbed
the "National Vietnam Veterans Readjustment Study (NVVRS)." Completed in 1988, the NVVRS found that 30.6 percent of male Vietnam
veterans, and 26.9 percent of female Vietnam veterans, "had full-blown
[PTSD] at some time during their lives," while 15.2 percent of men and
8.5 percent of women had PTSD when interviewed for the study.[55] In addition, 11.1 percent of men, and 7.8 percent of women studied currently
had "partial PTSD." The NVVRS also concluded that "the prevalence of
PTSD . . . is significantly, and often dramatically, higher among those with
high levels of exposure to combat."[56]

More veterans with PTSD and other mental issues were able to get
the help they needed because of the widespread recognition of Vietnam
veterans' readjustment difficulties. The downside of this heightened awareness was the formation of the crazed Vietnam veteran stereotype. Beginning in the early 1970s, stories of veterans who were supposedly turned
into murderous criminals by their Vietnam tours became a favorite topic
in the news media, and the psychotic veteran became a common character
in popular culture.[57] In a 1979 *Esquire* article titled, "The Violent Vet," Tim
O'Brien asserted that television shows and movies offered two distinct, yet
equally offensive, versions of the mentally damaged Vietnam veteran character. Television programs, he argued, generally portrayed veterans as de-
ranged killers, while Hollywood, "aiming for psychological understanding

and insight," produced veteran characters who were "baleful, explosive, spiritually exhausted, tormented, with brains like whipped cream."[58]

O'Brien was indignant about popular culture's portrayal of Vietnam veterans as mentally unbalanced, and his criticisms have been echoed by other prominent veterans.[59] It is all the more interesting, then, that a great number of memoirists readily admit that they experienced Vietnam-related psychological problems. Very few veterans explicitly say they had post-traumatic stress after they came home, but the psychological issues they list in their narratives often fall into one of the three classes of PTSD symptoms. Some were haunted by reoccurring war-related dreams, such as James R. McDonough, who dreamt about comrades who died in battle,[60] or Nathaniel Tripp, who dreamt about army helicopters landing in his suburban neighborhood.[61] A number of veterans felt alienated from family and friends when they came home, avoided social interactions, and felt as if their feelings were numbed. Smith became a virtual recluse when she came home, rarely leaving her bedroom and avoiding contact with her concerned parents and friends.[62] Bob Kerrey, the onetime governor of Nebraska, was evacuated to the United States after he was severely wounded in Vietnam, but requested he be sent to a hospital that was as far away from his family as possible.[63] Rod Kane labels himself a "combat bachelor" because his emotional issues forestalled potential postwar marriages.[64]

Perhaps the most common psychological symptoms reported in narratives are those that fall into the third PTSD category, "increased arousal." Many veterans had insomnia when they returned to the United States, were startled by fireworks and other loud noises, and could not "turn off" the constant state of vigilance that developed over months of combat duty in Vietnam. In the months following Bruce Weigl's return to the United States, he prepared for potential attackers when inside buildings by always choosing a seat facing the door, his back to the wall.[65] David Donovan reflexively looked for ambushes and booby traps more than a decade after coming home from Southeast Asia.[66]

Many people try to deal with PTSD by self-medicating with alcohol and drugs,[67] and several memoirists who had combat-related stress became substance abusers. Smith spent most of those solitary weeks in her room drowning her sadness in alcohol.[68] Weigl states on the first page of his memoir that he "lost whole years" of his life to drug addiction during a period of "black postwar grief."[69] Kane got drunk every night for a year after returning to the United States.[70] Robert Mason and Lewis Puller Jr.

devote large portions of their memoirs to the horrible years after Vietnam they spent trying to assuage psychological turmoil with alcohol.[71]

The first mental health professionals who focused on the post-traumatic stress of Vietnam veterans brought their patients together to talk about their problems in "rap groups."[72] This form of group therapy eventually became the preferred method of treatment for Vietnam veterans with war-related mental illnesses.[73] By 1981, almost two hundred "store-front vet centers" featuring group therapy existed around the country.[74] Several memoirists turned to this kind of treatment when their readjustment problems became unbearable. Former marine Albert French, for instance, writes at length in his memoir about participating in a therapeutic rap group. He became plagued by thoughts about comrades who died in battle almost twenty years after his tour ended. Desperate for help, French went to his local "Vietnam Veterans Center." He and a group of fellow combat veterans met at the center once a week and shared their troubles, from the anger they felt at spouses who did not understand their struggles, to the nightmares that kept them awake at night.

Rap group sessions were helpful to veterans because they involved talking to other veterans, the only people who could possibly relate to what they were going through. The members of French's group called themselves "brothers" because of their shared status as veterans, and he only felt comfortable with the therapist who led the meetings because he too had served in Vietnam.[75] Arthur Woodley Jr., an ex–Special Forces soldier, started a veterans group in his neighborhood to talk about the war and revive "the comradeship that [they] had in the service."[76] Robert Rawls had terrifying nightmares about the war, but could not talk to anyone about them, including his wife, except for other veterans in his rap group.[77] Memoirists who did not formally participate in group therapy also eased their postwar troubles by spending time with fellow veterans. Ron Kovic suggests that the first time he felt any relief from the crushing depression that characterized his post-Vietnam life was when he became an active member of Vietnam Veterans against the War (VVAW).[78]

Besides associating with others who served in Vietnam, memoirists used other means to heal psychological wounds and overcome readjustment setbacks. Several veterans suggest that they appreciated and benefited from the public events staged around the country in the 1980s aimed at giving Vietnam veterans the recognition they were supposedly denied years earlier. Kane and Donovan end their memoirs with accounts of joyfully marching in Reagan-era "welcome home parades."[79] Mason and Ketwig did not march, but happily watched such events from the side-lines.[80] Matthew Brennan says he finally "came home" from the war when he visited the Vietnam Veterans Memorial in Washington, D.C.[81] French cites a trip to a replica of the memorial set up near his home as a turning point in his recovery. Visiting "The Wall" gave him "a real good feeling" because it afforded him his first chance to "say goodbye" to friends who died in Vietnam.[82]

The theme of eventual recovery from postwar problems, psycholog-ical or otherwise, is also manifested in the great academic and profes-sional success achieved by memoirists. Of the fifty-one veterans whose memoirs serve as the basis of this book, thirty pursued higher education after they came home, seven of these garnering bachelor's degrees, and nineteen earning MBAs, PhDs, and other postgraduate degrees. A number of memoirists were famous before their memoirs were published, with most acquiring this status as either authors or politicians. Kerrey, John McCain, and Colin Powell all wrote Vietnam memoirs, and all went on after the war to play prominent roles in national politics. O'Brien, Weigl, Larry Heinemann, and several others produced critically acclaimed fic-tional works about the war before and after publishing their memoirs. Three others, French, Tobias Wolff, and Tracy Kidder, authored successful non-Vietnam novels before their memoirs were published. Several of the most celebrated memoirs, such as Caputo's *A Rumor of War* and Kovic's *Born on the Fourth of July,* were themselves the source of their authors' fame. All of the authors, of course, achieved the rare distinction of writing a published, notable book.

From the late 1960s onward, various commentators have spread the word that Vietnam veterans were unique in US history because they, un-like the veterans of earlier wars, were not received as heroes by the Ameri-can public. Vietnam veterans were not only scorned, so the story went, but they also endured psychological problems that were unknown among the returning soldiers of earlier generations. Adding to the strength of these ideas is that they are repeated by Vietnam veterans themselves in memoirs, oral histories, and other personal narratives.

These concepts, regardless of their prevalence, are nevertheless false. In the aftermath of virtually every war fought by the United States in its history, its soldiers experienced postwar difficulties that would be famil-iar to any reader of Vietnam narratives. When the victorious Continental Army left the battlefield in 1783, they were met with "few, if any, official welcomes . . . no homecoming parades, no flags flying nor bands playing,

[and] no smiles from many of the civilians whose fortunes had waxed with their liberties."[83] Veterans flooded the cities of the newly independent United States in search of work, but employment was scarce. When ex-soldiers became destitute, they could not, at least in the immediate postwar years, expect any help from the government they had fought to create. Such exasperated veterans led Shay's Rebellion, a 1786 armed uprising of poor farmers in western Massachusetts against a judicial system that had sent many of their kind to debtors' prisons.[84]

Decades later, when the bloody American Civil War finally ended, thousands of Union soldiers marched in victory parades in Washington, D.C., and other cities, and newspapermen, politicians, and ordinary Americans lavished admiration and gratitude upon the men who defeated the Southern rebels.[85] The glow of victory quickly faded, however, when many Northern veterans could not find work, became homeless, or were preyed upon by swindlers and thieves. Some former soldiers concealed their history of military service because veterans were seen by employers as "unstable, untutored, unmanageable—a bad risk."[86] Many veterans turned to crime to make ends meet. In the years following the end of the war, Union veterans filled jails from Massachusetts to Wisconsin. The situation was even worse for Confederate veterans who returned home to destroyed cities and a wrecked economy, and worse still for African American Union veterans whose service was rewarded with second-class citizenship and lynchings.[87]

Decades later, the "doughboys" who fought in World War I came home to "high unemployment and runaway inflation," and when the Great Depression descended on the United States in late 1929, things got much worse. In the spring of 1932, a group of destitute World War I veterans walked and "rode the rails" from Oregon to Washington, D.C., to drum up support for immediate government assistance to veterans in the form of cash "bonuses." These "bonus marchers" and their families set up camp in the nation's capital, where their ranks eventually grew from twenty thousand to forty thousand veterans. In July 1932, however, the marchers were chased out of Washington by US Army troops under the command of Gen. Douglas MacArthur, on orders from President Herbert Hoover.[88]

Vietnam veterans most often compare their own negative homecoming experiences to those of the World War II veterans who supposedly "returned home to a grateful nation happy, healthy, and respected."[89] There is definitely some truth to this idea, for the soldiers who fought in World War II received more postwar support than veterans of any previous American war. Unlike earlier generations of veterans, the men who served in World War II did not have to form advocacy groups after the war and spend years petitioning the government for pensions and other benefits.[90] On June 22, 1944, more than a year before the war ended, President Franklin D. Roosevelt, who felt that veterans were "entitled to definite action to help take care of their special problems," signed the Servicemen's Readjustment Act into law.[91] Better known as the "GI Bill," this measure provided veterans with fifty-two weeks of unemployment compensation, low-interest home and business loans, and financial assistance for education and job training.[92] The GI Bill was not perfect, but its programs nevertheless produced "a generation of well-educated professionals, businessmen, and homeowners who became the basis of a greatly strengthened American middle class."[93]

Although they were treated better than perhaps any other generation of veterans before or since, the homecoming experience for World War II veterans was not all ticker-tape parades and adoring crowds. In fact, most World War II troops came home alone from Europe or Asia, not in units, and few participated in victory parades.[94] In the early postwar years, veterans faced labor unrest, rising inflation, and a severe housing shortage.[95] Thousands of former fighting men lived with family and friends if they were lucky, or in "barns, trailers, decommissioned streetcars . . . even automobiles," if they were not.[96] A majority of GIs surveyed in 1945 agreed with the statement, "On the whole, I think the Army has hurt me more than it helped me."[97] A 1947 poll found that 48 percent of veterans thought the war had made their life worse, and that 41 percent believed military service had made them "more nervous, high-strung, restless . . . [and] tense."[98] Despite the "public euphoria" occasioned by the war's end, many Americans at the time worried that years of combat had turned GIs into killers or criminals.[99]

The mutual hostility that developed between veterans and nonveterans following World War II is reminiscent of the veteran–nonveteran conflicts that are prevalent in Vietnam veteran narratives. Conflict of this sort, however, goes back much further than World War II. In *When Johnny Comes Marching Home*, a 1944 history of American war veterans, Dixon Wecter argues that tensions existed between soldiers and civilians in the aftermath of every military conflict beginning with the Revolutionary War. As he astutely put it, soldiers invariably return home from the battlefield believing that civilians are indebted to them for the hardships they endured on the nation's behalf. Veterans, however, see their sacrifices as so great that civilians can never really pay off that debt.[100] During the latter years of the American Civil War, embittered Union soldiers thought Northern civilians were selfish and ungrateful. When they finally came home, many Union veterans, like many US military personnel who served in Vietnam, could only relate to other veterans.[101] Psychiatrist Jonathan Shay argues in his book, *Odysseus in America: Combat Trauma and the Trial of Homecoming*, that conflict between war veterans and civilians goes back at least to the days of Ancient Greece.[102]

Just as negative homecomings and conflicts with civilians were not unique to Vietnam veterans, neither was post-traumatic stress. Whereas Vietnam veterans were diagnosed with "post-Vietnam syndrome" and "post-traumatic stress disorder," similarly troubled veterans of World Wars I and II were labeled as victims of "shell shock" and "combat fatigue." Eric T. Dean Jr. persuasively argues in his book, *Shook over Hell: Post-traumatic Stress, Vietnam, and the Civil War*, that untold numbers of Civil War veterans were afflicted with the psychological disorder now known as PTSD.[103] Shay shows in *Odysseus in America* and an earlier book, *Achilles in Vietnam: Combat Trauma and the Undoing of Character*, that Achilles, Odysseus, and other legendary warriors chronicled in Homer's epic poetry also had combat-related mental illnesses.[104] Such studies make it clear that psychological trauma is not the byproduct of certain types of wars, but all wars.

Veterans cannot be blamed, however, for not including accurate historical details about the postwar experiences of earlier veterans in their narratives. For one thing, memoirs are inherently self-focused; veterans produce narratives to talk about *their* wartime experiences, not those of previous generations. Additionally, most Vietnam veterans, like most Americans in general, probably knew nothing about the readjustment problems that plagued ex-soldiers throughout history. By the time Baby Boomers were coming of age, the tensions and conflicts that occurred when the troops came home in the 1940s had long been forgotten. Many of the movies and television shows Vietnam veterans watched when they were growing up were about World War II and other conflicts. But most of these productions portrayed war as a glorious adventure, saying nothing about the postwar plights of former fighting men. In fact, as the celebration of the "Greatest Generation" in more recent years demonstrates, the idealization of the World War II era in American culture continues unabated into the present. Many Vietnam veterans had fathers, uncles, and neighbors who were real-life veterans of World War II, but such men were members of a generation that was encouraged to keep bad memories and inner conflicts bottled up inside and hidden from view.[105]

A good way to illustrate the falsity of the glorified version of World War II (and warfare in general) that was presented to future Vietnam veterans is to examine the life of World War II hero and postwar movie star, Audie Murphy. The son of Texas sharecroppers, Murphy joined the army at age seventeen with a falsified birth certificate. He fought in Europe from 1943 to 1945, then came back to the United States with the Medal of Honor and thirty-two other awards, making him the most decorated American soldier of the war. After the war, Murphy became a popular Hollywood actor, starring in over forty movies between 1948 and 1969, most of them war movies and westerns. He even played himself in a World War II picture, *To Hell and Back* (1955), which was based on his 1949 autobiography of the same name.

Several memoirists say that Murphy was one of their role models growing up. What they, or any of his other fans, did not know was that their hero came back from Europe with severe post-traumatic stress. Soon after Murphy returned home, his family noticed that there was something wrong with him: he was jittery, stressed out, nervous, and tortured by nightmares. As time went on, and Murphy became a star, his personal life only got worse. His nightmares got so bad that he occasionally woke up and grabbed the handgun he always kept at his bedside and fired at imaginary enemies in the darkness of his bedroom. On movie sets, at restaurants, and at home with his wife, Murphy went into rages that often ended with him physically assaulting someone or threatening people with firearms. In the years before he died in a 1971 plane crash, he talked about committing suicide and was arrested several times for beating up strangers.[106]

Veterans' narratives are also misleading in that they generally feature the theme of eventual postmilitary recovery and success. At first glance, government-sponsored studies of Vietnam veterans seemingly support the validity of this theme. The authors of the NVVRS asserted that their findings showed that "the majority of Vietnam theater veterans have made a successful reentry into civilian life and are currently experiencing few symptoms of PTSD or other readjustment problems."[107] Another study, *Legacies of Vietnam: Comparative Adjustment of Veterans and Their Peers,* published in 1981, determined that veterans had achieved some significant educational and workforce successes after they came home. Using surveys taken in the late 1970s, *Legacies* found that 70 percent of Vietnam veterans "resumed their educational careers following" military service,[108] and that most "did so within the first year following release."[109] According to the study, as of 1977 there "were no substantial differences between veterans and non-veterans in unemployment rates," and "veterans had higher median wages than non-veterans."[110] The study also determined that black veterans were better educated and had better jobs than African Americans who did not serve.[111]

Closer scrutiny of these studies, however, shows that the mental and physical health, education, and employment situations for Vietnam veterans were not entirely positive. Although the NVVRS concluded that the majority of veterans were not suffering from PTSD by 1988, the 26.3 percent of veterans who currently had either "full-blown" or "partial" PTSD represented a significant minority.[112] Furthermore, research has shown that, for many people, PTSD is irreversible, so it is likely that many of these veterans continued to endure symptoms after the late eighties. Unfortunately, the fact is that many veterans with PTSD, contrary to suggestions made in veterans' narratives, never recovered from the psychological injuries they incurred in Vietnam.[113]

Not all combat-related injuries, of course, were psychological. Thousands of American soldiers came home from Vietnam with physical wounds. Puller and several other memoirists were terribly injured during their tours. But these authors overcame their disabilities and achieved professional success. Scores of other wounded veterans were surely not so fortunate. Thousands of GIs returned to America with ailments caused by exposure to "Agent Orange." Beginning in 1961, the U.S military, seeking to "remove the foliage cover which had afforded concealment to the enemy," sprayed eighteen million gallons of chemical defoliants over South Vietnam.[114] Approximately 60 percent of the defoliant sprayed was "Agent Orange,"[115] a chemical which "contained TCDD-dioxin, the most toxic known substance."[116] Many veterans exposed to Agent Orange had "skin rashes, weakness of limbs, nervous disorders, liver disease . . . [and] cancer."[117] No memoirists say they were afflicted by debilitating Agent Orange–related illnesses after the war.[118] Considering that the hardest hit victims either died from their afflictions or were probably too ill to write memoirs, this is not surprising. The omission of significant discussions of Agent Orange from veteran narratives meant that readers were not reminded of one of the most depressing consequences of the war.

Although *Legacies of Vietnam* contained some positive findings, the authors of the study nevertheless concluded that "military duty in Vietnam had a negative effect upon postmilitary achievement."[119] Although most Vietnam veterans engaged in some kind of educational training after leaving the military, only 22 percent were college graduates by 1977. In comparison, 46 percent of nonveterans had graduated from college by that time, and nonveterans were more likely than veterans to have "pursue[d] post-graduate or professional training."[120] The study also found that "in the competition for high level jobs, non-veterans [were] markedly more successful than veterans," and that the professional success of nonveterans was due to their superior educational backgrounds.[121] Moreover, the "modest wage advantage" that white veterans held over their nonveteran peers was actually illusory, for the veterans surveyed were, on average, older than the nonveterans. This age difference was evidently an important factor, because when veterans were matched with nonveterans of the same age, their wage advantage disappeared.[122]

Although the *Legacies* study found that military service benefited African Americans in some ways, it nevertheless determined that many black veterans were faring badly in post-Vietnam America. The unemployment rate for black Vietnam-era veterans "was three times that of white veterans," and even higher, 22 percent, for African Americans who served in Vietnam.[123] Black Vietnam veterans had a high "career unemployment" rate,[124] and African American veterans were "less satisfied with their jobs than white veterans."[125] Although the study determined that African Americans who served in Vietnam had higher incomes than those who did not, the *Legacies* researchers found that black veterans nevertheless experienced a "drastic loss in real wages" in the late 1970s.[126]

Despite the claim that military service provides young men with valuable job skills, few Vietnam veterans were prepared to reenter the civilian economy when they left the military.[127] Men who served in the infantry and other combat positions were especially lacking in "skills transferable to the civilian job market."[128] Worse yet, the rapid deindustrialization of the American economy in the 1970s eliminated many of the jobs previously available to unskilled workers. As a result, scores of Vietnam veterans became unemployed after the war, which led in many cases to homelessness. African Americans, veterans included, were particularly hard hit by deindustrialization, which led to a rise in black homelessness. A disproportionate nonwhite presence in the infantry during the war was surely a factor in the appearance of young black and Latino veterans in the post-Vietnam-era homeless population.[129]

It is true that most Americans who served in Vietnam successfully reentered civilian life after they came home. But the NVVRS and *Legacies of Vietnam* show that the postwar fate of veterans was far from an unambiguous success story. A dominant theme in memoirs is the story of the veteran who initially encounters readjustment problems, but then recovers and goes on to achieve great professional success. This discrepancy between narratives and other sources on the subject of veterans' postwar lives is rooted in the demographics of memoirists. Veteran-authors were disproportionately white and middle class, and they generally entered the military with better educations than the average soldier who fought in Vietnam. When most memoirists came home, they, like many nonveterans, had a leg up on the majority of veterans who came from low-income households and had, at best, only graduated from high school. Consequently, readers primarily learned about how Vietnam veterans fared after the war from men and women who were better equipped to succeed in civilian life than the typical combat veteran.

---

Lewis Puller Jr. went to Vietnam as a young, patriotic Marine Corps officer, but returned home a psychological and physical wreck. He stepped on a Vietcong booby trap that mutilated his hands and blew off both of his legs only a few months after assuming command of his infantry platoon. Puller's memoir, *Fortunate Son*, chronicled his short, disillusioning tour in Vietnam, the long and painful recovery from his physical injuries, and his battles with depression and alcoholism. Like many other Vietnam veteran memoirs, *Fortunate Son* ends on a positive note, with Puller looking forward to moving on with his life, his troubles seemingly behind him. After the book was published in 1992, his good fortune continued. *Fortunate Son* won a Pulitzer Prize, and Puller shared the stage with President Bill Clinton during a 1993 Memorial Day ceremony. The original cover of *Fortunate Son* described the book as a story about "the healing of a Vietnam vet," and that seemed an apt description until early May 1994, when Puller, abusing drugs and again beset by depression, killed himself in his Virginia home.[130]

Because Puller's sad passing did not take place until after his book was published, the readers of *Fortunate Son* knew much about Puller's post-Vietnam life, but they did not get the full story. In several ways, veteran narratives are like his tragic story: they tell a lot, but not everything about the return of Vietnam veterans to America. Memoirs correctly explain to readers that ex-soldiers encountered many difficulties after they came home. But they did not inform them that returning to the civilian world has always been hard for warriors. In addition, evidence suggests that stories of abusive antiwar protestors are, at best, hyperbolic. Memoirists

94    forthrightly acknowledge the psychological afflictions they faced, but the same authors incorrectly suggest that veterans always eventually overcame their problems and moved on to success in civilian life.

# 6 The Political Content of Veteran Narratives

In May 1985, the Asia Society sponsored a conference in New York on "The Vietnam Experience in American Literature." Academics, publishers, and representatives from other fields spoke at the event, but the most important participants were writers, most of them Vietnam veterans, who had produced novels, memoirs, poetry, and oral histories about the war. Political scientist Timothy J. Lomperis explained in his published commentary on the proceedings that similar events were held earlier in the decade, but they did not live up to expectations. The organizers of these earlier conferences, he said, had set "modest agendas" and structured discussions around "manageable subtopics." But participants, according to Lomperis, invariably discarded these plans in favor of pursuing chaotic, "grandiose" discussions about the "lessons" of the war.[1] The 1985 Asia Society conference was also divided into subtopics, such as "combat literature" and "fact and fiction in the literature," and from the outset participants were admonished not to repeat the mistakes of the past and veer into arguments about "the lessons of Vietnam."[2]

From the moment the conference started, however, it was clear that this warning would not be heeded. The keynote speaker was James Webb, Vietnam veteran, future US Senator, and author of the semiautobiographical Vietnam War novel, *Fields of Fire*. He began the conference by chastising writers for romanticizing America's enemies during the war, and for ignoring the expansionist policies of the Communist regime that had ruled a reunited Vietnam since 1975. Webb went on to say that "our literature" had depicted Vietnam veterans as "men . . . dragged into the war zone against their will, later as losers, finally as victims," when statistics and surveys showed that most veterans were well-educated homeowners

95

who supported "the bombing of North Vietnam" and "the use of napalm." Most veterans, he added, had volunteered and were "glad they served their country."[3] Webb also stated that he believed in "the validity of our effort in Vietnam," and that only "our flawed government policy made the war unwinnable."[4]

At the time, Webb was a high-level official in the US Department of Defense, so many at the conference regarded his speech as "a partisan and political defense of the Reagan administration's interpretation of the war as a 'noble crusade.'"[5] W. D. Ehrhart, an author who joined the Vietnam Veterans Against the War (VVAW) after his combat tour ended, drew applause when he said that even if Webb's assessment of post-1975 Vietnam was correct, it did not change the fact that the war was "unspeakably evil and immoral."[6] Another former VVAW activist, Ron Kovic, said Webb "was trying to undo everything that I and others had done," and "negate . . . the suffering of thousands and thousands of Americans and Vietnamese."[7] He went on to call what he saw as a Reagan-era revival of militarism the "Nazification of my country," and speculated that "maybe Hitler is in the White House right now."[8]

The heated, ideologically charged arguments that broke out during the conference, however, demonstrated that Webb was not alone in his feelings about the war and its aftermath. Memoirist Frederick Downs agreed with Webb's contention that publishers in the immediate postwar years had been unwilling to publish Vietnam War books that were not sufficiently antiwar in tone. During a panel titled "Images of Asia and Asians in the Literature," veteran-author Al Santoli loudly reiterated Webb's sentiments about Communist depredations in 1980s Southeast Asia, and asserted that the publishing industry refused to print anything about the war that did not adhere to "the Ho Chi Minh point of view."[9]

There was much conflict in the United States during the Vietnam War between "hawks" and "doves" over America's military endeavors in Southeast Asia. After the shooting war ended another "war" began: the struggle over how the war would be remembered.[10] As the Asia Society conference shows, this battle perhaps reached its apex during the 1980s, with some arguing that the war was a "noble cause," while others saw it as an awful mistake. Although the battle over the nation's collective memory of the war gradually decreased in intensity as years passed, this struggle nevertheless continued after the 1980s and into the present day.[11]

There is a reoccurring theme in veteran narratives that they are above the rancorous debates over the war that occurred during the conflict and after it ended. Some authors assert that their war stories are nothing more than straightforward accounts of personal experiences. Philip Caputo states in the first paragraphs of *A Rumor of War* that his book "is simply a story about war," and "has nothing to do with politics, power, strategy, influence, national interests, or foreign policy."[12] Tim O'Brien makes a similar point when he asserts in his oft-quoted short story, "How to Tell a True War Story," that a "true war story . . . does not instruct, nor encourage virtue, nor suggest models of proper human behavior."[13] Samuel Hynes perfectly sums up this attitude by stating that veterans' personal narratives do not engage in the polemics that surround wars and their aftermaths, but instead, "simply tell us what it is like. . . . They bear witness."[14]

Veteran-writers may claim that they are simply dispassionate recorders of past events, but the vitriolic proceedings of the Asia Society conference are just one indication that many memoirists have been fully engaged in public memory battles. Many veterans' narratives make overt political or ideological comments about the war and how it has been remembered. But all veterans who produce personal narratives, purposefully or not, affect collective memory just by telling readers what they experienced in Vietnam. Even Caputo, O'Brien, and other veterans who want their works to exist outside the ongoing contest over history and memory become part of it because their narratives continue to influence large numbers of people.

Despite the prevalence of political and ideological elements in veteran narratives, relatively little attention has been paid to this important topic. Notable exceptions are the literary scholars who contend that almost all veteran narratives represent powerful cases for why the Vietnam War was a monstrous atrocity that should never be repeated.[15] There is some truth to this argument, but it is too simplistic and does not take into account the many nuances in veterans' statements and depictions of the war. Most of these scholars came to these conclusions by analyzing only a handful of veteran narratives, and their analyses usually made no distinctions between fiction and nonfiction.

Veteran memoirs, for the most part, offer a decidedly negative interpretation of the Vietnam conflict. Some directly criticize the war, and most portray it in ways that amount to implicit condemnations. Yet, memoirists are also generally hostile towards the civilian antiwar movement, and hold traditional ideas about patriotism and military service. Besides discussing memoirists' political stances on the war, this chapter will assess the print media's role in shaping the public's collective understanding of the war. It then addresses the question of whether ordinary veterans' views on the war paralleled or deviated from that of ex-soldiers who wrote memoirs about their experiences.

———

Which Vietnam memoirs influential periodicals chose to review, and the nature of the reviews themselves, played an important role in determining the success of a book and how many people read it. This in turn affected whether a particular book had any significant impact on collective memory. A survey of veterans' narratives reviewed from 1967 to 2005 in three of the most prominent, nationally read publications, the *New York Times,* the *Washington Post,* and *Time,* demonstrates that the books that got the most attention were those that portrayed the war in a generally negative manner. Prominent publications usually avoided books that represented Vietnam, as Webb and Reagan did, as a just undertaking undermined by poor military strategy and the actions of traitorous peace advocates. But such publications also ignored memoirs that espoused a more extreme, unambiguous antiwar message. The rare reviews of books that took clear left- or right-wing stances on the war were either dismissive, or at least neutral, when compared with how less-prominent (or more ideologically oriented) periodicals dealt with the same works.

An analysis of the publishing history of veterans' memoirs is the best way to begin the discussion of how the mainstream media has elevated some types of books over others. The first Vietnam veteran memoir published by a major company was Donald Duncan's 1967 book, *The New Legions.*[16] Duncan went to South Vietnam in 1964 as a member of the Green Berets. But during his eighteen-month stint there he became convinced that the war was wrong, and when he left the military he joined the antiwar movement. Duncan was eventually hired by *Ramparts,* a New Left magazine, to serve as their military editor, and in February 1966 he authored an article about his Vietnam experiences for that publication titled "The Whole Thing Was a Lie!"[17] Both the article and *The New Legions,* unlike many subsequent veteran narratives, were not written ostensibly to "just tell it like it was." Instead, they were political tracts in which Duncan used his experiences to support his arguments against the war.

Aside from *The New Legions,* most veteran memoirs were not published until after the war ended. The handful of narratives that reached bookstores in the early 1970s, like other types of Vietnam War books published during this period,[18] usually fell into one of two categories:

antiwar pieces akin to *The New Legions* or works that supported the war. On the antiwar side were books such as Terry Whitmore's *Memphis, Nam, Sweden: The Story of a Black Deserter* (1971)[19] and *A Hero's Welcome: The Conscience of Sergeant James Daly Versus the United States Army* (1975).[20] Representing the pro-war side were primarily books written by former POWs who were staunch advocates of America's cause in Vietnam, such as James N. Rowe's *Five Years to Freedom* (1971)[21] and Robinson Risner's *The Passing of the Night: My Seven Years as a Prisoner of the North Vietnamese* (1973).[22] Memoirs published in this era make up only a small fraction of the fifty-eight most prominent veteran narratives, and not all of them garnered enough attention from critics, readers, or scholars to warrant wide circulation.

Perhaps veteran memoirs were scarce during this period because veteran-writers needed time after their tours ended to process their experiences and learn how to put them into writing.[23] Some commentators claim that many veteran-authored books never reached the public in the immediate postwar years because publishers rejected any manuscripts that were not sufficiently antiwar in content.[24] *Publishers Weekly* reported in the late 1960s that many in the industry were against the war, but did not indicate that anyone rejected books on an ideological basis.[25] Others, however, claim that publishing companies avoided any type of Vietnam book during these years because they believed readers were sick of the war and would not buy such titles.[26] Various scholars and other commentators buttress this notion by referring to the immediate postwar period as a time when Americans tried to put the war behind them and forget it ever happened.[27]

The dearth of published veteran narratives, whatever caused it, ended in the late 1970s. This change began with the great critical and popular success achieved by Kovic's 1976 memoir, *Born on the Fourth of July*.[28] *A Rumor of War* was released to similar acclaim a year later. In 1978, Hollywood released *Coming Home* and *The Deer Hunter*, further signaling a growing willingness to confront the war.[29] During the 1980s, renewed interest in the conflict reached a crescendo, as Vietnam during this decade suffused movies, television shows,[30] political discourse, and other aspects of American culture.[31] Eager to feed off this trend, publishers put out hundreds of veteran-authored memoirs, novels, and oral histories over the next couple of decades. By the early 1990s, bookstores contained "Vietnam shelves" in their history sections, and a large percentage of the titles on display were authored by veterans.[32]

The great majority of the veteran memoirs published since about 1990 have been what Philip D. Beidler calls "Vietpulp": cheap paperback novels, memoirs, biographies, and popular histories of low literary quality that often focus on the exploits of elite combat units.[33] Such books are mostly apolitical, as they center on combat and do not often address any of the war's larger issues. With few exceptions, Vietpulp-type memoirs were not award winners or best sellers and were not reviewed in the most influential periodicals or consulted by scholars. As a result, only a few books that could be called Vietpulp earned a spot among the most prominent Vietnam veteran narratives.

Most prominent veteran narratives are ostensibly, and often expressly, apolitical; they supposedly just "tell it like it was" and nothing more. The same goes for the most popular oral histories. But unlike most Vietpulp, the majority of these books are actually far from apolitical. Eleven memoirists, all of them former POWs, express unambiguous support for the war. These men depict the war as a clear struggle between good and evil. This is understandable considering that they were held in poor conditions and tortured by their North Vietnamese captors. Such authors lauded President Richard Nixon and his controversial handling of the war and portrayed American peace protestors as dupes of Communist propaganda or outright villains.

The most dominant, obvious message in the veteran narrative genre, however, is that the war was, at best, a horrific mistake and, at worst, a terrible crime. One of the most common themes in the genre is the idealistic young American who goes to Vietnam and has disillusioning experiences that turn him against the war. This theme began with *Born on the Fourth of July,* continued with *A Rumor of War,* and was subsequently repeated in many other narratives. A smaller number of well-known memoirs, such as O'Brien's *If I Die in a Combat Zone,* are written by authors who opposed the war, ended up in Vietnam anyway, and then had experiences that reinforced their original views.[34] Kovic, Caputo, and other important memoirists joined the VVAW or other antiwar groups when they came home from Southeast Asia. Several others did not participate in the peace movement but were openly sympathetic with its actions.[35]

Many memoirists were unambiguous in their antipathy towards the war. O'Brien writes in *If I Die* that he "was persuaded the war was wrong" before he left for Vietnam and was just as persuaded when he was writing his book years later.[36] He calls himself a "coward" for going to Vietnam even though he opposed the war.[37] Several other memoirists, such as Tobias Wolff and Bruce Weigl, suggest that young men who avoided military service during the war were brave, or at least intelligent.[38] Nathaniel Tripp calls the war "wrong, stupid, and futile,"[39] and admits that his Vietnam experiences made him hate the United States to the extent that he considered moving to another country.[40] Michael Norman says that while other Vietnam veterans he knows "would carry a gun again if the call came," he would instead "shoot the caller."[41]

Reinforcing these direct statements against the war are the negative depictions of the conflict discussed in chapter 2. Many veterans, rather than romanticizing their combat experiences, focused on mutilated corpses, ghastly injuries, and the fear that gripped men engaged in combat. The particular kind of war they fought in Vietnam, with its booby traps and hit-and-run ambushes, caused extraordinary aggravation, and the tactics used by the American military often seemed nonsensical. Adding to the frustration were the civilians, who are represented as enemy collaborators and dollar-loving opportunists, and the ARVNs, who were supposedly too stupid to fight their own battles. And, as chapter 5 demonstrates, a large number of veterans acknowledge they had post-traumatic stress and went through other Vietnam-related tribulations long after their combat tours ended.

Negative depictions of the war were not limited to narratives that express unbridled hatred of the war. In a 1986 *Journal of American History* review essay, George C. Herring identifies two veteran memoirs, David Donovan's *Once a Warrior King: Memories of an Officer in Vietnam,* and James R. McDonough's *Platoon Leader,* as "revisionist."[42] Like many Reagan-era conservatives, Donovan denounces the Communist government of postwar Vietnam and blames the "perfidious" American public for the defeat of US forces in Southeast Asia.[43] As Herring notes in his article, however, both Donovan and McDonough also paint, at times, a bleak picture of the war.[44] Donovan suggests that the average GI held all Vietnamese in contempt,[45] and McDonough writes of soldiers driven insane by combat and American officers who hid from battle.[46] Both memoirists portray South Vietnamese government officials and military men as cruel or incompetent.[47]

There are elements of veteran memoirs, however, that clash with their overall negative portrayal of the war. Although a number of the best-known memoirists either sympathized with the antiwar movement or actually participated in it themselves, antiwar civilians are commonly depicted as malicious soldier-hating hippies. Lynda Van Devanter, for example, observed a 1969 Thanksgiving Day fast in Vietnam to show her solidarity with antiwar protestors back in the United States. But later in her book she tells the story about the stereotypical antiwar civilian who spat on her.[48] As chapter 5 shows, however, there is no credible evidence that GIs were verbally or physically assaulted by protestors on a regular basis. Memoirists are further misleading in their suggestion that war opponents were all hippies or left-wing radicals. This was never the case.[49] Participants in the 1967 March on the Pentagon "included . . . middle-class liberals, student radicals, hippies, civil rights workers, black power advocates, Vietnam veterans, [and] even some federal workers."[50] On October 15, 1969, millions of people took "a one-day pause in their usual business" to observe the "Moratorium" against the war.[51] Opposition to the war was "so mainstream" in its final years that "establishment" Democratic politicians, such as Senators Edward Kennedy and Edmund ("Ed") Muskie, were its most conspicuous critics.[52]

Besides disliking protesters, many memoirists, including those who clearly loathed the war, are proud of their service, enjoyed some aspects of their combat tours, and continue to hold conventional patriotic values. Caputo asserts in the prologue to *A Rumor of War* that "anyone who fought in Vietnam . . . will have to admit he enjoyed the compelling attractiveness of combat."[53] He adds that "nostalgia" for his own tour prevented him from hating the war as much as others who worked in the antiwar movement.[54] Robert Mason and William Broyles Jr. both met with Vietcong and NVA veterans during postwar trips to Vietnam. Despite their mostly negative feelings about the conflict, both memoirists were rankled by their former adversaries' boasts about defeating America.[55] Lewis Puller Jr. was tempted to join VVAW activists who threw their medals over the fence in front of the US Capitol building in 1971, but could not bring himself to do it. His medals and what they represented were still too dear to throw away.[56]

Although many veterans depict the war in a negative light or make unambiguous statements against it, Ehrhart's four memoirs are noteworthy for the clear antiwar message they present. His first volume, *Vietnam-Perkasie: A Combat Marine Memoir*, covers his tour in Vietnam,[57] while the subsequent memoirs deal with his postwar experiences. Ehrhart joined the marines in 1966 as a patriotic young man who wanted to help protect South Vietnam from Communist aggression, but months of combat eroded the values that had led him to volunteer. He explains in his second memoir, *Passing Time: Memoir of a Vietnam Veteran against the War*, that his feelings about the war reached a turning point in 1971. In that year the

US government's secret history of the Vietnam War, the *Pentagon Papers,*
became public. These documents convinced Ehrhart that the war was not
a mistake, as he previously believed, but a "deliberate attempt to hammer
the world by brute force into the shape perceived by vain, duplicitous
power brokers."[58] He was outraged and radicalized by these revelations,
and joined the antiwar movement soon afterwards, determined to stop the
war that had turned him into, in his own estimation, a "murderer."[59]

Ehrhart's memoirs do not simply convey the message that the Vietnam
War was wrong, but, rather, that warfare itself is fundamentally immoral.
He has candidly stated that his books are "tool[s] for political education,"
and that the purpose of his writing is to prevent future wars and spare
future generations the horrors he witnessed in Vietnam.[60] The broad scope
of Ehrhart's goals and concerns is evident in many of his works, including *Passing Time,* which includes a chapter-long radical interpretation of
United States history. Through a reconstructed discussion between himself
and another VVAW activist, Ehrhart presents American history as a long
series of injustices, from the expulsion of Native Americans from their
lands by white settlers, to the US government's Cold War policies in Latin
America and Asia.[61] Ehrhart states that these events show that the United
States has always acted out of complete self-interest, and has never cared
"about freedom or justice or democracy for anybody."[62]

Although Ehrhart's books have not done well commercially, his work
is constantly cited by scholars interested in the Vietnam War and the literature that came out of it. Historian H. Bruce Franklin calls "[Ehrhart] the
preeminent figure in this literature—treasured for his nonfiction, enor-
mously influential as the foremost anthologist of Vietnam War poetry, and
himself unsurpassed as a poet."[63] He also speculates that Ehrhart is not
better known outside academic circles because he rejects both the noble
cause interpretation of Vietnam and its "liberal alternative," the idea that
the war was a "horrible mistake."[64] Ehrhart instead posits that the war
was engendered by the purposeful actions of shadowy, "duplicitous power
brokers."[65] This conception, Franklin argues, is unacceptable to those who
control "corporate publishing and the major media."[66] The leaders of these
industries, he claims, are akin to the elites who planned and carried out the
war and are unwilling to disseminate ideas about the conflict that diverge
from a moderate viewpoint.[67]

Franklin's theory is at least partly supported by an analysis of how the
*New York Times,* the *Washington Post,* and *Time* magazine have dealt with
veteran memoirs over the decades. These media outlets, which are read by

millions of Americans, did not review most veteran narratives that conveyed an explicit antiwar message, and the few such books reviewed were given unfavorable or neutral receptions. Of the three periodicals surveyed, only *Time* reviewed Duncan's *The New Legions*. That review was only one paragraph long, and its author dismissively ended the piece by saying that "the book says as much about the author's state of mind as about Viet Nam."[68] Strangely, the *Time* reviewer made no reference to the political content of this hyperpolitical book, but did sardonically note that Duncan worked for "the anti-almost-everything magazine *Ramparts*."[69] Ehrhart's books were rarely reviewed by this group of publications. The one exception, a short 1995 *Washington Post* review of Erhart's *Busted: A Vietnam Veteran in Nixon's America,* was mostly positive. But it nevertheless ended with this comment: "It's easy to laugh along with Ehrhart, but hard to derive from his tale any lasting thoughts."[70]

It is possible to see what is missing from mainstream media coverage of antiwar memoirs by looking at how *The Nation,* a left-leaning publication, dealt with such books. In 1967, *The Nation* reviewed *The New Legions* at length, and its reviewer properly highlighted the polemical nature of the book.[71] In 1975, mainstream reviewers ignored *A Hero's Welcome,* the memoir of James Daly, an African American who, while held as a POW in North Vietnam, joined a group of antiwar prisoners who called themselves the "Peace Committee." *A Hero's Welcome* was reviewed in *The Nation,* however, and its reviewer said that the book was written "with humor and sensitivity," and that it gave Americans "a rare close-up of the national enemy we spent a decade hating and killing."[72] The reviewer also hinted at a possible reason why Daly's book did not receive much attention, stating that it "contradicts nearly everything the American people were told about the [American POWs] by Nixon and his spokesmen, the Pentagon, and the television networks during the war."[73] In 1995, *The Nation* printed a laudatory, lengthy review of *Busted,* noting that the "the singular achievement" of the book is that, while providing a personal perspective on the Vietnam conflict, it also addresses the larger, complicated issues surrounding the war, including its "complex link to US geopolitical ambitions."[74]

Franklin, however, was mistaken in suggesting that the media was only biased against Vietnam War books that expressed leftist sentiments. The three mainstream publications surveyed in this chapter also showed a bias against veteran memoirs that conveyed right-wing views of the war. This bias is best illustrated by examining how the *National Review,* the leading conservative magazine in the United States, covered these types of books. Everett Alvarez's memoir, *Chained Eagle: The Heroic Story of the First American Shot Down over North Vietnam,* was not reviewed by the *New York Times,* the *Washington Post,*[75] or *Time,* but it was afforded a glowing review in the *National Review.* The reviewer proclaimed that "every American" should read *Chained Eagle* and other POW memoirs that similarly exude patriotism and denounce the antiwar movement, even if Hollywood, in his estimation, avoided such Vietnam stories.[76] A few years earlier, the *National Review* praised another conservative-minded memoir, *In Love and War: The Story of a Family's Ordeal and Sacrifice during the Vietnam Years,* cowritten by former POW James Stockdale and his wife, Sybil.[77] The *Times*[78] and *Post* reviews of the book were mostly positive, but far more neutral in tone, although the *Post* reviewer does flippantly suggest that the Stockdales, who both endured terrible hardships during James's captivity, "loved" the war.[79]

---

The engagement of veteran-writers in the struggle for the collective memory of the Vietnam War is on display in their memoirs. Even those who do not make clear-cut statements for or against the war became involved in this memory battle as soon as their experiences were published. Their portrayals of the war, whether meaning to or not, inevitably affected readers' conceptions of the conflict. The overall depiction of the war that memoirists conveyed to their readers was overwhelmingly negative. The same veterans, however, are often proud they served, say their tours were positive in some respects, and voice animosity towards the antiwar movement. Books that convey these messages are the majority in the ranks of the most popular veterans' narratives partly because editors and the media select them over works that espouse overtly left- or right-wing political messages.

Interestingly, the government studies mentioned in chapter 5, *Myths and Realities* and *Legacies of Vietnam,* found that Vietnam veterans as a whole hold similarly complex, contradictory feelings about the war. *Myths and Realities* determined that "on balance, Vietnam era veterans believe our military involvement in Vietnam was a mistake,"[80] and 59 percent agreed with the idea that American "troops were asked to fight a war [they] could never win."[81] A full 71 percent of veterans said that the statement, "I found I actually liked the thrill of being in a war,"[82] did *not* correspond to their own feelings at all. Only 5 percent said it matched their sentiments "very closely."[83] The negative tone of these results was, in some respects, echoed in the surveys of veterans taken as part of *Legacies of Vietnam.* Almost 43 percent of these veterans opposed the war while serving in Vietnam, and 13.5 percent were neither for nor against the conflict because they did not understand it. Additionally, 44.2 percent believed that the war had "a negative effect . . . on the Vietnamese."[84]

Closer examination of these studies, however, shows that veterans' feelings about their tours were not all negative. *Myths and Realities* concluded that most respondents were proud to be Vietnam veterans, were glad that they served their country, and would do so again if asked.[85] Most likewise "rejected the statement that 'it is shameful what my country did to the Vietnamese people.' "[86] These results indicated, according to the study's authors, that veterans "remain surprisingly patriotic,"[87] and that "the representation of these veterans as consumed by guilt . . . and ashamed to be recognized as Vietnam veterans . . . is a myth."[88] As for *Legacies of Vietnam*, although its authors thought it significant "that nearly six out of ten Vietnam veterans were participating in a war which they either opposed . . . or did not understand," this still meant that 43.6 percent supported the war while in Vietnam.[89] *Legacies* respondents were also more likely to have supported the war than nonveterans or veterans who served during the war years, but not in Vietnam. These latter two groups were also "substantially more likely" to "perceive a negative effect of the war on the Vietnamese" than Vietnam veterans.[90]

These studies suggest that most veterans, like most prominent memoirists, do not hold extreme positions on war-related issues. Ordinary veterans, like the small minority of their population that produced personal narratives, had convoluted feelings that could not be clearly ascribed to one side or the other in debates concerning the war. The most successful memoirs, then, may have owed some of their popularity to decisions made by editors and reviewers, but the messages they conveyed were nevertheless reflective of veterans' views in general. The concurrence of the two groups' opinions is probably related to the fact that the majority of memoirists had Vietnam experiences similar to those of typical combat soldiers. The authors' backgrounds may have been exceptional in many respects, but they too went through bewildering combat tours that left them with ambiguous outlooks on the war.

# 7

## Those Who Came Before and After

In the spring of 2003, Nathaniel Fick, a young Marine Corps lieutenant, was among the US forces leading the drive to Baghdad, Iraq's capital. Somewhere on the road to Baghdad, Fick's unit reached the outskirts of the Qalat Sukkar military airfield. Fick had so far succeeded in his main objective, keeping his men unhurt and alive, but his first experiences with war had left him numbed and bewildered. His platoon had come under attack from both enemy fighters and fellow marines who mistook them for Iraqis. It felt to Fick like they were "driving a hundred miles an hour down a highway in a blinding snowstorm."[1] By the time his unit made it to Qalat Sukkar, a combination of "fatigue, darkness, stress, and a vague mission" had enveloped them in "a fog."[2]

Fick's unit was tasked with reconnoitering the airfield in preparation for a larger assault by British paratroopers. Fick saw men, apparently carrying rifles, running in the distance upon reaching the installation. Muzzle flashes told the marines that they were receiving enemy fire. The platoon fired back and their radios were "flooded" with excited reports of armed men on the move and sightings of Iraqi "tanks and guns in the trees."[3] The marines nevertheless quickly took control of the airfield; the British assault was canceled. Just as they began to relax someone noticed a small group of people approaching them. The Americans readied themselves for another firefight, but the people were just civilians dragging bundles through the desert. Fick discovered the bundles contained two teenaged boys, alive but riddled with bullets. He quickly realized what was going on: "Those weren't rifles we had seen but shepherd's canes, not muzzle flashes but sun reflecting on a windshield . . . We'd shot two children."[4]

Fick's account of the marines' terrible mistake at Qalat Sukkar, re-counted in his 2005 memoir, *One Bullet Away: The Making of a Marine Officer*, is compelling in its own right. But his story is also noteworthy because it is remarkably similar to another horrible mistake made by ma-rines. More than thirty years before Fick went to war, Ron Kovic, as he recounts in *Born on the Fourth of July*, took part in a nighttime ambush of supposed Vietcong guerrillas. His platoon struggled to operate in the fog of war from the onset. It was rainy and dark and they were not completely confident in their mission. Kovic and his comrades spied figures in the distance that they incorrectly judged to be enemy fighters carrying rifles. The operation was marked by chaos and confusion; the "keyed up" pla-toon started wildly firing their weapons before ordered to do so. When the smoke cleared, the marines discovered that they had shot children, not enemy soldiers. Both platoons, Fick's and Kovic's, were emotionally devas-tated by their actions. Both groups of men believed,[5] in Fick's words, that US marines "don't shoot kids."[6]

It is striking how closely the Fick and Kovic anecdotes match up, but this connection is not anomalous. Veteran narratives of wars that oc-curred before and after America's conflict in Southeast Asia are analogous in numerous ways to Vietnam memoirs. This chapter explores the link-ages between Vietnam narratives and those produced by ex-soldiers who fought in World War II, the Korean War, the Gulf War, and the wars in Iraq and Afghanistan that followed the terrorist attacks of September 11, 2001. World War II is a fitting starting point since that conflict looms so large in the narratives of subsequent wars. There is a dearth, moreover, of notable memoirs written by Americans who fought in World War I.[7] Veterans of the Civil War and even earlier conflicts wrote about their experiences as well, but a deep analysis of pre-twentieth-century accounts is beyond the scope of this book. Non–Vietnam War books were selected accord-ing to the same criteria that informed Vietnam memoir selection. The non-Vietnam narratives were all commercially published and prominent because they were best sellers, written by famous people, or reviewed by influential newspapers and magazines.

Great differences, of course, separate the American wars of the twen-tieth and early twenty-first centuries. World War II mobilized a compara-tively huge portion of the US population, and was fought in European forests, North African deserts, and Asian jungles. The defeat of the Axis powers brought a definitive ending to the Second World War that veter-ans of the Vietnam War and later conflicts could only dream about. The

Korean War was often fought in the frigid cold, and by the time it ended in 1953, the opposing armies were engaged in a kind of static, trench warfare reminiscent of World War I. The Gulf War of 1991 was famously brief, and US casualty numbers were tiny compared to other conflicts. In their early phases, the post-9/11 wars featured conventional battles between nation-state militaries. But American troops fighting in the latter years of these same conflicts grappled with fighters who employed Vietcong-like guerrilla tactics.

The similarities linking veteran narratives across the generations, however, are more numerous and more profound than their differences. What accounts for this situation? One factor behind cross-narrative parallels is the influence of Vietnam writers over authors who fought in other wars. David Kieran argues that "the most noteworthy Second World War memoirs" published since the end of the Vietnam conflict "appropriated and re-deployed the conventions of Vietnam memoirs."[8] One of the World War II veteran-authors he cites, Paul Fussell, calls "W.D. Ehrhart's *Vietnam-Perkasie: A Combat Marine's Memoir* . . . an inspiring model of clear-sightedness and artistic energy" in his own memoir.[9] Fussell also quotes Philip Caputo, Tim O'Brien, and other Vietnam memoirists in the book.[10] Kieran likewise asserts that the most influential Iraq and Afghanistan (IA) memoirists are "deeply indebted to their predecessors from the Vietnam era."[11] This newest generation of veteran-authors, he says, so extensively "appropriate the tropes" of Vietnam narratives that their memoirs sometimes read like post-9/11 versions of Caputo's *A Rumor of War* or O'Brien's *If I Die in a Combat Zone*.[12] Fick's description of his PTSD symptoms, for example, "seems taken directly from Caputo."[13]

There are, however, two other more important reasons behind the similarities shared by memoirs of different wars. The first reason is that combat soldiers' wartime experiences have not changed in many fundamental ways since at least the 1940s. In other words, many of the things Vietnam memoirists saw and felt actually were amazingly similar to what veteran-authors of earlier and later wars saw and felt. The second reason is that memoirist demographics have also changed little since the 1940s. Like Vietnam authors, most memoirists of other wars were white, college educated, and former officers. Memoirists across the generations, then, also consistently reported the same things because the same types of people were usually doing the reporting.

Vietnam veteran-authors commonly note that their prewar conceptions of combat were based on novels, comic books, and, especially, movies. Many Baby Boomer memoirists grew up "playing war" and admiring male relatives and neighbors who fought in World War II. Very similar scenarios play out in the narratives of soldiers who fought in other wars. A young Audie Murphy decided to become a soldier after listening to a neighbor talk about his stint as a World War I "dough boy."[14] Fussell was fascinated by his veteran father's Great War mementos and staged mock battles in the backyard with his boyhood friends.[15] Many Generation X and Millennial veterans, like their Vietnam-era counterparts, were inspired by World War II movie heroics in their formative years. But *Saving Private Ryan* (1998), rather than a John Wayne movie, was the WWII film of choice for this latest generation of soldiers. Fictionalized accounts of other conflicts also intrigued post-Vietnam veterans. Craig Mullaney bonded with a fellow cadet at West Point over their shared "obsession with *Braveheart, Gladiator*," and other action movies.[16] He, like other IA troops, also enjoyed *Gates of Fire,* a novel based on the legendary 480 BCE "last stand" of Spartan warriors against Persian invaders.[17]

The Vietnam War, however, is the historical conflict most referenced in IA narratives. It is common for memoirists of America's most recent wars to highlight the Vietnam-era military service of family members, neighbors, and superior officers. Encounters with Vietnam veterans and references to Vietnam War movies are scattered throughout IA narratives. Anthony Swofford, a veteran of the Gulf War, gathered around the TV with his platoon mates to watch *Apocalypse Now, Platoon*, and other Vietnam movies before deploying to Saudi Arabia.[18] *Full Metal Jacket*, director Stanley Kubrick's 1986 film about Vietnam-era marine recruits, is cited many times by veteran-authors. Memoirist Benjamin Busch had Kubrick's movie on his mind when he commenced Marine Corps officer training in 1989.[19] Fick was thinking about *Full Metal Jacket* on his own first day of officer training about a decade later.[20]

Other sources indicate that *Full Metal Jacket* has greatly influenced soldiers and would-be soldiers since it was released. In 1995, journalist Thomas Ricks observed recruits endure several months of "boot camp" at Parris Island, South Carolina, the legendary Marine Corps training facility. He says that a group of trainees considered administering a ritualized beating called a "blanket party" to another recruit. They learned of this practice from "*Full Metal Jacket*, which most rented . . . and viewed before leaving for Parris Island."[21] The US Army discovered several years later that

*Full Metal Jacket* was the movie young Americans most associated with the army, despite the film's focus on the Marine Corps.[22] A fictional veteran quoted in *Redeployment*, Iraq veteran Phil Klay's short story collection, asserts that "more Marines have joined the Corps because of *Full Metal Jacket* than because of any fucking recruiting commercial."[23]

Some IA GIs continued to think about their favorite war movies even after reaching real war zones. Fick's "first reaction was to laugh" during a firefight in Iraq because it reminded him of a scene from a Vietnam War movie.[24] He adds that some marines, imitating their Vietnam movie heroes, stenciled "Born to Kill" on their helmets and "half jokingly" referred to Iraqis as "'gooks' or 'Charlie.'"[25] David Bellavia quoted *We Were Soldiers,* a 2002 film about an early Vietnam War battle, during a heated engagement with Iraqi insurgents.[26] Mullaney planned to give an inspiring speech to his men in Afghanistan which included a few "gung ho slogans from *Apocalypse Now*."[27] Sean Parnell says GIs in Afghanistan spent their downtime immersed in another arena of fictional combat: war-themed video games.[28]

Other IA soldiers thought about the exploits of real-life US military heroes while fighting overseas. Fick notes in *One Bullet Away* that history is the "religion" of the US Marine Corps.[29] The history of "the Corps" is taught to recruits and they are told to emulate the exploits of legendary marine heroes when they go into battle themselves.[30] One of Donovan Campbell's men asked if "the marines who fought at Iwo Jima and Okinawa" would be proud of their platoon after its first real taste of battle in the streets of Ramadi, Iraq.[31] Not only marines, however, are preoccupied with history. Bellavia, a former army infantryman, refers to the Second Battle of Fallujah (Iraq) as equal in significance to D-Day and the momentous World War I battle of Verdun.[32] Parnell, another former army infantryman, references the Civil War, World War II, the Korean War, and other conflicts in his memoir.[33]

Prewar fascination with war movies sometimes led to postwar disillusionment. Vietnam memoirists often angrily recount the ways in which their own battlefield experiences clashed with what they learned about war from popular culture. This same bitterness is evident in memoirs of other conflicts. Several veteran-authors seem guilty or even disappointed that their wars did not measure up to the epic engagements of the past. James Brady disparages his Korean War service because "the biggest fight" he participated in only involved a handful of enemy troops.[34] Shortly after returning to the United States from Iraq, Kayla Williams met a Vietnam veteran whose platoon was nearly wiped out during his tour.[35] Since no one in her "entire company" had died she felt it was "wrong" to "think that what [she] experienced in Iraq was tough or difficult."[36] Swofford and his comrades were angry and confused when the Gulf War ended because their "entire ground war lasted as long as a long-range jungle patrol" in Vietnam.[37]

One of the biggest discrepancies between real and cinematic warfare was the prevalence of combat-related psychological problems among soldiers. Most memoirs contain several stories about men and women who, in the terminology of World War II GIs, "cracked up" in battle.[38] Brady says that Korean War troops called such breakdowns getting "shook,"[39] while John Muirhead, who flew a B-17 bomber during World War II, calls such episodes "the clanks."[40] A member of Muirhead's crew experienced a mental collapse immediately upon their bomber's return from a mission over Nazi-occupied territory. The stricken man sweated heavily, trembled, and "soiled himself" because he was justly terrified that the Germans would one day shoot them down.[41] Williams witnessed a GI go through a "psychotic break" in Iraq. She tried to help the man as he cried, "curled up" in a fetal position, and punched himself.[42] Williams herself was so depressed in the last months of her tour that she seriously considered suicide.[43] Numerous other pre- and post-Vietnam memoirists say they personally experienced significant psychological issues during their combat tours. Mullaney "began to have more nightmares about the firefights" he had experienced over the previous year shortly before leaving Afghanistan.[44] He worried he was "going crazy."[45]

Most memoirists record encounters with foreign civilians in their books. Meetings between GIs and European, Asian, or Australian citizens are almost uniformly positive experiences in World War II memoirs. Joyous French people shouted "Vive les Americains!" when Donald Burgett's paratroop unit drove German occupiers out of a Normandy town. When he was wounded, the boat that ferried him back to England was met at the dock by a crowd of grateful British citizens.[46] Italians poured into the streets and turned the American advance through Rome into a jubilant victory parade when Harold L. Bond and thousands of other GIs liberated the city.[47] Troops who fought the Japanese had far fewer interactions with civilians, but several Pacific Theater memoirists were treated like heroes when their units rested in Australia between combat deployments. American servicemen, such authors say, were randomly invited into Australian homes and treated as honored guests. Australian children even asked ordinary GIs for their autographs.[48]

Servicemen bound for Vietnam, with World War II in mind, often expected to be greeted as liberators by the Vietnamese. The pimps, prostitutes, and guerrilla-harboring peasants they interacted with in Southeast Asia, however, did not resemble the gleeful foreigners who mobbed US troops in old newsreel footage. Interactions with foreign civilians documented in Korean War and post-Vietnam narratives are more similar to the Vietnam experience than to the World War II ideal. Brady, a former officer, had to deal with irate Korean village leaders who claimed two American soldiers raped their kinswomen. He threatened to destroy a different village if its inhabitants did not stop its infiltration by Chinese Communists. Acting just like the peasants in so many Vietnam War narratives, the Koreans disingenuously protested their ignorance about the infiltrators and pledged their loyalty to the Americans.[49]

Swofford's unit only briefly glimpsed wealthy Saudis as they passed by in expensive cars. These rare sightings fueled his suspicions that oil-rich Arabs unduly benefited from US participation in the Gulf War.[50] His resentments echo those of Vietnam veterans who rethought the virtue of their war because most Vietnamese seemed unappreciative of the sacrifices American soldiers made on their behalf. Post-9/11 narratives are even more evocative of Vietnam books in the way they describe GI–civilian relations. IA memoirists, like Vietnam GIs, were constantly pestered by street children begging for food, money, and cigarettes. The broken English shouted at Americans by young Afghan and Iraqi beggars was even similar to the patois of young Vietnamese panhandlers. Daily negative interactions with civilians eventually led Williams and every other GI she knew to hate *all* Iraqis.[51]

The development of a loathing for "hajjis" (a derogatory term for Iraqis widely used by GIs)[52] that Williams experienced is instantly recognizable to readers of Vietnam War narratives. Some American soldiers grew to hate all "gooks" by the time their Vietnam tours ended, and this kind of enmity sometimes led to atrocities. No war crimes at the level of the My Lai massacre are recounted in IA narratives, but they do contain other types of atrocity stories. Swofford watched another marine repeatedly hack at an Iraqi corpse with an entrenching tool in the aftermath of America's 1991 victory over Iraq. He says similar acts were perpetrated by other GIs, including blowing up Iraqi bodies with explosives for amusement.[53] In April 2004, media outlets published photographs taken at the Abu Ghraib prison which depicted shocking abuse of Iraqi prisoners by US military guards. An interrogation witnessed by Williams suggests that

mistreatment of Iraqi detainees was not limited to Abu Ghraib. US personnel trying to "break" a prisoner thought it would be easier to humiliate
him with Williams, "a blonde American female," looking on. Interrogators
struck the prisoner and flicked lit cigarettes at him, and she claims that the
installation where this took place was later investigated because one man
died in its custody and another was badly injured.[54]

IA narratives as a whole, however, feature fewer atrocity stories than
Vietnam memoirs. But World War II narratives, especially those written
by Pacific Theater veterans, contain numerous accounts of GIs perpetrat-
ing war crimes, most of them involving enemy corpses. E. B. Sledge saw
a marine urinate into the mouths of dead Japanese soldiers, another take
a Japanese hand as a trophy, and several others pry gold fillings out of the
mouths of enemy bodies.[55] Another veteran of the Pacific War, Robert
Leckie, served with a marine dubbed "Souvenirs" for his post-firefight
hunts for Japanese fillings.[56] James J. Fahey witnessed fellow sailors scram-
ble to extricate Japanese body parts from the wreckage of kamikaze planes
that slammed into the deck of a US Navy destroyer. One trophy hunter
found a "Jap rib . . . cleaned it up" and planned to give it to his sister, who
wanted "part of a Jap body."[57]

Sex has long been a crucial component of what Samuel Hynes calls
"the soldiers' tale." He accurately notes that veteran memoirs suggest that
"sex was everywhere" in Vietnam. Hynes wrongly asserts, however, that
World War II memoirists left sex out of their books.[58] Most World War II
veterans write about sex in less graphic language than their Vietnam successors, but it is nevertheless present in their narratives. Memoirs published
during the war and in the early postwar years are tame in terms of sexual
content, but even these narratives obliquely comment on the sex lives of
GIs. Even Murphy, the boyish war hero, included jokes about venereal
disease and prostitutes in his 1949 memoir, *To Hell and Back*.[59] World War
II narratives published in latter decades are just as frank in discussing sex
as Vietnam memoirs. William Manchester includes detailed descriptions of
several sexual encounters in his 1980 memoir, *Goodbye, Darkness*.[60] Elmer
Bendiner mentions in *The Fall of Fortresses*, also published in 1980, that he
cheated on his newly pregnant wife while stationed in England during
World War II. He says many servicemen, bachelors and married men alike,
were driven, like himself, "to the palliative of sex" by fear.[61]

Like their Vietnam successors, World War II authors often portray females they met overseas, regardless of their race, as one-dimensional figures
whose primary function was to provide sexual pleasure to GIs. Bendiner,

a former B-17 navigator, says American airmen categorized English girls they dated as either "whores or cockteasers . . . depending on whether the speaker had won or lost the endless chase."[62] E. J. Kahn Jr., whose 1943 memoir was published during the war, explains to his readers that "Australian girls . . . are neither as well dressed, nor as good-looking . . . as American girls," but are sufficient to "abet loneliness in American soldiers."[63] Gregory "Pappy" Boyington, a Medal of Honor recipient, similarly notes that while "Australian girls didn't have anything on the girls back home," GIs pursued female companionship anyway when stationed "down under" out of necessity.[64]

Although European and (presumably Caucasian) Australian women are objectified in World War II narratives, Asians are afforded even less respect. American troops harshly judged the physical appearances of non-white females long before GIs derided Vietnamese women for their supposed inferiority to "round-eyes." American soldiers, according to Kahn, paid no attention to the women of Papua New Guinea because they "were an unseemly bunch" characterized by "eccentric shapes."[65] He underscores the racism of this assessment by wryly observing that "native" females did not look like Dorothy Lamour, a white American movie star.[66] Boyington proclaims that the most attractive women he saw during a visit to Singapore were "mixed breeds."[67] He, like many GIs who served in Southeast Asia decades later, evidently believed that Asian women could not be truly beautiful unless they possessed some Caucasian ancestry. Martin Russ reveals that racist, superficial assessments of Asian women took place during the Korean War as well. He says it did not matter that Korean prostitutes fell short of American standards of beauty because any woman looked appealing to an amorous fighting man far from home.[68]

GIs who served in Afghanistan, Iraq, or elsewhere in the Middle East had far fewer opportunities to interact with local women than Americans who fought in earlier wars. Swofford, as a fan of Vietnam War films, always assumed that access to prostitutes was an essential perk of going to war. But during the Gulf War he and thousands of other Americans were stationed in remote desert areas on the Saudi Arabia–Iraq border. GIs in "sexless Saudi" almost never saw women of any kind, let alone prostitutes.[69] Fictional GIs in another Klay short story, "In Vietnam They Had Whores," compare what they have heard about Vietnam to their own situation in Iraq. The men dream about nonexistent "Iraqi whorehouses" and are dumbstruck when they spot a woman in their "chow hall."[70] Sex, however, is not absent from post-Vietnam narratives. IA memoirists say that GIs commonly bragged about sexual escapades and possessed pornographic magazines and videos. Williams asserts that sexual relationships between male and female GIs were commonplace, even in Iraq.[71] Mullaney was amazed to see condoms on sale and "crowds of male and female soldiers . . . on the prowl" at Kandahar Airfield in Afghanistan.[72]

Williams's memoir, *Love My Rifle More Than You*, provides another perspective on combat soldiers' preoccupation with sex. Her experiences as a female soldier in Iraq are reminiscent of those recounted by Lynda VanDevanter and other American women who served in Vietnam. Mutual love and respect existed between Williams and her male comrades, but she nevertheless faced frequent sexual harassment. Male soldiers blatantly leered at her body, taunted her with crude sexual jokes, and propositioned her for sex. On one occasion she fought off a sexual assault. Williams maintains that servicewomen, whether stationed in Iraq or elsewhere, were placed in one of two categories by male troops: "bitch" or "slut." A bitch was someone who refrained from sexual activities with other GIs; a slut did not. The former group was viewed as aloof and conceited, while the latter was seen as immoral and untrustworthy. Women GIs, therefore, were castigated by their male peers no matter what they did.[73]

Another linkage between veteran–authors of different wars is two specific groups of people they disliked during their combat tours. The first category of people is noncombat soldiers. The idea that American combat troops had more in common with Vietcong guerrillas than REMFs is expressed in several Vietnam narratives. Brady makes an almost identical statement in his memoir, *The Coldest Winter*. He realized one day that he "understood" enemy soldiers better than American sailors aboard navy vessels patrolling the Korean coastline. The sailors were safe and warm while Brady and his Chinese and Korean adversaries faced death and freezing temperatures every day.[74] Support troops were referred to as "Fobbits" by post-9/11 GIs, an epithet derived from Forward Operating Base (FOB), a military term for the heavily defended safe areas where noncombat GIs spent most of their time.[75] After months of battling the Taliban in the Afghan countryside, Mullaney was astonished when confronted with the creature comforts offered to the thousands of Fobbits stationed at Kandahar Airfield. He admits that "it was impossible not to resent the standard of living" his "less bloodied comrades" enjoyed while his platoon endured so much violence and deprivation.[76]

Former officers are overrepresented among veteran-writers, but officers, especially those of high rank, are nonetheless the other commonly disparaged group. Manchester describes his regimental commander as a buffoon and tells an anecdote about a bumbling, inexperienced lieutenant who died when he foolishly exposed himself to enemy machinegun fire.[77] Brady castigates American generals who initiated a "silly, flamboyant," and ineffectual plan designed to break the stalemate on the Korean peninsula.[78] Parnell took a flight to Bagram Airfield after months of hot, dirty fighting in the Afghan "boonies." Soon after arrival, his weather-beaten uniform was called a "disgrace" by an appalled major. The major was not in the infantry and "wore no combat badges," which made him, in Parnell's mind, just one of the many other Fobbits who inhabited the airfield.[79] After days of street fighting in Fallujah, Bellavia and his platoon mates were finally allowed to rest at a US military base. But soon after the fatigued troops arrived at the base they were informed by an officer that they needed to clean their uniforms and make ready for an inspection by a general. Bellavia declares that he regards a lieutenant he fought alongside as a "brother," but has no respect for generals and other high-ranking officers who stayed far away from combat.[80]

Most fighting men and women stationed overseas dream of returning home to their loved ones, but, as so many Vietnam narratives illustrate, soldiers' homecomings can be painful. Many GIs developed an ambivalent attitude about the "folks back home" before their tours even ended. Sledge, for instance, wished clueless civilians back in the United States would get bombed so they could understand the terror felt by "their boys" fighting overseas.[81] No veterans of pre- or post-Vietnam conflicts say they were treated poorly when they came home, let alone spat upon. But, like Vietnam veterans, many veterans of other wars had difficulty interacting with civilians when they got back to the United States. Mullaney says he "felt . . . acutely conscious of standing apart from [his] civilian peers" at a cocktail party he attended after returning from Afghanistan.[82] When Williams returned to America, she "did not want to be around non-Army people" and thought civilians "were selfish" and "didn't understand anything."[83] Civilians also enraged her by incorrectly assuming that she had not been a "real" soldier or done anything noteworthy in Iraq because she is a woman.[84]

Dealing with ignorant civilians, however, was not the worst problem faced by ex-soldiers over the decades. Murphy declares at the end of *To Hell and Back* that he "will not be defeated" by his horrible memories of the war and "learn to live again."[85] Sadly, severe mental torment prevented Murphy from fulfilling his vow.[86] *To Hell and Back* nevertheless eschewed any real discussions of these difficulties, and for decades most other Second World War veteran-authors followed suit. This all changed in the post-Vietnam era. World War II writers of this period, as David Kieran contends, employed "the language and discourses of Vietnam memoirs" to describe their own postwar troubles.[87] Such authors, most notably Fussell, Sledge, and Manchester, say that after they returned from combat they jumped at loud noises, had reoccurring nightmares, and wept for no apparent reason.[88]

Fussell says that "no one had heard yet of post-traumatic stress disorder" when he came home from Europe, "but for the first couple of years after the war [he] experienced something close to it."[89] Conversely, the tribulations of Vietnam veterans and the existence of PTSD were common knowledge by the time IA memoirists sat down and wrote about their combat tours. The acceptance of these issues is evident in the many IA narratives that forthrightly discuss postwar battles with PTSD. After Fick came home, he cried, had nightmares, and reflexively looked for roadside bombs while driving on American streets. He eventually improved, but for a time feared he was "losing [his] mind."[90] Marcus Luttrell, former Navy SEAL and author of the best-selling memoir *Lone Survivor*, doubts he "will ever sleep through the night again" because he hears the screams of a friend who died in Afghanistan every time he closes his eyes.[91] Williams's second memoir, *Plenty of Time When We Get Home*, focuses on the several horrendous years in which she and her Iraq veteran husband experienced post-traumatic stress.[92]

It is necessary to scrutinize the content of war memoirs to determine what exactly ex-soldiers say about their childhoods, their combat experiences, their postwar civilian lives, and other matters. But it is equally important, as was shown with Vietnam memoirs in previous chapters, to determine *how* they were written. Exploring this subject exposes additional linkages between Vietnam narratives and those of other conflicts. Sex, death, war wounds, and other controversial topics were addressed in essentially every veteran memoir published from 1942 onward. But the ways in which ex-soldiers wrote about these sensitive issues changed over the decades.

There is virtually no profanity in World War II memoirs published in the 1940s, sex is only hinted at, and battlefield injuries and deaths are generally not described in detail. Memoirs published during the war were especially free from provocative material. This is understandable since such books were obviously meant to serve, at least in part, as pro-war propaganda. The late 1950s were a turning point in the veteran memoir genre. Two narratives published during this period, Russ's *The Last Parallel* (1957) and Boyington's *Baa Baa Black Sheep* (1958), were far more graphic and vulgar than veteran memoirs published in earlier years. Russ devotes the first several pages of *The Last Parallel* to his predeployment quest to lose his virginity,[93] a goal he eventually accomplished "among the sooty weeds next to a railroad siding."[94] He later explains that "the word 'fuck' [is] used three times as often as it usually is" in many conversations between marines.[95] Like numerous Vietnam memoirists, Russ uses this word himself throughout his book. Boyington, a World War II fighter pilot, unashamedly writes about drunken wartime trips to brothels, and mentions seeing GIs waiting in line outside a makeshift bordello in New Caledonia.[96]

Scores of Vietnam War memoirs featuring graphic descriptions of sex and violence have been published since the mid-1970s. Many have been best sellers or critics' favorites. As a result, the style and content of veteran narratives have become less determined by publisher censorship or writer self-censorship. This state of affairs has in turn paved the way for less sanitized depictions of pre-Vietnam conflicts to be published. Some World War II memoirs published in the 1980s are nearly as profane and explicit as Vietnam narratives.[97] World War II bomber crews, according to Bendiner, peppered most of their conversations with a variety of swear words. Sledge's 1981 memoir, *With the Old Breed*, describes fighting in the Pacific as an exercise carried out among putrefying corpses, writhing maggots, unburied human excrement, and massive swarms of flies.[98] Manchester's *Goodbye, Darkness* includes the description of a marine whose face became "juicy shapeless red pulp" after he was hit by a mortar round.[99] A few pages later he describes being "encompassed" by the "flesh, blood, brains, and intestines" of another marine struck down by Japanese firepower.[100]

Swofford's *Jarhead*, the first major American memoir of a post-Vietnam conflict, is replete with frank talk about sex. He writes about watching pornographic videos, wanting to "screw" his girlfriend while in boot camp, and his adolescent desire to "chase prostitutes through the world's brothels."[101] Shortly before the start of the ground offensive against Iraq, a sergeant told Swofford and the other marines in his charge to remove all "foreign matter" from their personal belongings. "By foreign matter [the sergeant meant] letters from women or girls other than our wives or girlfriends, and also pornography and other profane materials." The sergeant did not want such items shipped home to the relatives of marines killed in combat.[102] *Jarhead*, in addition to its blunt treatment of sex, features vivid descriptions of corpses and war wounds, something it has in common with post-9/11 narratives. Parnell, for instance, saw a soldier covered with the "blood, chunks of skin, and tendons" of a comrade who was hit by an RPG (rocket-propelled grenade).[103]

Post-9/11 memoirs generally contain fewer discussions of sex than those of other conflicts. The male memoirists of America's latest wars say little about women at all, but when they do it is often about a loving, patient wife or girlfriend waiting back home. Campbell "prayed and cried throughout the night" with his wife Christy before shipping out for the Middle East.[104] He mentions how difficult it was for her to hear about fierce fighting in Ramadi on the news when she knew he was stationed in that city.[105] Like Campbell, Mullaney recognizes that the woman in his life suffered during his tour. Meena, his fiancée, experienced the daily torture of waiting for a phone call telling her that he was dead or wounded.[106] Such stories of stable, committed relationships are rare in the narratives of earlier wars.

As chapter 6 demonstrates, Vietnam memoirists generally had mixed feelings about their tours even though their overall depiction of the war was decidedly negative. Narratives about other wars often convey similarly complicated messages. Manchester, for instance, states that his "feelings about the Marine Corps are still highly ambivalent, tinged with sadness and bitterness, yet with the first enchantment lingering."[107] This uncertainty is evident throughout his book. Manchester begins *Goodbye, Darkness* with a distressing story about "the first man [he] slew," a Japanese sniper.[108] After shooting the man at close range with his pistol, Manchester vomited and tearfully told the dead man he was sorry. Many of his anecdotes about the war match the disturbing and depressing tone of the sniper story. But at other points Manchester reveals obvious pride in his military service and the martial prowess displayed by the marines who beat the Japanese at Guadalcanal, Okinawa, and elsewhere.[109] He also gloats about the impossibility of "the generation of the 1980's" ever equaling the patriotism and toughness of the World War II generation.[110]

Many World War II memoirists, like Manchester, describe their combat tours as a string of horrific, dispiriting episodes. *To Hell and Back* is the story of one of the war's greatest heroes, and it features much comic banter between Murphy and his army buddies, but it is also the story of how almost all of these buddies eventually died in battle. The tone of *To Hell and Back* becomes increasingly somber as it progresses. Celebrations heralding the war's end in Europe only caused a dejected Murphy to reminisce about his many slain comrades.[111] He never, however, seriously questions the righteousness of the cause for which he fought. Other World War II memoirists are similarly certain that the war was terrible yet necessary,[112] and this belief tempers negative descriptions of the conflict. Bendiner, for instance, expresses sadness for the women, children, forced laborers, and other innocents who were likely killed by bombs dropped from his B-17. He states several times, however, that as horrible as these deaths were, they paled in comparison to the crimes committed by Hitler's regime. And because the horror of Nazi rule had to be stopped, the Allied "cause was just."[113]

Vietnam War memoirists were far less confident in the cause that sent them to Southeast Asia in the 1960s and early 1970s. Many veteran-authors unambiguously declared that America's war in Vietnam was absurd and unwinnable, highlighting the ARVN's aversion to combat, the widespread collusion of civilians with the Vietcong, and other factors. IA memoirists were often just as disillusioned with the causes that sent them into battle. Swofford believes the United States went to war with Iraq in 1991 solely to protect the interests of Saudi, Kuwaiti, and American oil tycoons.[114] Williams declares that Saddam Hussein's regime was not linked to the 9/11 attacks, as officials in the US government alleged, and that the American case for going to war in 2003 was based on "lies."[115] Both Fick and Campbell scorn US authorities who bungled the occupation of Iraq by issuing foolish and counterproductive decrees that contributed to the chaos following the ouster of the Hussein government.[116]

Scathing statements about the falsity of America's reasons for going to war, combined with stories about Iraqi civilians shooting at GIs or supposed Afghan allies selling weapons to the Taliban, cast a poor light on post-Vietnam military interventions. But most IA memoirists display the same ambivalence expressed by veterans of earlier conflicts. Campbell wrote his memoir, *Joker One*, to publicize marine heroics he witnessed during the fight for Ramadi, the US military's bloodiest operation, he proudly notes, since the Vietnam War.[117] A prominent theme of post-9/11 narratives is the profound bonds of friendship that develop between combat soldiers. Authors who served in Iraq or Afghanistan often experienced an unsettling feeling when they left the military: they were glad to be out of danger, but simultaneously yearned to be with their brother and sister soldiers again on the battlefield. Memoirists describe such thoughts as strange and confusing, but such emotional turmoil was not a new phenomenon; veterans of World War II, Korea, and Vietnam all wrote about feeling the same way.

An important question remains concerning pre– and post–Vietnam War narratives: who wrote them? These memoirists are remarkably similar to their Vietnam counterparts; they are, on average, white, middle-class, college-educated, former junior officers. All of the World War II and Korean War memoirists discussed in this chapter are white. Millions of African American men served in the US military during World War II, although most were restricted to labor battalions. Government and military leaders believed, in the words of Secretary of War Henry Stimson, that African Americans "'lacked the moral and mental qualifications' for combat."[118] Some black troops saw combat, but their heroics were mostly ignored by the mainstream press.[119] Polls taken in the 1940s showed that "more than half of black troops questioned why they had to fight," and a "majority . . . believed black people overall would not be much better off after the war."[120] This cynicism is understandable since black GIs served in segregated units and often trained at Southern military bases surrounded by racist white civilians.[121] American authorities enforced segregation overseas as well, explaining to allied nations that this practice was necessary to "protect white women."[122]

World War II veteran-authors say very little about race, racism, or even the existence of black soldiers. Muirhead, whose only mention of African Americans is an offhand reference to "one of the black mess men," talks more about black troops than other World War II memoirists.[123] One likely reason African Americans barely appear in white-authored narratives is the fact that most black troops were assigned to segregated labor units, and all the memoirists served in combat positions. The authors, then, probably had limited contact with African American GIs. In 1948, President Harry Truman issued Executive Order 9981, which desegregated the American armed forces. African Americans were fighting alongside whites by the end of the Korean War. The two white authors of Korean War memoirs studied in this chapter, however, say relatively little about the newly integrated military in which they served. Russ describes one soldier he meets as a "Negro," and another as a "colored guy," but says nothing else about race relations in the 1950s Marine Corps.[124] Brady notes that "in 1951 and 1952 you never saw a Negro officer," and many white marines (especially Southerners) expressed racist attitudes about African Americans.[125] But Brady's treatment of racial matters only amounts to a few paragraphs. He does not even mention that the integrated units in which he served did not exist a few years earlier.

IA narratives suggest that the US military of the twenty-first century is a racially and ethnically diverse organization. Memoirists mention comrades who are first- and second-generation immigrants from the Philippines, Mexico, Nigeria, Russia, Haiti, and other nations. Andrew Exum and Parnell both served with Vietnamese American soldiers whose fathers fought in the ARVN.[126] Exum's platoon was composed of "white, black, Hispanic, [and] Asian" members, but they nevertheless became "a family" after serving together in Afghanistan.[127] A navy corpsmen attached to Campbell's unit, "Doc" Camacho, was fluent in English but "spoke Spanish as his first language."[128] The most popular member of Campbell's platoon was Todd Bolding, an African American affectionately nicknamed "Black Man." When Bolding died in combat, Campbell and his platoon mates were inconsolable.[129]

All of the IA memoirists, however, are white, and they say little about racial issues. Minority GIs nevertheless faced significant issues during the post-Vietnam era. Large numbers of African Americans, for instance, joined the armed forces after the war ended in 1973. Many black Americans saw joining up as a smart economic decision, but a majority also opposed post-Vietnam military conflicts, especially the second war in Iraq.[130] A willingness to join the armed forces combined with a distaste for military adventurism amounts to what Kimberly L. Philips calls "one of the paradoxes of US history."[131] What was it like to fight in Iraq when most people in your community were against the war? That is a question, among untold others related to the experiences of nonwhite GIs, that cannot yet be answered by reading the most popular IA memoirs.

The mobilization of manpower carried out by the federal government during World War II was on a larger scale than the drive to secure enough men to fight the Vietnam conflict. The sheer numbers needed to wage a world war was one reason why more men from the upper and middle classes were drawn into World War II. Another reason for this phenomenon was the matter of "personal honor." Men from all levels of 1940s society, even those at its pinnacle, considered it their manly, patriotic duty to join the armed forces in time of war. Winthrop Rockefeller, grandson of billionaire John D. Rockefeller, volunteered for military service, for example, soon after the Japanese attack on Pearl Harbor.[132] Still another reason for the broad participation of men from fortunate backgrounds in World War II was a draft system that was, in Beth Bailey's words, "fairly inclusive and relatively egalitarian."[133] Throughout most of World War II, it was relatively difficult to obtain an educational deferment, which meant that the college plans of thousands of young men were interrupted by military service. An ability to pay college tuition gave middle- and upper-class men an easy way to avoid military service during the Vietnam era; this was not the case in the 1940s.[134]

Although the presence of wealthy and middle-class men in the military was not so extraordinary during the 1940s as it was in later decades, a disproportionate number of World War II memoirists nevertheless came from privileged backgrounds. Fussell was drafted into the army out of college and grew up during the Great Depression in a rich household in a "highly privileged suburb."[135] Sledge dropped out of college to join the marines and his father was a medical doctor.[136] One of his platoon mates was surprised by his toughness because Sledge, in his estimation, was "sort of a rich kid compared to some guys."[137] Kahn was a Harvard graduate who was writing for the *New Yorker* when he was drafted.[138] Ralph Ingersoll, the author of *The Battle Is the Pay-Off,* was a Yale graduate and the well-known editor of *PM,* a leftist newspaper, when he was drafted.[139] Bond, author of *Return to Cassino,* arrived in war-torn Italy as a second lieutenant and a college graduate. When he realized some of his men were "almost illiterate," he helped them write letters, and was delighted when a transfer to a new job enabled him "to be able to speak of books and ideas" with other officers who were "college men."[140]

Bailey states in her 2009 book, *America's Army: The Making of the All-Volunteer Force,* that "though a great many Americans . . . still see the army as the final refuge for those with no other options, it is not."[141] The poor are underrepresented in today's army because they are more likely to have criminal records, health problems, and inadequate educations that make them ineligible for military service. And the majority of upper- and upper-middle-class youths do not want to join the armed forces. This situation, Bailey explains, makes the army of the early twenty-first century a "fairly solidly middle class" institution.[142] The extraordinary premilitary educations of many IA memoirists, however, indicate that a disproportionate number have exceptional backgrounds. Campbell graduated from Princeton University,[143] Busch from Vassar College,[144] and Fick from Dartmouth College;[145] all three are elite, private institutions. Mullaney came from a working-class family, but graduated from West Point and attended Oxford University on a Rhodes scholarship. He surmises that his "ivory tower peers" would likely never have any contact with the types of Americans who comprised his platoon in Afghanistan.[146]

Veteran-authors of both pre- and post-Vietnam conflicts are also conspicuous in the educational and professional achievements they accrued after they came home from war. Fussell earned a PhD from Harvard

University after leaving the army and, like fellow PhDs Sledge and Bond, later became a college professor. Leckie, Bendiner, Manchester, and Brady were all successful writers before their memoirs were published. Fick was enrolled in both Harvard's Business School and its John F. Kennedy School of Government when *One Bullet Away* was published in 2005; he has twice worked as a CEO for major companies since 2007. Campbell attended Harvard Business School as well, graduating with an MBA in 2007, and Exum was awarded a PhD in 2011 by King's College London. Mullaney was appointed to teach history at the United States Naval Academy while still in the army. He later held important positions in business and government. Before and after Busch's second tour in Iraq, he worked as an actor in significant roles on several television series, most notably HBO's *The Wire*. Murphy became a movie star, and Luttrell's *Lone Survivor* was released as a Hollywood film of the same name in 2013.

Most memoirists, however, like their equally distinguished Vietnam-era counterparts, fought as junior officers or, less often, enlisted men. Fussell, who served as a second lieutenant in Europe, describes himself as "a grunt with gold bars," referring to the uniform insignia that indicate officer status.[147] The many other former lieutenants among veteran-authors would likely proudly identify with Fussell's description of himself. A common theme in the veteran memoir genre is the author's gradual transformation from a "green" lieutenant to a respected and trusted leader. An integral component of this concept is the formation of a strong bond between the lieutenant and his platoon. Several months into Parnell's tour he was given the opportunity to go "on leave" to the United States. He had mixed feelings about the visit because while he longed to see his family back in the United States, he also did not want to leave his men in Afghanistan, his other "family." After a few days on leave Parnell learned that a member of his platoon had been killed. In his grief he realized that his real "home" was now with his platoon mates, not in America.[148] The details of Parnell's story are unique, but his realizations are present in practically every ex–junior officer's memoir published since World War II.

Fick states that "the homecoming story is a cliché" before describing his own return to America from Iraq. His account is indeed stereotypical, but it is nevertheless remarkable because it so closely resembles, at least in the beginning, a typical *Vietnam* veteran homecoming tale. Fick ended his combat tour aboard a commercial airplane, and the GI passengers cheered when the plane left Kuwait. During the long journey home he reveled in things he had missed while fighting in the Iraqi desert: appetizing food, attractive female flight attendants, and green grass spied during a layover in Germany. When the pilot announced that Fick's plane had entered US airspace the troops cheered again.[149] Pretty stewardesses, civilian airliners, and effusive GIs are all hallmarks of the average Vietnam memoirist's story about taking the "freedom bird" back to "the world." During Fick's first night back in the United States he marveled at the "dark brown face [that] stared back from the bathroom mirror," and took two showers "just because [he] could."[150] Decades earlier, soldiers newly arrived from Southeast Asia did these same things.

The linkages between Fick's return home and the homecoming stories of so many Vietnam writers is further evidence that some things for combat soldiers never change. An analysis of pre–World War II narratives would likely uncover comparable connections. But another reason for such similarities is the preponderance of certain types of people among veteran-writers. Parallels between narratives are surely more likely to occur if author demographics rarely stray from a certain set of characteristics. Historians are fortunate that numerous literate, college-educated men and women have written down their battlefield experiences over the last sixty years or so. But the full story of the veteran experience goes untold when the stories of working-class people, African Americans, enlisted men, and others are underrepresented.

# Conclusion
## *The Vietnam Memoir Legacy*

When the Civil War ended in 1865, the memories of the soldiers who fought in it, Union and Confederate alike, seemed, in the words of Gerald F. Linderman, to go into a kind of "hibernation" for the ensuing fifteen years.[1] These men witnessed unspeakable carnage and suffered great privations, and many apparently just wanted to forget all they had been through. The veterans' collective silence during these fifteen years was abetted by a general feeling that the nation should move on and leave the horrors of the preceding years behind it. The 1880s, however, brought a great revival of interest in the Civil War. The public craved information about the conflict, and more ex-soldiers wanted to tell their stories. In the last two decades of the century, thousands of Northern and Southern veterans recorded their war narratives in memoirs, magazines, and "formal papers" presented at the meetings of veterans' organizations.[2]

Although many Americans became fascinated with the Civil War in the 1880s, few "wanted to recollect the horror or the meaning of the war."[3] Veterans, David W. Blight explains, participated in this selective remembering by "clean[ing] up the battles and the campaigns of the real war, render[ing] it exciting and normal all at once."[4] By focusing on glorified recollections of combat and eschewing "the political meanings" of the war, especially its racial underpinnings, the nation moved closer towards sectional reconciliation as the century drew to a close. Another consequence of this reformulation of memory was a rebirth of militarism. Men who decried the horrors of war as soldiers in the 1860s extolled it in the 1890s as a cure for the "softness" and materialism supposedly destroying society during this era of massive urbanization and industrialization. Consequently, when war broke out between the United States and Spain in 1898, thousands of young men reared on romantic tales of Civil War heroics eagerly signed up for a chance at battlefield glory.[5]

Another hibernation period followed America's defeat in Vietnam. There was a widespread sentiment throughout much of the 1970s that the country needed to forget the painful tribulations of the Vietnam era and look to the future. This all changed in the 1980s. Americans during the Reagan era suddenly became interested in all things Vietnam, and book publishers, filmmakers, and even politicians eagerly fed the demand. Similar to the Civil War revival of a century earlier, much of the Vietnam-related cultural material produced during this period depicted the war unrealistically and avoided or misrepresented its political aspects. Some representations were appropriately serious, but such renderings were outweighed by cartoonish action movies, comic books, pulp novels, and television shows. A new genre of films, with *Rambo: First Blood Part II* at the forefront, focused on the exploits of ex-soldiers sent back to Southeast Asia to rescue secretly held American POWs. On television, the popular series *The A-Team* chronicled the adventures of four former Vietnam War commandos who traveled America helping the unfortunate and fighting injustice.

Most Vietnam veteran-memoirists, however, have not participated in trivializing the war in which they fought. Veteran authors have instead written about shattered limbs, exposed intestines, slain women and children, and the terror of being under fire. While dealing forthrightly with the brutalities of war, veteran narratives also expose the racist and sexist attitudes held by many GIs in Vietnam. And all of this was rendered in graphic, vulgar, sometimes obscene language that is a far cry from the "purple prose" produced by many Civil War memoirists.[6] Also unlike Civil War veterans, Vietnam memoirists did not shy away from the larger issues surrounding the war. The latter generation of veterans candidly stated whether they thought military strategies in Vietnam were wrong or even if the war itself was wrong.

Some scholars believed in the 1980s that veteran-authored Vietnam War literature could stem resurgent militarism and prevent the United States from wading into future military quagmires. This, of course, did not happen. American soldiers have been involved in many armed conflicts, both big and small, since Saigon fell in 1975. The success of Vietnam memoirs, however, did make it easier for the men and women who fought in America's post-Vietnam wars to tell their stories. It is unlikely that Iraq and Afghanistan memoirists would have written about their experiences with such brutal honesty and in such a realistic style if an example had not

been first set by Vietnam authors. Vietnam authors likewise paved the way
for World War II and Korean War veterans who wanted to write memoirs
that were less sanitized than narratives published before the 1970s.

Vietnam veteran memoirs, however, have their faults. Five of the Vietnam War books George Herring reviewed for the *Journal of American History* are veteran memoirs or other types of personal narratives. Herring says
that "a major weakness of the books reviewed . . . especially the memoirs,
is inevitable lack of historical perspective."[7] He thus concludes that people
"who confine their Vietnam reading to this kind of book will get only a
fragmentary and misleading view of the broader historical forces that gave
the war its peculiar dynamism and do so much to explain its outcome
and consequences."[8] Many more Vietnam memoirs and oral histories were
published after Herring made these statements in 1986, but, as this book
has shown, they still ring true. But by "telling it like it was" and encouraging other generations of ex-soldiers to do the same, veteran memoirists
have nevertheless enhanced our understanding of the true nature of war.

# Notes

*Introduction*

1. Robert Mason, *Chickenhawk* (New York: Penguin, 2005), 17–51.

2. Ibid., 42.

3. Ibid., 140.

4. Ibid., 131.

5. Ibid., 242–43, 390–92, 415–16, 434–39, 451–62.

6. Robert Mason, *Chickenhawk Back in the World: Life after Vietnam* (New York: Viking, 1993), 5–87.

7. Ibid, 87.

8. Edwin McDowell, "Publishing: Vietnam Rediscovered," *New York Times*, December 2, 1983, C25.

9. Mason, *Chickenhawk Back in the World*, 92.

10. Ibid., 86–87, 225–26, 241–48, 317–19; and Mason, *Chickenhawk*, 479.

11. McDowell, "Publishing: Vietnam Rediscovered," C25.

12. "4 Writers Try to Make Sense of the Vietnam-Book Boom," *New York Times*, August 4, 1987, C17.

13. Ibid.

14. Merritt Clifton, *Those Who Were There: Eyewitness Accounts of the War in Southeast Asia, 1956–1975, & Aftermath* (Paradise, CA: Dustbooks, 1984).

15. Paul Fussell, *The Great War and Modern Memory* (New York: Oxford University Press, 2000), 327.

16. Samuel Hynes, *The Soldiers' Tale: Bearing Witness to Modern War* (New York: Penguin Press, 1997), 1–3.

17. Ibid., 1.

18. Phil Klay, *Redeployment* (New York: Penguin Press, 2014), 170.

132          19. Philip H. Melling, *Vietnam in American Literature* (Boston: Twayne Publishers, 1990), 49–55.

20. Ibid., 54.

21. Ibid., 53.

22. Ibid., 54.

23. Ibid., 53.

24. Ibid., 54.

25. Jerry Lembke, *The Spitting Image: Myth, Memory, and the Legacy of Vietnam* (New York: New York University Press, 1998), 11–26; and Andrew J. Bacevich, *The Limits of Power: The End of American Exceptionalism* (New York: Metropolitan Books, 2008), 128–31.

26. David Kieran, *Forever Vietnam: How a Divisive War Changed American Public Memory* (Boston: University of Massachusetts Press, 2014), 219.

27. Ibid., 205, 219, 228, 233.

28. Meredith H. Lair, *Armed with Abundance: Consumerism and Soldiering in the Vietnam War* (Chapel Hill: The University of North Carolina Press, 2011), 218–19.

29. Examples of books that espoused this conception of veteran-authored Vietnam War literature include: Thomas Myers, *Walking Point: American Narratives of Vietnam* (New York: Oxford University Press, 1988), 5–13, 26–31; Andrew Martin, *Receptions of War: Vietnam in American Culture* (Norman: University of Oklahoma Press, 1993), 77–78; Julia Bleakney, *Revisiting Vietnam: Memoirs, Memorials, Museums* (New York: Routledge, 2006), 39–40, 46; and Tobey C. Herzog, *Vietnam War Stories: Innocence Lost* (New York: Routledge, 1992), 5–6.

30. Susan Jeffords, *The Remasculinization of America: Gender and the Vietnam War* (Indianapolis: Indiana University Press, 1989).

31. Herman Beavers, "Contemporary Afro-American Studies and the Study of the Vietnam War," *Vietnam Generation* 1, no. 2 (1989): 6–13; and Perry D. Luckett, "The Black Soldier in Vietnam War Literature and Film," *War, Literature, and the Arts* 1, no. 2 (1989–1990): 1–27.

32. Jacqueline Lawson, "'She's a Pretty Woman . . . for a Gook': The Misogyny of the Vietnam War," in *Fourteen Landing Zones: Approaches to Vietnam War Literature*, ed. Philip K. Jason, 17–34 (Iowa City: University of Iowa Press, 1991), 19.

33. See Christian G. Appy, *Working-Class War: American Combat Soldiers and Vietnam* (Chapel Hill: The University of North Carolina Press, 1993), 343–44; Marilyn B. Young, *The Vietnam Wars, 1945–1990* (New York: HarperCollins, 1991), 375–79; and George C. Herring, *America's Longest War: The United States and Vietnam, 1950–1975* (New York: John Wiley & Sons, 1979), 145, 154, 156, 162, 266.

34. The only existing work of historical scholarship that regards veterans' narratives as a separate topic, or examines the potential effects of such works on

collective memory, is a 1986 *Journal of American History* review of nonfiction Vietnam War books by Herring. George C. Herring, "Vietnam Remembered," *Journal of American History* 73, no. 1 (June 1986): 152–64.

35. Peter S. Kindsvatter, *American Soldiers: Ground Combat in the World Wars, Korea, and Vietnam* (Lawrence: Kansas University Press, 2003), 405–15.

36. David Thelen, "Memory and American History," *Journal of American History* 75, no. 4 (March 1989): 1119.

37. Ibid.

38. Lair, *Armed with Abundance*, 18.

### Chapter 1: Who Were the Vietnam Veteran Memoirists?

1. Lewis B. Puller Jr., *Fortunate Son* (New York: Grove Weindenfeld, 1991), 1–33, 73, 77, 78.

2. William Broyles Jr., *Brothers in Arms: A Journey from War to Peace* (New York: Alfred A. Knopf, 1986), 9–10.

3. Ibid., 135.

4. Philip Caputo, *A Rumor of War* (New York: Owl Books, 1996), 27.

5. Ibid., 28.

6. Appy, *Working-Class War*, 25–35, 44–46.

7. Lair, *Armed with Abundance*, 5, 15–18, 25–31.

8. Appy, *Working-Class War*, 167. See also Lawrence M. Baskir and William A. Strauss, *Chance and Circumstance: The Draft, the War and the Vietnam Generation* (New York: Vintage Books, 1978), 51–53.

9. Baskir and Strauss, *Chance and Circumstance*, 54–55.

10. Ibid., 52–59.

11. Appy, *Working-Class War*, 25–26, 45–46.

12. Ibid., 24. "Officers comprised 11 percent of the total number of men in Vietnam."

13. James Westheider, *Fighting on Two Fronts: African Americans and the Vietnam War* (New York: New York University Press, 1997), 11–14.

14. C. D. B. Bryan, "Growing Up the Hard Way," *New York Times*, August 15, 1976.

15. Clifton, *Those Who Were There*, vii–viii.

16. Philip K. Jason, ed., *Fourteen Landing Zones: Approaches to Vietnam War Literature* (Iowa City: University of Iowa Press, 1991), x.

17. Philip D. Beidler, *Late Thoughts on an Old War: The Legacy of Vietnam* (Athens: University of Georgia Press, 2004), 123–38.

18. Beavers, "Contemporary Afro-American Studies," 6–13; Luckett, "The Black Soldier," 1–27.

134    19. Ron Milam, *Not a Gentleman's War: An Inside View of Junior Officers in the Vietnam War* (Chapel Hill: The University of North Carolina Press, 2009), 5–8.

20. Baskir and Strauss, *Chance and Circumstance*, 3.

21. The exception is General William C. Westmoreland, the onetime commander of all US forces in Vietnam. He was born in 1914.

22. Loren Baritz, *Backfire: A History of How American Culture Led Us into Vietnam and Made Us Fight the Way We Did* (New York: William Morrow, 1985), 276–77; Appy, *Working-Class War*, 27.

23. "Record Counts by Age and Time of Death or Declaration of Death," Combat Area Casualties Current File (CACCF), National Archives and Records Administration, obtained from www.archives.gov.

24. Broyles Jr., *Brothers in Arms*, 136.

25. Bruce Weigl, *The Circle of Hahn: A Memoir* (New York: Grove Press, 2000), 1–6.

26. Appy, *Working-Class War*, 27.

27. For a detailed explanation of channeling see Baskir and Strauss, *Chance and Circumstance*, 14–28.

28. Ibid., 17.

29. Ibid., 15.

30. Appy, *Working-Class War*, 25–26, 45–46.

31. Baskir and Strauss, *Chance and Circumstance*, 29–51.

32. Ibid., 52–56. See also Westheider, *Fighting on Two Fronts*, 37–39.

33. Ibid., 52.

34. Ibid., 57.

35. Ibid., 52–56.

36. Westheider, *Fighting on Two Fronts*, 37–39.

37. Appy, *Working-Class War*, 25.

38. John Helmer, *Bringing the War Home: The American Soldier in Vietnam and After* (New York: The Free Press, 1974), 303.

39. The education levels of two memoirists could not be determined.

40. Caputo, *A Rumor of War*, 221.

41. Colin Powell, *My American Journey* (New York: Random House, 1995), 25.

42. Everett Alvarez Jr. and Anthony S. Pitch, *Chained Eagle: The Heroic Story of the First American Shot Down over North Vietnam* (New York: Donald I. Fine, 1989), 55.

43. Milam, *Not a Gentleman's War*, 18–21.

44. Ibid., 26.

45. Appy, *Working-Class War*, 24.

46. Tobias Wolff, *In Pharaoh's Army: Memories of the Lost War* (New York: Alfred A. Knopf, 1994), 42–58.

47. Frederick Downs, *The Killing Zone: My Life in the Vietnam War* (New York: WW Norton & Company, 1978), 15, 29, 230.

48. Appy, *Working-Class War*, 25–26, 45–46.

49. Joseph W. Callaway Jr., *Mekong First Light* (New York: Presidio Press/Ballantine Books, 2004), 19.

50. Robert Mason, *Chickenhawk*, 21.

51. Lynda Van Devanter with Christopher Morgan, *Home Before Morning: The Story of an Army Nurse in Vietnam* (New York: Beaufort Books, 1983), 28.

52. Ron Kovic, *Born on the Fourth of July* (New York: Akashic, 2005), 57–74.

53. Appy, *Working-Class War*, 80–82.

54. Ibid., 82.

55. Westheider, *Fighting on Two Fronts*, 11–14.

56. Several other books written by nonwhite veterans were also published, but because they received comparatively little recognition, they were not included in the primary group of memoirs. These books, however, are analyzed in chapter 3.

57. Westheider, *Fighting on Two Fronts*, 120–23.

58. Appy, *Working-Class War*, 28–29.

59. Helmer, *Bringing the War Home*, 34.

60. Appy, *Working-Class War*, 29, 45–47.

61. Ibid., 28.

62. Helmer, *Bringing the War Home*, 34.

63. Ibid., 110.

64. W. D. Ehrhart, *Vietnam-Perkasie: A Combat Marine Memoir* (Amherst: University of Massachusetts Press, 1995), 8–10.

65. Michael Norman, *These Good Men: Friendships Forged from War* (New York: Crown Publishers, 1989), 76.

66. Charles R. Anderson, *Vietnam: The Other War* (Novato, CA: Presidio Press, 1982), 52–53.

67. Rod Kane, *Veteran's Day: A Combat Odyssey* (New York: Orion; Pocket Book, 1990), 1–6.

68. Nathaniel Tripp, *Father, Soldier, Son: Memoir of a Platoon Leader in Vietnam* (South Royalton, VT: Steerforth Press, 1996), 22.

69. Herring, *America's Longest War*, 183, 187.

70. Van Devanter and Morgan, *Home Before Morning*, 78–79.

71. Lair, *Armed with Abundance*, 8.

72. Ibid., 5, 15–18, 25–31.

73. Beidler, *Late Thoughts*, 123–38.

74. David Donovan, *Once a Warrior King: Memories of an Officer in Vietnam* (New York: McGraw-Hill, 1985), vii, 32–36.

75. John McCain, *Faith of My Fathers* (New York: Random House, 1999), 180.

76. Craig Howes, *Voices of the Vietnam P.O.W.s: Witnesses to their Fight* (New York: Oxford University Press, 1993), 4. An estimated 629 US military personnel were held prisoner at one time or another by enemy forces during the Vietnam War.

77. Milam, *Not a Gentleman's War*, 5.

78. Ibid., 6–8.

79. Downs, *The Killing Zone*, 231–37.

80. Puller, *Fortunate Son*, 157–61.

81. Richard A. Gabriel and Paul L. Savage, *Crisis in Command: Mismanagement in the Army* (New York: Hill and Wang, 1978), 55.

82. Ibid., 11–17, 65–66.

83. Samuel P. Huntington, *The Soldier and the State: The Theory and Politics of Civil-Military Relations* (Cambridge, MA: The Belknap Press of Harvard University Press, 1964), 17.

84. Ibid., 13.

85. Morris Janowitz, *The Professional Soldier: A Social and Political Portrait* (Glencoe, IL: The Free Press, 1960), 80, 104–7, 137, 175–78, 218–19.

86. Appy, *Working-Class War*, 49, 235–37. The Marine Corps was the only service branch that offered a two-year enlistment option to recruits during the Vietnam era.

87. Gabriel and Savage, *Crisis in Command*, 131.

88. Elizabeth Kastor, "The Combat Bachelor's War Within; Rod Kane's 'Veteran's Day,' Transcript of a 20-Year Obsession with Vietnam," *Washington Post*, 19 April 1990, E1.

89. It is difficult to make a quantified analysis of the demographics of the veterans included in most oral history compilations, but most of the veterans featured in these books seem to have served in regular army and Marine Corps units, and were from poor and working-class backgrounds. One of these books, *Bloods: An Oral History of the Vietnam War by Black Veterans*, was exclusively devoted to the accounts of African American veterans. Wallace Terry, *Bloods: An Oral History of the Vietnam War by Black Veterans* (New York: Ballantine, 1985 ).

*Chapter 2: Combat Conditions and the Vietnamese People*

1. John Ketwig, *And a Hard Rain Fell: A G.I.'s True Story of the War in Vietnam* (New York: Macmillan, 1985), 3–36, 45–47.

2. Ibid., 55.

3. Ibid., 57.

4. Ibid., 57–60.

5. Ibid., 70–72.

6. Ibid., 72.

7. Ibid., 62–65.

8. Ibid., 63.

9. Ibid., 76.

10. Ibid., 138–42.

11. Ibid., 142.

12. Many scholars and other commentators have argued that Vietnam veterans have been portrayed as victims in one way or another in American culture. Susan Jeffords names numerous groups that have been portrayed as victimizers of US troops in representations of the war, including Vietnamese civilians and ARVN soldiers. Jeffords, *Remasculinization of America*, 116–43.

13. Kovic, *Born on the Fourth of July*, 64–65; and Caputo, *A Rumor of War*, 6.

14. Ehrhart, *Vietnam-Perkasie*, 7–8.

15. Puller Jr., *Fortunate Son*, 114.

16. Larry Heinemann, *Black Virgin Mountain: A Return to Vietnam* (New York: Doubleday, 2005), 8–9.

17. Caputo, *A Rumor of War*, 120.

18. Charles R. Anderson, *The Grunts* (San Rafael, CA: Presidio Press, 1976), 145.

19. Caputo, *A Rumor of War*, 120.

20. Ibid., 118.

21. Young, *The Vietnam Wars*, 74–77, 82–84, 144–46, 162–66. For more on Westmoreland and the strategies he employed in Vietnam, see his autobiography: William C. Westmoreland, *A Soldier Reports* (Garden City, NY: Doubleday, 1976).

22. Ibid., 163.

23. Ibid.

24. Herring, *America's Longest War*, 153–54.

25. Young, *The Vietnam Wars*, 186–87.

26. Alain Enthoven, "Memorandum for Secretary of Defense, 4 May 1967," *The Pentagon Papers*, IV, 462, in Helmer, *Bringing the War Home*, 26.

27. Anderson, *The Grunts*, 37, 79.

28. Kane, *Veteran's Day*, 27.

29. Tripp, *Father, Soldier, Son*, 62.

30. Young, *Vietnam Wars*, 173–75.

31. Caputo, *A Rumor of War*, 153–208.

32. Ibid., 168.

33. Ibid., xix, 168.

34. Ibid., xx.

35. Puller, *Fortunate Son*, 97–98, 114–16, 145–57.

36. Al Santoli, *Everything We Had: An Oral History of the Vietnam War by Thirty-Three American Soldiers Who Fought It* (New York: Ballantine, 1983), 50.

37. Tripp, *Father, Soldier, Son*, 15–16.

38. Appy, *Working-Class War*, 222, 243–45.

39. Matthew Brennan, *Brennan's War: Vietnam 1965–69* (Novato, CA: Presidio Press, 1985), 211.

40. Appy, *Working-Class War*, 243–45.

41. Ibid., 202.

42. Ibid., 203.

43. Ibid., 204.

44. Herring, *America's Longest War*, 140, 152–53, 185, 209.

45. Brennan, *Brennan's War*, 61–62.

46. Puller, *Fortunate Son*, 130.

47. Kovic, *Born on the Fourth of July*, 195–203.

48. Young, *The Vietnam Wars*, 172.

49. Ibid., 70.

50. Ibid., 72.

51. Ibid., 71–73, 160.

52. Ibid., 160; and Appy, *Working-Class War*, 114.

53. Appy, *Working-Class War*, 114.

54. Broyles Jr., *Brothers in Arms*, 220.

55. Sandra C. Taylor, *Vietnamese Women at War: Fighting for Ho Chi Minh and the Revolution* (Lawrence: University Press of Kansas, 1999), 38, 61, 71, 87–89; Karen Gottschang Turner with Phan Thanh Hao, *Even the Women Must Fight: Memories of War from North Vietnam* (New York: John Wiley and Sons Inc., 1998), 20–23, 33.

56. Taylor, *Vietnamese Women at War*, 95–96.

57. Tim O'Brien, *If I Die in a Combat Zone, Box Me Up and Ship Me Home* (New York: Delta, 1989), 114.

58. Herring, *America's Longest War*, 212; and Young, *The Vietnam Wars*, 243. For a full account of the My Lai Massacre see Seymour M. Hersh, *My Lai 4: A Report on the Massacre and Its Aftermath* (New York: Random House, 1970).

59. Deborah Nelson, *The War behind Me: Vietnam Veterans Confront the Truth about U.S. War Crimes* (New York: Basic Books, 2008), 1–3.

60. Ibid., 3.

61. Ibid.

62. Young, *The Vietnam Wars*, 255–56.

63. "Transcript: Kerry Testifies Before Senate Panel, 1971," from NPR.org, 25 April 2006, obtained 12 Dec. 2008.

64. Young, *The Vietnam Wars*, 256.

65. Philip Knightly, *The First Casualty: The War Correspondent as Hero and Myth-Maker from the Crimea to Iraq*, 3rd ed. (Baltimore, MD: The Johns Hopkins University Press, 2004), 431.

66. Ibid., 434.

67. Ibid., 435.

68. Broyles, *Brothers in Arms*, 252.

69. Donovan, *Once a Warrior King*, 223–24.

70. Caputo, *A Rumor of War*, 315–37.

71. Mason, *Chickenhawk*, 434–35.

72. Downs, *The Killing Zone*, 171–72.

73. Anderson, *The Grunts*, 121–22.

74. Michael Lee Lanning, *Vietnam, 1969–1970: A Company Commander's Journal* (College Station: Texas A&M University Press, 2007), 249; and Stanley Goff, Robert Sanders, and Clark Smith, *Brothers: Black Soldiers in the Nam* (Novato, CA: Presdio Press, 1982), 142.

75. Brennan, *Brennan's War*, 82, 162.

76. Mason, *Chickenhawk*, 387, 395–96.

77. Weigl, *The Circle of Hahn*, 132–33; Kane, *Veteran's Day*, 59; Alfred S. Bradford, *Some Even Volunteered: The First Wolfhounds Pacify Vietnam* (Westport, CT: Praeger Publishing, 1994), 125.

78. Downs, *The Killing Zone*, 71–72.

79. Puller, *Fortunate Son*, 145.

80. Broyles, *Brothers in Arms*, 202.

81. Johnnie M. Clark, *Guns Up!* (New York: Ballantine Books, 2002), 65.

82. Kindsvatter, *American Soldiers*, 192

83. Ibid., 192–93.

84. Ibid., 193.

85. Ibid., 199.

86. Ibid., 193–94, 201–13; and Appy, *Working-Class War*, 103, 106–7. For more on racism and atrocities in the Pacific Theater of World War II see John W. Dower, *War without Mercy: Race and Power in the Pacific War* (New York: Pantheon Books, 1986).

87. Mason, *Chickenhawk*, 218.

88. Appy, *Working-Class War*, 204.

89. Herring, *America's Longest War*, 67.

90. Michael Bilton and Kevin Sim, *Four Hours in My Lai* (New York: Viking, 1992), 36.

91. Ibid.

140

92. Frances Fitzgerald, *Fire in the Lake: The Vietnamese and the Americans in Vietnam* (Boston: Little, Brown and Company, 1972), 173–75.

93. Young, *The Vietnam Wars*, 219.

94. Ibid., 218–19.

95. Herring, *America's Longest War*, 187.

96. Andrew F. Krepinevich, *The Army and Vietnam* (Baltimore: The Johns Hopkins University Press, 1986), 250.

97. Caputo, *A Rumor of War*, 109–10, 304–5.

98. Santoli, *Everything We Had*, 62–63.

99. William Calley and John Sack, *Lieutenant Calley: His Own Story* (New York: Viking Press, 1971), 8–9, 23, 59, 78–80, 84–85, 88–94, 101–3.

100. Christian G. Appy, using fictional and nonfictional veteran narratives, also found that mutual enmity was often evident in the interactions between American soldiers and begging Vietnamese children. Appy, *Working-Class War*, 133–35.

101. James R. McDonough, *Platoon Leader* (Novato, CA: Presidio, 1985), 20.

102. Ibid., 20.

103. Downs, *The Killing Zone*, 77.

104. Kovic, *Born on the Fourth of July*, 212.

105. Puller, *Fortunate Son*, 141.

106. Downs, *The Killing Zone*, 202.

107. Broyles, *Brothers in Arms*, 136.

108. Caputo, *A Rumor of War*, 107.

109. Broyles, *Brothers in Arms*, 220–21.

110. Puller, *Fortunate Son*, 82–85.

111. Wolff, *In Pharaoh's Army*, 188–89.

112. Caputo, *A Rumor of War*, 107.

113. Fitzgerald, *Fire in the Lake*, 348–53; and Appy, *Working-Class War*, 289–91.

114. Fitzgerald, *Fire in the Lake*, 344–45; and Young, *The Vietnam Wars*, 174–77.

115. Young, *The Vietnam Wars*, 177.

116. Ibid.

117. Appy, *Working-Class War*, 289–91.

118. Le Ly Hayslip and Jay Wurts, *When Heaven and Earth Changed Places* (New York: Doubleday, 1989), 86–97, 168–74, 184–85, 256–326.

119. Neil Sheehan, *A Bright Shining Lie: John Paul Vann and America in Vietnam* (New York: Random House, 1988), 124, 309–11.

120. Ibid., 310.

121. Ibid., 311.

122. Fitzgerald, *Fire in the Lake*, 7–16.

123. Martha Hess, *Then the Americans Came: Voices from Vietnam* (New York: Four Walls Eight Windows, 1993), 193.

124. Fitzgerald, *Fire in the Lake*, 103–7, 143–45, 158–63, 299; and Young, *The Vietnam Wars*, 60–69, 103.

125. David Chanoff and Doan Van Toai, *Portrait of the Enemy* (New York: Random House, 1986), 42–43.

126. Young, *The Vietnam Wars*, 70–71.

127. Sheehan, *A Bright Shining Lie*, 192–93.

128. Robert K. Brigham, *ARVN: Life and Death in the South Vietnamese Army* (Lawrence: University Press of Kansas, 2006), 13–18.

129. Krepinevich, *The Army and Vietnam*, 20–22.

130. Andrew Wiest, *Vietnam's Forgotten Army: Heroism and Betrayal in the ARVN* (New York: New York University Press, 2008), 22–23, 26–28.

131. Krepinevich, *The Army and Vietnam*, 78–79.

132. Ibid., 79.

133. Wiest, *Vietnam's Forgotten Army*, 28.

134. Ibid., 36.

135. Ibid., 36–38.

136. Ibid., 49.

137. James H. Willbanks, *Abandoning Vietnam: How America Left and South Vietnam Lost Its War* (Lawrence: University Press of Kansas, 2004), 22–32, 123, 173–75, 189, 202–3.

138. Ibid., 122.

139. Ibid., 175.

140. Ibid., 84–87, 102–17.

141. Ibid., 114.

142. Ibid., 122–60.

143. Ibid., 156.

144. Ibid., 157, 184–87, 235–77.

145. Wiest, *Vietnam's Forgotten Army*, 6.

146. Ibid., 96–125.

147. Ibid., 218.

148. Ibid.

149. Willbanks, *Abandoning Vietnam*, 107, 112, 149–55, 157–58, 243, 251, 253, 255, 266–67.

150. Ibid., 267.

151. Ibid.

152. Ibid., 28, 55, 68, 88–89, 116, 155–57, 190, 205–7, 255, 276; Wiest, *Vietnam's Forgotten Army*, 21, 24–26, 33, 36–39, 44–45, 268–69.

153. Wiest, *Vietnam's Forgotten Army*, 21.

154. Ibid., 21, 24–25, 36–39, 44–45, 268–69; Willbanks, *Abandoning Vietnam*, 88, 116, 205–7.

155. Willbanks, *Abandoning Vietnam*, 205.

156. Ibid., 207.

157. Ibid., 156, 255, 276.

158. Wiest, *Vietnam's Forgotten Army*, 268.

159. Willbanks, *Abandoning Vietnam*, 110, 112–13, 116, 193, 200–202, 229, 235–37.

160. Ibid., 149–50; Wiest, *Vietnam's Forgotten Army*, 63, 269.

161. Brigham, *ARVN*, 7.

162. Ibid., 7–8, 11, 27–44, 50.

163. Ibid., 27.

164. Wiest, *Vietnam's Forgotten Army*, 39.

165. Willbanks, *Abandoning Vietnam*, 204–5.

166. Appy, *Working-Class War*, 113.

167. Ibid., 113–16; Krepinevich, *The Army and Vietnam*, 174.

168. Krepinevich, *The Army and Vietnam*, 23, 48–49, 209–10; Wiest, *Vietnam's Forgotten Army*, 86.

169. Ibid., 210.

170. Theodore H. White, *The Making of the President, 1968* (New York: Atheneum, 1969), 16–17.

171. Robert S. McNamara with Brian VandeMark, *In Retrospect: The Tragedy and Lessons of Vietnam* (New York: Times Books, 1995), 43. For all of McNamara's comments on the American leadership's ignorance of the Vietnamese see pages 32–33, 321–23.

172. Lair, *Armed with Abundance*, 5.

173. Ibid., 74–79, 84–86, 134, 158–59, 188–90.

174. Wiest, *Vietnam's Forgotten Army*, 86.

175. Ketwig, *And a Hard Rain Fell*, 39.

176. Ibid., 63.

177. Ibid., 63–66.

### Chapter 3: Race and Racism

1. Richard Ogden, *Green Knight, Red Mourning* (New York: Pinnacle Books, 2002), 13–17, 190–92, 199.

2. Ibid., 183–203, 221–23, 257–58.

3. O'Brien, *If I Die in a Combat Zone*, 168.

4. Two major films have been made about the experiences of African American soldiers in Vietnam: *The Walking Dead*, directed by Preston A. Whitmore II (1995)

and *Dead Presidents*, directed by Albert Hughes and Allen Hughes (1995). No major films have focused on the experiences of other nonwhite groups. Many other Vietnam War movies feature black characters, but some have criticized the portrayal of these soldiers and allege that nonwhites are never present in large enough numbers. See "Blacks Blast Movie and TV Industries' Perpetuation of Old Stereotyped Images," *Jet*, 28 November 1988, 64.

5. Herman Beavers stated in 1989 that "one is hard pressed to find in Afro-American literature more than three novels that center on the Vietnam experience." Beavers, "Contemporary Afro-American Studies," 8. As of 1997, only six of the six hundred published Vietnam novels were authored by African Americans, only three of them veterans. All of these books were published before 1986, and none achieved any kind of commercial success. Jeff Loeb, "MIA: African American Autobiography of the Vietnam War," *African American Review* 31, no. 1 (Spring 1997): 105. Five novels about Mexican American soldiers in Vietnam have been published since 1988, four of them authored by Chicano veterans. None of these books evidently achieved much recognition either. John Alba Culter, "Disappeared Men: Chicana/o Authenticity and the American War in Viet Nam," *American Literature* 81, no. 3 (September 2009): 585.

6. See Westheider, *Fighting on Two Fronts*; Herman Graham III, *The Brothers' Vietnam War: Black Power, Manhood, and the Military Experience* (Gainesville: University Press of Florida, 2003); Kimberly L. Philips, *War! What Is It Good For? Black Freedom Struggles and the U.S. Military from World War II to Iraq* (Chapel Hill: The University of North Carolina Press, 2012).

7. There is only one book-length scholarly study of non–African American, nonwhite soldiers who served in Vietnam: Tom Holm, *Strong Hearts, Wounded Souls: Native American Veterans of the Vietnam War* (Austin: University of Texas Press, 1996). A shorter piece of historical scholarship about nonblack, nonwhite soldiers is: Lea Ybarra, "Perceptions of Race and Class among Chicano Vietnam Veterans," *Viet Nam Generation* 1, no. 2 (1989): 69–93.

8. Loeb, "MIA: African American Autobiography," 105–23.

9. Carolyn Kitsch, *Pages from the Past: History and Memory in American Magazines* (Chapel Hill: The University of North Carolina Press, 2005), 93.

10. For general information about the Black Power movement see Peniel E. Joseph, *Waiting 'Till the Midnight Hour: A Narrative of Black Power in America* (New York: Henry Holt and Company, 2006); and William L. Van Deburg, *New Day in Babylon: The Black Power Movement and American Culture, 1965–1975* (Chicago: University of Chicago Press, 1992).

11. Van Deburg, *New Day in Babylon*, 102–6.

12. Graham, *The Brothers' Vietnam War*, 1–14.

144

13. Westheider, *Fighting on Two Fronts*, 8–12, 21–22; Nikolas Kozloff, "Vietnam, the African American Community, and the *Pittsburgh New Courier*," *Historian* 63 (Spring 2001): 521–22, 525, 528, 532–33.

14. Simeon Booker, "Negroes in Vietnam: 'We Are Americans Too,'" *Ebony*, November 1965, 98.

15. R. W. Apple Jr., "Negro and White Fight Side by Side," *New York Times*, 3 January 1966, 7.

16. "Armed Forces: Democracy in the Foxhole," *Time*, 26 May 1967.

17. "Huckleberry Finn in Vietnam," *New Republic*, 6 January 1968.

18. Samuel Vance, *The Courageous and the Proud* (New York: W. W. Norton and Company, 1970), 158.

19. Santoli, *Everything We Had*, 157.

20. Goff, Sanders, and Smith, *Brothers*, 131.

21. Ibid., 122–23, 131.

22. "South Viet Nam: Soul Alley," *Time*, 14 December 1970.

23. Ibid.

24. Charles C. Moskos Jr., *The American Enlisted Man: The Rank and File in Today's Military* (New York: Russel Sage Foundation, 1970), 125.

25. From the beginning of the American occupation of Japan, for instance, prostitutes were apportioned "into separate districts . . . reserved for use by U.S. officers, white enlisted men and black enlisted men." John Dower, *Embracing Defeat: Japan in the Wake of World War II* (New York: W. W. Norton & Company, 1999), 130. In a Vietnam-era example of such forced segregation, African American troops stationed near Anjong-ni, South Korea, rioted in July 1971 because they were denied access to bars and prostitutes. Stuart H. Loory, *Defeated: Inside America's Military Machine* (New York: Random House, 1973), 219–220.

26. Moskos, *The American Enlisted Man*, 125.

27. Wallace Terry II, "Bringing the War Home," *Black Scholar*, November 1970, 14. A short summary of the findings and observations Terry included in this article later appeared in "Black Power in Viet Nam," *Time*, 19 September 1969.

28. Terry Whitmore and Richard P. Weber, *Memphis, Nam, Sweden: The Story of a Black Deserter* (Jackson: University Press of Mississippi, 1997), 98–99.

29. Van Deburg, *New Day in Babylon*, 43.

30. For information on the ideological precursors and origins of the Black Power movement see the first five chapters of Joseph's *Waiting Till the Midnight Hour*, 1–117.

31. Van Deburg, *New Day in Babylon*, 43–45, 51–53, 113–16, 129–45.

32. Manny Garcia, *An Accidental Soldier: Memoirs of a Mestizo in Vietnam* (Alberquerque: University of New Mexico Press, 2003), 123.

33. Lea Ybarra, ed., *Vietnam Veteranos: Chicanos Recall the War* (Austin: University of Texas Press, 2004), 71; Charley Trujillo, *Soldados: Chicanos in Vietnam* (San Jose, CA: Chusma House Publishers, 1990), 125–26, 140.

34. Westheider, *Fighting on Two Fronts*, 94–113. For more on the *Kitty Hawk* riot, and racial unrest in the US Navy during the war in general, see John Darrell Sherwood, *Black Sailor, White Navy: Racial Unrest in the Fleet During the Vietnam War Era* (New York: New York University Press, 2007).

35. Ed Emanuel, *Soul Patrol* (New York: Ballantine Books, 2003), 244–45.

36. Garcia, *An Accidental Soldier*, 101.

37. Whitmore and Weber, *Memphis, Nam, Sweden*, 52–53.

38. James A. Daly and Lee Bergman, *Black Prisoner of War: A Conscientious Objector's Vietnam Memoir* (Lawrence: University Press of Kansas, 2000), 107, 133, 148. Originally published as *A Hero's Welcome: The Conscience of Sergeant James Daly Versus the U.S. Army* (Indianapolis, IN: Bobbs-Merrill, 1975).

39. Trujillo, *Soldados,* 162. The last name of this particular veteran is not given.

40. Juan Ramirez, *A Patriot After All: The Story of a Chicano Vietnam Vet* (Albuquerque: University of New Mexico Press, 1999), 85, 110–11.

41. Ybarra, *Vietnam Veteranos*, 71; Trujillo, *Soldados*, 125–26, 140; and Ramirez, *A Patriot After All*, 94.

42. Carina A. Del Rosario, ed., *A Different Battle: Stories of Asian Pacific American Veterans* (Seattle: Wing Luke Asian Museum, 1999), 60.

43. Ybarra, *Vietnam Veteranos*, 69. The last names of the veterans interviewed for *Vietnam Veteranos* are not provided.

44. Del Rosario, *A Different Battle*, 40, 48, 80, 103.

45. Roy P. Benavidez and Oscar Griffin, *The Three Wars of Roy Benavidez* (San Antonio, TX: Corona Publishing Company, 1986), 4–5.

46. Arthur Egendorf, et al., *Legacies of Vietnam: Comparative Adjustment of Veterans and Their Peers* (Washington, DC: US Government Printing Office, 1981), 392.

47. Emmanuel, *Soul Patrol*, 130.

48. Ybarra, *Vietnam Veteranos*, 39–41.

49. Ibid., 41–42.

50. Ibid.

51. Dwight W. Birdwell, *A Hundred Miles of Bad Road: An Armored Cavalryman in Vietnam, 1967–1968* (Novato, CA: Presidio Press, 2000), 139.

52. David Parks, *G.I. Diary* (Washington, DC: Howard University Press, 1984), 52.

53. Hersh, *My Lai 4*, 16–18, 23–24, 30–31.

54. Bilton and Sim, *Four Hours in My Lai*, 5–8, 62, 78–79, 97–101, 115, 117, 126–27, 157–58, 160–61.

55. Ibid., 7.

56. Ibid., 135–41.

57. Van Deburg, *New Day in Babylon*, 99–100.

58. Joseph, *Waiting*, 180–181.

59. Ibid., 194.

60. Westheider, *Fighting on Two Fronts*, 153–57.

61. Terry, "Bringing the War Home," 8.

62. The only minority memoir produced by a veteran who could be deemed an enemy sympathizer was *Black Prisoner of War*, by James Daly, an army infantryman who was captured by the Vietcong in 1966. Daly became sympathetic to the cause of his captors, embraced Communism, and joined a group of antiwar POWs called the "Peace Committee" that issued condemnations against the war to the world media. Daly was charged with collaboration with the enemy by the US government when he returned to the US, but was acquitted.

63. Terry, *Bloods*, 137.

64. Westheider, *Fighting on Two Fronts*, 156–57.

65. Whitmore and Weber, *Memphis, Nam, and Sweden*, 71.

66. James E. Jackson Jr., "18 Months as a Prisoner of the Vietcong," *Ebony*, August 1968, 118.

67. Terry, *Bloods*, 63.

68. Ybarra, *Vietnam Veteranos*, 40, 146.

69. Leroy TeCube, *A Year in Nam: A Native American Soldier's Story* (Lincoln: University of Nebraska Press, 1999), xvi.

70. Holm, *Strong Hearts*, 19.

71. Goff, Sanders, and Smith, *Brothers*, 67–70.

72. The *New York Times* reported in January 1966 that "the all-volunteer 173 Airborne Division have as many as six Negroes among every 10 men." Apple Jr., "Negro and White," 7. Later that year, *Ebony* reported that African Americans comprised "more than a third of the 101's [Airborne Division] crack 1 Brigade in Vietnam." "Birdmen with Black Rifles," *Ebony*, October 1966, 37.

73. Holm, *Strong Hearts*, 19; Ralph Guzman, "Mexican American Casualties in Vietnam," *La Raza* 1, no. 1 (1971): 12.

74. Terry, *Bloods*, 237–38.

75. Ibid., 18.

76. Terry, "Bringing the War Home," 12.

77. Parks, *G.I. Diary*, 76.

78. Garcia, *Accidental Soldier*, 42.

79. Emmanuel, *Soul Patrol*, 125.

80. Fenton A. Williams, *Just Before the Dawn: A Doctor's Experiences in Vietnam* (New York: Exposition Press, 1971), 114.

81. Santoli, *Everything We Had*, 161.

82. Westheider, *Fighting on Two Fronts*, 12–13. Besides the Pentagon's conscious efforts to lessen the presence of blacks on the frontlines, the reduction of the African American death rate was also partly due to changes in American military strategy implemented in the war's later stages. During this period, US forces in Vietnam shifted their focus from ground combat to airpower. Since far more black servicemen were involved in ground combat than the air war, fewer African American troops were in Vietnam after the strategy shift occurred.

83. Racial category list is from the United States National Archives and Records Administration, Combat Area Casualties Current File (CACCF). Obtained online at http://www.archives.gov/research/vietnam-war/casualty-statistics.html. There was also a sixth racial category: "Unknown or Not Reported."

84. Native Americans comprised 1.4 percent of the US population in the Vietnam era, and approximately .4 percent of American soldiers killed in Vietnam. United States National Archives and Records Administration, Combat Area Casualties Current File (CACCF). Obtained online at http://www.archives.gov/research/vietnam-war/casualty-statistics.html.

85. Holm, *Strong Hearts*, 11.

86. Guzman, "Mexican American Casualties in Vietnam," 12.

87. Van Deburg, *New Day in Babylon*, 100.

88. Westheider, *Fighting on Two Fronts*, 4, 12–14, 37. Tom Holm surmises that Native Americans were also disproportionately involved in combat because substandard educations caused them to generally do poorly on the AFQT. (Holm, *Strong Hearts*, 10, 19).

89. Goff, Sanders, and Smith, *Brothers*, 11.

90. Emanuel, *Soul Patrol*, 58.

91. Ibid., 86–87.

92. Vance, *The Courageous and the Proud*, 9.

93. Emmanuel, *Soul Patrol*, 129.

94. Trujillo, *Soldados*, 128.

95. Holm, *Strong Hearts*, 151–52.

96. Delano Cummings, *Moon Dash Warrior: The Story of an American Indian in Vietnam, A Marine from the Land of the Lumbee* (Livermore, ME: Signal Tree Publications, 2001), 6, 37, 54, 75.

97. Terry, *Bloods*, 23.

98. Vance, *The Courageous and the Proud*, 76, 101, 133.

99. Peter Goldman, *Report From Black America* (New York: Simon and Schuster, 1970), 45.

100. Trujillo, *Soldados*, 80, 128, 157.

101. Jeffords, *Remasculinization of America: Gender and the Vietnam War* (Bloomington, IN: Indiana University Press, 1989), 54.

102. Beavers, "Contemporary Afro-American Studies," 9–13.

103. Downs, *The Killing Zone*, 37.

## Chapter 4: Men, Women, and Vietnam

1. Michael Lee Lanning, *The Only War We Had: A Platoon Leader's Journal of Vietnam* (New York: Ivy Books, 1987).

2. Lanning, *Vietnam, 1969–1970.*

3. Lanning, *The Only War We Had*, 5, 11–12, 38–39, 47–48.

4. Ibid., 232–33.

5. Ibid., 241.

6. Ibid., 79, 238–39.

7. Lanning, *Vietnam, 1969–1970*, 21.

8. Karen Dixon Vuic, *Officer, Nurse, Woman: The Army Nurse Corps in the Vietnam War* (Baltimore: The Johns Hopkins University Press, 2010), 140.

9. Jeffords, *Remasculinization of America.*

10. Heather Marie Stur, *Beyond Combat: Women and Gender in the Vietnam War Era* (New York: Cambridge University Press, 2011).

11. Caputo, *A Rumor of War*, 107–8.

12. Robert Hemphill, *Platoon, Bravo Company* (Fredericksburg, VA: St. Martin's Paperbacks, 2001), 39–41.

13. Stur, *Beyond Combat*, 29.

14. R. W. Apple Jr., "Lodge Worried over Behavior of G.I.'s in Saigon," *New York Times*, 13 August 1966, 3.

15. E. W. Kenworthy, "Fulbright Issues a Warning to U.S.," *New York Times*, 6 May 1966, 2.

16. Bernard Weinraub, "Pleiku, Open to G.I.'s, Is Problem City," *New York Times*, 12 August 1968, 3.

17. Stur, *Beyond Combat*, 49, 53–54, 59.

18. Nu-Anh Tran, "South Vietnamese Identity, American Intervention, and the Newspaper Chinh Luan," *Journal of Vietnamese Studies* 1, no. 1–2 (February 2006): 179, 186–90.

19. "Hanoi Asks Nun to Rehabilitate Ex-prostitutes," *New York Times*, 6 February 1977, L9.

20. Stur, *Beyond Combat*, 35–36, 45–53, 60–61.

21. Charles Winick and Paul M. Kinsie, *The Lively Commerce: Prostitution in the United States* (Chicago: Quadrangle Books, 1971), 246, 258–60.

22. David H. Hackworth and Julie Sherman, *About Face* (New York: Simon and Schuster, 1989), 771–83.

23. Ibid., 132.

24. Ibid.

25. Terry, *Bloods*, 25–26.

26. Jonathan Randal, "Red-Light Limits Opposed in Saigon," *New York Times*, 14 November 1966, 13; Susan Brownmiller, *Against Our Will: Men, Women, and Rape* (New York: Fawcett Columbine, 1975), 93–95.

27. "Disneyland East," *Time*, 6 May 1966.

28. Ibid.

29. "Five-Day Bonanza," *Time*, 22 December, 1967. The ten R&R cities were Hong Kong, Bangkok, Honolulu, Tokyo, Taipei, Singapore, Manila, Penang, Kuala Lumpur, and Sydney.

30. Charles H. Turner, "When Johnny Comes Marching to Hawaii on R&R," *New York Times*, 21 March 1971, XX1.

31. Mason, *Chickenhawk*, 325.

32. O'Brien, *If I Die in a Combat Zone*, 101.

33. Tracy Kidder, *My Detachment: A Memoir* (New York: Random House, 2005), 116–17.

34. Sidney Gruson, "'R and R' Tours on Taiwan: American Servicemen Bring a Mixed Blessing to the Island," *New York Times*, 14 February 1968, 6.

35. Loory, *Defeated*, 225–26.

36. Anderson, *Vietnam: The Other War*, 175–82; and Mason, *Chickenhawk*, 325–28.

37. Winick and Kinsie, *The Lively Commerce*, 247–59.

38. Loory, *Defeated*, 216–30.

39. Brownmiller, *Against Our Will*, 93–94.

40. Kathryn Marshall, *In the Combat Zone: An Oral History of American Women in Vietnam, 1966–1975* (Boston: Little, Brown, 1987), 76.

41. Mary Reynolds Powell, *A World of Hurt: Between Innocence and Arrogance in Vietnam* (Cleveland, OH: Greenleaf Enterprises, 2000), 145.

42. Winnie Smith, *American Daughter Gone to War: On the Frontlines with an Army Nurse in Vietnam* (New York: Pocket Books, 1994), 223–24.

43. Appy, *Working-Class War*, 237.

44. "Sydney Greets U.S. Servicemen from Vietnam," *New York Times*, 6 October 1967, 5; and Robert Trumbull, "For R and R, It's Australia First, Last, Always," *New York Times*, 10 January 1969, 10.

150

45. "Cleaning Up Saigon," *Time*, 1 December 1969.

46. Trumbull, "For R and R, It's Australia," 10.

47. "Fulbright Declares He Regrets Charge of U.S. 'Arrogance,' " *New York Times*, 18 May 1966, 8.

48. Mason, *Chickenhawk*, 234–35.

49. Ogden, *Green Knight, Red Mourning*, 118.

50. Anderson, *Vietnam: The Other War*, 182.

51. The lone exception was Donald Duncan, a former Green Beret who wrote the first published Vietnam veteran memoir, *The New Legions*. Duncan became disillusioned with the war and the military while in Vietnam, and became an active participant in the antiwar movement after he returned to the United States. He presents the negative effects of the sex trade on Vietnamese society as one of many reasons why US involvement in Vietnam is wrong. Duncan, *The New Legions* (New York: Random House, 1967), 224–25.

52. Mark Baker, *Nam: The Vietnam War in the Words of the Soldiers Who Fought There* (New York: Berkley Books, 1983), 119. All of the veterans quoted in *Nam* are anonymous.

53. Hynes, *The Soldiers' Tale*, 181.

54. Wolff, *In Pharaoh's Army*, 30–35; and Anderson, *The Grunts*, 82–107.

55. Broyles Jr., *Brothers in Arms*, 206–7.

56. Michael Norman, for instance, writes in his memoir, *These Good Men*, about Jim, a "naïve and vulnerable man" in his unit who married a bar girl while in Thailand during R&R. Jim really loved the girl, but Norman believed she was most likely using the marriage as a means to get to America. Norman, *These Good Men*, 151–52.

57. Ketwig, *And a Hard Rain Fell*, 110–12, 117, 130.

58. Goff, Sanders, and Smith, *Brothers*, 184–89.

59. US Commissioner of Immigration and Naturalization, *Annual Reports, 1947–75* in Bok-Lim Kim, "Asian Wives of U.S. Servicemen: Women in the Shadows" *Amerasia* 4, no.1 (1977): 99.

60. Robert S. McKelvey, *The Dust of Life: America's Children Abandoned in Vietnam* (Seattle: University of Washington Press, 1999), 3–4, 44–45. A US government study found that Vietnamese mothers of Amerasian children usually had relationships with the fathers of their children that were "more than transitory affairs or 'one night stands.'" (45) The majority of women said they lived with, and were financially supported by, their American lovers, and "nearly 63 percent expected to join the father after he first left Vietnam." (45)

61. Broyles Jr., *Brothers in Arms*, 206–7.

62. John D'Emilio and Estelle B. Freedman, *Intimate Matters: A History of Sexuality in America* (New York: Harper and Row, 1998), 256–65; and Beth Bailey, *Sex in the Heartland* (Cambridge, MA: Harvard University Press, 1999), 117–20.

63. Alfred C. Kinsey, Wardell B. Pomeroy, and Clyde E. Martin, *Sexual Behavior in the Human Male* (Philadelphia: W.B. Saunders Company, 1948), 597–609.

64. D'Emilio and Freedman, *Intimate Matters*, 256–65; and Bailey, *Sex in the Heartland*, 117–20.

65. Duncan, *The New Legions*, 225.

66. Anderson, *Vietnam: The Other War*, 136.

67. Downs, *The Killing Zone*, 82.

68. O'Brien, *If I Die in a Combat Zone*, 110.

69. Clark, *Guns Up!*, 199.

70. Bradford, *Some Even Volunteered*, 60–61.

71. Tripp, *Father, Soldier, Son*, 192.

72. Kali Tal, "The Mind at War: Images of Women in Vietnam Novels by Combat Veterans," *Contemporary Literature* 31, no.1 (Spring 1990): 77, 80–85.

73. Santoli, *Everything We Had*, 59–61.

74. Goff, Sanders, and Smith, *Brothers*, 184–89.

75. Tal, "The Mind at War," 77.

76. Ehrhart, *Vietnam-Perkasie*, 157–71.

77. Hayslip and Wurts, *When Heaven and Earth Changed Places*, 168–69, 173–74, 224–27, 255, 262, 274–84, 279–302, 323–25.

78. Brownmiller, *Against Our Will*, 97–101.

79. Lawson, "She's a Pretty Woman," 19.

80. Ketwig, *And a Hard Rain Fell*, 70–73.

81. Terry, *Bloods*, 248.

82. Clark, *Guns Up!*, 199–201.

83. Tal, "The Mind at War," 82–84; and Karen Stuhldreher, "State Rape: Representations of Rape in Vietnam," *Vietnam Generation* 5, no. 1–4 (1994): 155–58.

84. See Taylor, *Vietnamese Women at War*, 38, 61, 71, 87–89; and Gottschang Turner and Thanh Hao, *Even the Women Must Fight*, 20–23, 33.

85. Brennan, *Brennan's War*, 48.

86. Clark, *Guns Up!*, 201; and Donovan, *Once a Warrior King*, 218.

87. Vuic, *Officer, Nurse, Woman*, 17–18.

88. Stur, *Beyond Combat*, 97–103.

89. Ibid., 103.

90. "Miss 'Black America' takes Soul to Vietnam," *Ebony*, May 1970, 88–94.

91. Ehrhart, *Vietnam-Perkasie*, 51.

92. Trumbull, "For R and R, It's Australia," 10.

93. Baker, *Nam*, 118.

94. "Five Day Bonanza," *Time*.

95. Ehrhart, *Vietnam-Perkasie*, 81.

96. Lanning, *The Only War We Had*, 239.

97. Stur, *Beyond Combat*, 80.

98. Bradford, *Some Even Volunteered*, 108–9.

99. Mason, *Chickenhawk*, 341–42.

100. Bradford says in his memoir that he met a Donut Dolly who bragged that she charged an American general $5,000 for sex, and hoped to make $100,000 from prostitution before she left Vietnam. Bradford, *Some Even Volunteered*, 108. Clark claims that he paid a Red Cross volunteer for sex during his tour, and that this woman also said she planned to make thousands of dollars as a prostitute while in Vietnam. Clark, *Guns Up!*, 216–23.

101. Vuic, *Officer, Nurse, Woman*, 149–54.

102. Ibid., 150.

103. Ibid., 141–42.

104. Ibid., 142.

105. Powell, *A World of Hurt*, 12.

106. Smith, *American Daughter*, 14.

107. Ibid., 81.

108. Lynn Hampton, *The Fighting Strength: Memoirs of a Combat Nurse in Vietnam* (New York: Warner Books, 1992), 14, 86.

109. Stur, *Beyond Combat*, 92–93.

110. Marshall, *In the Combat Zone*, 68–72.

111. Appy, *Working-Class War*, 250.

112. O'Brien, *If I Die in a Combat Zone*, 44.

113. Broyles, *Brothers in Arms*, 145.

114. Ehrhart, *Vietnam-Perkasie*, 131–36.

115. Broyles, *Brothers in Arms*, 205–6.

### Chapter 5: The Return Home and Life after Vietnam

1. Van Devanter with Morgan, *Home Before Morning*, 1–208.

2. Ibid., 208.

3. Ibid.

4. Ibid.

5. Ibid., 209–10.

6. Ibid., 211.

7. Ibid., 220–86.

8. Ibid., 249.

9. Ibid., 272–74.

10. Ibid., 303.

11. Baker, *Nam*, 239–96.

12. Peter Biskind, "The Vietnam Oscars," *Vanity Fair*, March 2008.

13. Van Devanter with Morgan, *Home Before Morning*, 209.

14. Caputo, *A Rumor of War*, 337.

15. W. D. Ehrhart, *Passing Time: Memoir of a Vietnam Veteran Against the War* (Amherst: University of Massachusetts Press, 1995), 7. Originally published as *Marking Time* (New York: Avon Books, 1986).

16. Frederick Downs, *Aftermath: A Soldier's Return to America from Vietnam* (New York: Norton, 1984), 95.

17. Smith, *American Daughter*, 253.

18. Santoli, *Everything We Had*, 133. Several other veterans' narratives also contain references to civilians insensitively asking veterans if they had killed anyone in Vietnam, including Baker, *Nam*, 259; Weigl, *The Circle of Hahn*, 154; and Kane, *Veteran's Day*, 75.

19. Clark, *Guns Up!*, 320–21.

20. Mason, *Chickenhawk*, 463.

21. Baker, *Nam*, 247–48.

22. Bob Greene, *Homecoming: When the Soldiers Returned from Vietnam* (New York: Putnam, 1989), 8–16.

23. For letters detailing stories of Vietnam veteran harassment that include spitting see Greene, *Homecoming*, 17–85. For letters detailing stories of veteran abuse that did not include spitting see Greene, *Homecoming*, 75–250.

24. Ibid., 24.

25. Ibid., 23.

26. Ibid., 24.

27. Thomas D. Beamish, Harvey Molotch, and Richard Flacks, "Who Supports the Troops? Vietnam, The Gulf War, and the Making of Collective Memory," *Social Problems* 42, no. 3 (August 1995): 350.

28. Ibid., 351.

29. Ibid.

30. Ibid., 353.

31. Lembke, *The Spitting Image*, 72–73.

32. Ibid., 73.

33. Ibid., 6, 37–48, 67–68, 72–73.

34. Terry H. Anderson, *The Movement and the Sixties* (New York: Oxford University Press, 1995), 332.

35. Ibid., 229–30, 319–21, 332, 417; and H. Bruce Franklin, *Vietnam and Other American Fantasies* (Amherst: University of Massachusetts, 2000), 62–70, 106–9.

36. Franklin, *Vietnam and Other Fantasies*, 106–7. For more information on Vietnam-era GI activism see David Cortright, *Soldiers in Revolt: The American Military Today* (New York: Anchor Press, 1975).

37. Veterans Administration, *Myths and Realities: A Study of Attitudes toward Vietnam Era Veterans* (Washington: US Government Printing Office, 1980), 39, 87.

38. Ibid., xxxviii.

39. Greene, *Homecoming*, 10; H. Bruce Franklin echoes these questions by doubting that "men just back from combat" would have "meekly walked away without attacking or even reporting" people who spat on them. Franklin, *Vietnam and Other Fantasies*, 62.

40. Appy, *Working-Class War*, 304.

41. Ibid., 304. There is at least one case in which two different memoirists' homecoming stories are suspiciously similar to each other. In the epilogue of the 2002 edition of Johnnie M. Clark's popular memoir, *Guns Up!*, he says that he was arrested after "decking" one of the "war protestors" that met the plane that brought him home from Vietnam in 1969. Clark says that he was quickly released from custody, however, because the policemen who arrested him were "old Marines" who sympathized with his plight (Clark, *Guns Up!*, 320–21). A more obscure memoir, James T. Gillam's *War in the Central Highlands of Vietnam, 1968–1970: A Historian's Experience*, published in 2006, ends with essentially the same story. Gillam also says that he punched an antiwar civilian shortly after disembarking from his plane, and that he too was quickly released because "one of the cops was a veteran." James T. Gillam, *War in the Central Highlands of Vietnam, 1968–1970: A Historian's Experience* (Lewiston, NY: The Edwin Mellen Press, 2006), 317.

42. The first published accounts of returning soldiers being spat upon and abused by American civilians appeared in *Nam: The Vietnam War in the Words of the Soldiers Who Fought There*. Baker, *Nam,* 241–68.

43. Murray Polner, *No Victory Parades: The Return of the Vietnam Veteran* (New York: Holt, Rinehart and Winston, 1971), xiv.

44. Eric T. Dean Jr., *Shook over Hell: Post-traumatic Stress, Vietnam, and the Civil War* (Cambridge, MA: Harvard University Press, 1997), 7–8, 12, 19; Lembke, *The Spitting Image*, 102–5.

45. In 1987, "25,000 Vietnam veterans marched in a New York City ticker-tape parade attended by one million people," and similarly large-scale events of this type were held in Chicago and Houston around the same time. Smaller "welcome home" parades were held in towns and cities across the nation, from Modesto, California to Northfield, Vermont. Dean, *Shook over Hell*, 19–20.

46. Lembke, *The Spitting Image*, 9, 80, 144–48, 176–77.

47. *First Blood*, directed by Ted Kotcheff (1982); quoted in Lembke, *The Spitting Image*, 176–77.

48. *Hamburger Hill*, directed by John Irvin (1987).

49. *Rambo: First Blood Part II*, directed by George P. Cosmatos (1985); quoted in Lembke, *The Spitting Image*, 177.

50. Ibid., 11–26. Beamish, Molotch, and Flacks, "Who Supports the Troops?," 344–46.

51. Lynda Boose, "Techno-muscularity and the 'Boy Eternal': From the Quagmire to the Gulf," in *Cultures of United States Imperialism*, eds. Amy Kaplan and Donald E. Pease (Durham, NC: Duke University Press, 1993), 583–601; Tom Engelhardt, *The End of Victory Culture: Cold War America and the Disillusioning of a Generation* (New York: BasicBooks, 1995), 4–15; Jeffords, *Remasculinization of America*, xi–xv, 116–43, 168–69; and Richard Slotkin, *Gunfighter Nation: The Myth of the Frontier in Twentieth-Century America* (New York: Atheneum, 1992), 624–54.

52. Dean, *Shook over Hell*, 14–22, 40–44; and Lembke, *The Spitting Image*, 101–15.

53. Richard A. Kulka et al., *Trauma and the Vietnam War Generation: Report of Findings from the National Vietnam Veterans Readjustment Study* (New York: Brunner/Mazel, 1990), 31.

54. Ibid., 31–32.

55. Ibid., xxvii.

56. Ibid.

57. Lembke, *The Spitting Image*, 107, 110; and Dean, *Shook over Hell*, 14, 20–22.

58. Tim O'Brien, "The Violent Vet," *Esquire*, December 1979, 96.

59. For example, see James Webb, "Viet Vets Didn't Kill Babies and They Aren't Suicidal," *Washington Post*, 6 April 1986, C1.

60. McDonough, *Platoon Leader*, 4–5.

61. Tripp, *Father, Soldier, Son*, 1–4.

62. Smith, *American Daughter*, 248–50.

63. Bob Kerrey, *When I Was a Young Man: A Memoir* (New York: Harcourt, 2002), 196, 214.

64. Kane, *Veteran's Day*, 328.

65. Weigl, *The Cirlce of Hanh*, 133.

66. Donovan, *Once a Warrior King*, 306.

67. Kulka et al., *Trauma and the Vietnam War Generation*, 283.

68. Smith, *American Daughter*, 244–92.

69. Weigl, *The Circle of Hanh*, 1.

70. Kane, *Veteran's Day*, 76.

156

71. Mason, *Chickenhawk*, 469–474; Mason, *Chickenhawk Back in the World*, 14–17, 20–27, 386–87; Puller Jr., *Fortunate Son*, 331–60.

72. Lembke, *The Spitting Image*, 105–6.

73. For a list of articles and books that chronicle the genesis of Vietnam veteran rap groups, or advocate their use, see Michael E. Reeves and Michael J. Maxwell, "The Evolution of a Therapy Group for Vietnam Veterans on a General Psychiatry Unit," *Journal of Contemporary Psychotherapy* 17, no. 1 (Spring 1987): 23–24.

74. Dean, *Shook over Hell*, 15. In 1979, the US government officially appropriated funds for "vet centers" with the creation of the "Vietnam Veterans' Outreach Program." Lembke, *The Spitting Image*, 109.

75. Albert French, *Patches of Fire: A Story of War and Redemption* (New York: Anchor Books, 1998), 158–74.

76. Terry, *Bloods*, 256.

77. Santoli, *Everything We Had*, 158.

78. Kovic, *Born on the Fourth of July*, 147–48.

79. Kane, *Veteran's Day*, 343–45; and Donovan, *Once a Warrior King*, 312.

80. Mason, *Chickenhawk Back in the World*, 366–67; Ketwig, *And a Hard Rain Fell*, 301.

81. Brennan, *Brennan's War*, 275.

82. French, *Patches of Fire*, 177.

83. Richard Severo and Lewis Milford, *The Wages of War: When America's Soldiers Came Home from Valley Forge to Vietnam* (New York: Simon and Schuster, 1989), 26.

84. Ibid., 22–28, 59–63. On homelessness among veterans following wars during the colonial period and the American revolution, see also Kenneth L. Kusmer, *Down and Out, On the Road: The Homeless in American History* (New York: Oxford University Press, 2002), 14, 16.

85. Dean, *Shook over Hell*, 94–97. Many Civil War veterans who marched in such parades, however, later recalled that they had found such parades tedious and unnecessary.

86. Severo and Milford, *The Wages of War*, 137; and Kusmer, *Down and Out*, 36–38.

87. Ibid., 139–40, 163–68.

88. Ibid., 241–79; Kusmer, *Down and Out*, 202–3.

89. Thomas Childers, *Soldier from the War Returning: The Greatest Generation's Troubled Homecoming from World War II* (Boston: Houghton Mifflin Harcourt, 2009), 3–4.

90. Dean, *Shook over Hell*, 268.

91. Severo and Milford, *The Wages of War*, 288.

92. Ibid., 287–90.

93. Ibid., 290.

94. Lembke, *The Spitting Image,* 119–20.

95. Michael D. Gambone, *The Greatest Generation Comes Home: The Veteran in American Society* (College Station: Texas A&M University Press, 2005), 23–24.

96. Childers, *Soldier from the War Returning,* 7.

97. Samuel A. Stouffer et al., *The American Soldier: Combat and Its Aftermath* (Princeton: Princeton University Press, 1949), 2:610–12.

98. Ibid., 610–12.

99. Childers, *Soldier from the War Returning,* 6–8.

100. Dixon Wecter, *When Johnny Comes Marching Home* (Cambridge, MA: Houghton Mifflin, 1944), 51–52.

101. Gerald F. Linderman, *Embattled Courage: The Experience of Combat in the American Civil War* (New York: The Free Press, 1987), 216–40.

102. Jonathan Shay, *Odysseus in America: Combat Trauma and the Trials of Homecoming* (New York: Scribner, 2002), 12–18, 120–53.

103. Dean, *Shook over Hell,* 26–40, 91–179.

104. See Jonathan Shay, *Achilles in Vietnam: Combat Trauma and the Undoing of Character* (New York: Atheneum, 1994); Shay, *Odysseus in America,* 149–53.

105. Childers, *Soldier from the War Returning,* 8.

106. Don Graham, *No Name on the Bullet: A Biography of Audie Murphy* (New York: Viking, 1989), 23, 122–24, 145–50, 174, 189–90, 202, 216, 220–21, 226, 257, 271–325.

107. Kulka et al., *Trauma and the Vietnam War Generation,* xxvii.

108. Egendorf et al., *Legacies of Vietnam,* 7. From 1970 to 1972, the Vietnam veteran unemployment rate was significantly higher than the national unemployment rate, but "by 1973 returning vets had been reabsorbed into the economy." Dean, *Shook over Hell,* 10–11.

109. Egendorf et al., *Legacies of Vietnam,* 8. The study also found that "two-thirds of all veterans worked full time" while "enrolled in educational training . . . in spite of the fact that the majority of veterans were full-time students."

110. Ibid., 7.

111. Ibid., 7–9.

112. Kulka, *Trauma and the Vietnam War Generation,* xxvii.

113. Shay, *Odysseus in America,* 149–50.

114. Paul Feeny and Jim Allaway, "The Ecological Impact of the Air War," in *Vietnam and America: A Documented History,* eds. Marvin E. Gettleman et al. (New York: Grove Press, 1985), 464.

115. Ibid., 466.

116. Ibid., 464.

117. Fred A. Wilcox, *Waiting for an Army to Die: The Tragedy of Agent Orange* (New York: Random House, 1983), 13. See also Feeny and Allaway, "The Ecological Impact," 463–64.

118. One veteran-author, Rod Kane, mentions at the end of his memoir that he has skin rashes possibly caused by exposure to Agent Orange. Kane, *Veteran's Day*, 254–55.

119. Egendorf et al., *Legacies of Vietnam*, 8.

120. Ibid., 13.

121. Ibid., 7.

122. Ibid., 9, 17, 187.

123. Ibid., 8.

124. Ibid.

125. Ibid., 7.

126. Ibid., 9.

127. Marjorie J. Robertson, "Homeless Veterans: An Emerging Problem?," in *The Homeless in Contemporary Society*, eds. Richard D. Bingham, Roy E. Green, and Sammis B. White (Newbury Park, CA: Sage Publications, 1987), 64, 74, 79.

128. Ibid., 74.

129. Kusmer, *Down and Out*, 239–47.

130. Catherine S. Manegold, "Suicide of a Veteran, Amid Pain and Fame," *New York Times*, 14 May 1994, 9.

### Chapter 6: The Political Content of Veteran Narratives

1. Timothy J. Lomperis, *"Reading the Wind": The Literature of the Vietnam War* (Durham, NC: Duke University Press, 1987), 4.

2. Ibid., 5.

3. Ibid., 16–17.

4. Ibid., 17. For all of Webb's speech see pages 13–19.

5. Ibid., 6.

6. Ibid., 20.

7. Ibid., 26.

8. Ibid., 31.

9. Ibid., 22, 72–73.

10. Jason, *Fourteen Landing Zones*, xii.

11. National politics is one arena of American life in which the Vietnam War remained a prominent topic long after the 1980s. Bill Clinton was criticized during and after his successful run for the presidency because he evaded the draft and opposed the war during his college years, and the Vietnam-era military service (or lack thereof) of candidates continued to be a reoccurring theme in ensuing

presidential elections. Julia Bleakney argues in *Revisiting Vietnam: Memoirs, Memorials, Museums*, however, that the Vietnam War has faded from importance in the nation's collective memory since the 9/11 attacks, with World War II reassuming its position as the preeminent war in the nation's consciousness. Bleakney, *Revisiting Vietnam*, 26–29.

12. Caputo, *A Rumor of War*, xiii.

13. Tim O'Brien, "How to Tell a True War Story," in *The Things They Carried: A Work of Fiction* (Boston: Houghton Mifflin, 1990), 76.

14. Hynes, *The Soldiers' Tale*, 30.

15. Examples of books that espoused this conception of veteran-authored Vietnam War literature include Myers, *Walking Point*, 5–13, 26–31; Andrew Martin, *Receptions of War*, 77–78; Bleakney, *Revisiting Vietnam*, 39–40, 46; and Herzog, *Vietnam War Stories*, 5–6.

16. Duncan, *The New Legions*.

17. Donald Duncan, "The Whole Thing Was a Lie!" *Ramparts* 4, no. 10 (February 1966): 12–24.

18. Jeffrey Walsh, *American War Literature, 1914 to Vietnam* (New York: St. Martin's Press, 1982), 2; Zalin Grant, "Vietnam as Fable," *New Republic*, 25 March 1978, 22–23.

19. Whitmore and Weber, *Memphis, Nam, Sweden*.

20. Daly and Bergman, *Black Prisoner of War*, 107, 133, 148.

21. James N. Rowe, *Five Years to Freedom* (New York: Ballantine/Presidio Press, 2005).

22. Robinson Risner, *The Passing of the Night: My Seven Years as a Prisoner of the North Vietnamese* (Old Saybrook, CT: Konecky & Konecky, 1973).

23. Clifton, *Those Who Were There*, viii.

24. Ibid., ix; Lomperis, *"Reading the Wind,"* 22; Brian Mitchell, "Jonah Speaks," review of *Chained Eagle: The Heroic Story of the First American Shot Down over North Vietnam* by Everett Alvarez and Anthony S. Pitch, *National Review*, 19 March 1990, 51; and McDowell, "Publishing: Vietnam Rediscovered." A few early veteran-authors said that publishers rejected their writings *because* of their strong antiwar sentiments. Caroline Slocock, "Winning Hearts and Minds: The Ist Casualty Press," *Journal of American Studies* 16, no. 1, (1982): 111–12.

25. "Publishers and Librarians Sign Vietnam Protest," *Publishers Weekly* 193 (January 1968): 24–25; and "Publishers Rally in Support of Vietnam Moratorium," *Publishers Weekly* 196 (October 1969): 36–37.

26. Lomperis, *"Reading the Wind,"* 45; McDowell, "Publishing: Vietnam Rediscovered," C25; "Vietnam-Book Boom," *New York Times*, C17; Slocock, "Winning Hearts and Minds," 112–14; and Grant, "Vietnam as Fable," 22.

27. Lomperis, *"Reading the Wind,"* 4; Peter Marin, "Coming To Terms with Vietnam," *Harper's*, December 1980, 41; Alf Louvre and Jefferey Walsh, eds., *Tell Me Lies about Vietnam: Cultural Battles for the Meaning of the War* (Philadelphia: Open University Press, 1988), 5–6; and James C. Wilson, *Vietnam in Prose and Film* (Jefferson, NC: McFarland & Company, 1982), 1–2.

28. Kovic, *Born on the Fourth of July*; and Clifton, *Those Who Were There*, x.

29. Biskind, "The Vietnam Oscars."

30. Dean Jr., *Shook over Hell*, 19–21; Louvre and Walsh, *Tell Me Lies about Vietnam*, 2.

31. Young, *The Vietnam Wars*, 314–16, 328–29.

32. Jason, *Fourteen Landing Zones*, xi.

33. Beidler, *Late Thoughts on an Old War*, 123–38.

34. O'Brien, *If I Die in a Combat Zone*. Other examples include Wolff, *In Pharaoh's Army*; Ketwig, *And a Hard Rain Fell*; and Heinemann, *Black Virgin Mountain*.

35. Examples of veteran-memoirists who joined the antiwar movement when they returned home include Caputo, *A Rumor of War*, xvi, 342; W. D. Ehrhart, *Passing Time*, 82–97; Rod Kane, *Veteran's Day*, 120–74; Kovic, *Born on the Fourth of July*, 147–181; Norman, *These Good Men*, 99–100; and Tripp, *Father, Soldier, Son*, 228.

36. O'Brien, *If I Die in a Combat Zone*, 17.

37. Ibid., 66.

38. Wolff, *In Pharaoh's Army*, 8, 117–28; Weigl, *The Circle of Hahn*, 131. Others include Kerrey, *When I Was a Young Man*, 136; and Ketwig, *And a Hard Rain Fell*, 116.

39. Tripp, *Father, Soldier, Son*, 85.

40. Ibid., 201.

41. Norman, *These Good Men*, 9.

42. Herring, "Vietnam Remembered," 161.

43. Donovan, *Once a Warrior King*, 307–8.

44. Herring, "Vietnam Remembered," 157–58, 161.

45. Donovan, *Once a Warrior King*, 28–33.

46. McDonough, *Platoon Leader*, 17–19, 24–26.

47. Ibid., 76, 114–15; Donovan, *Once a Warrior King*, 46, 98, 123–27, 133.

48. Van Devanter with Morgan, *Home Before Morning*, 159, 211. Other examples of veterans who worked in, or sympathized with the antiwar movement, but also offered negative portrayals of the movement included Norman, *These Good Men*, 99–100; Ketwig, *And a Hard Rain Fell*, 68, 77, 116, 151–52; Heinemann, *Black Virgin Mountain*, 27, 35; and Ehrhart, *Passing Time*, 7, 88–97.

49. This depiction of the antiwar movement harkens back to the media's portrayal of the movement during much of the war. In its coverage of peace

demonstrations, the media inevitably singled out the most newsworthy participants: "flamboyant" and militant protestors who waved the Vietcong flag and did other provocative things. Todd Gitlin, *The Whole World Is Watching: Mass Media in the Making & Unmaking of the New Left* (Berkeley: University of California Press, 2003), 181–83.

50. Anderson, *The Movement and the Sixties*, 124, 171, 178.

51. Ibid., 330.

52. Ibid., 396. See also, 380–81.

53. Caputo, *A Rumor of War*, xvii.

54. Ibid, xvi.

55. Mason, *Chickenhawk Back in the World*, 381; and Broyles Jr., *Brothers in Arms*, 94.

56. Puller Jr., *Fortunate Son*, 262–63.

57. Ehrhart, *Vietnam-Perkasie*.

58. Ehrhart, *Passing Time*, 172.

59. Ibid., 175.

60. Ronald Baughman, "Interview with W. D. Ehrhart (6 June 1991)," in *Dictionary of Literary Biography Documentary Series*, vol. 9, *American Writers of the Vietnam War*, ed. Ronald Baughman, 72 (Detroit, MI: Gale Research Inc., 1991). At the 1985 Asia Society conference on Vietnam War literature mentioned in this chapter's introduction, Ehrhart announced that his chief motive in writing was to "affect the course of [his] country." Lomperis, *"Reading the Wind,"* 32.

61. Ehrhart, *Passing Time*, 177–84.

62. Ibid., 181.

63. W. D. Ehrhart, *Busted: A Vietnam Veteran in Nixon's America*, with a foreword by H. Bruce Franklin (Amherst: University of Massachusetts Press, 1995), xi.

64. Ibid., xviii.

65. Ibid., xix.

66. Ibid., xx.

67. Ibid.

68. "Books: Viet Nam in Print," *Time*, 17 Nov. 1967, 116.

69. Ibid.

70. David Greenberg, review of *Busted: A Vietnam Veteran in Nixon's America* by W. D. Ehrhart, *Washington Post,* 24 December 1995, X04.

71. Alan Samuels, "I Quit! From Solo to Chorus," review of *The New Legions* by Donald Duncan, *Nation*, 26 September 1967, 284–85.

72. Roger Neville Williams, "What Sergeant Daly Saw," review of *A Hero's Welcome: The Conscience of Sergeant James Daly vs. The United States Army* by James A. Daly and Lee Bergman, *Nation,* 27 December 1975, 699.

73. Ibid.

74. Michael Uhl, "On the Lam from Vietnam," review of *Busted: A Vietnam Veteran in Nixon's America* by W. D. Ehrhart, *Nation*, 18 September 1995, 286.

75. The *Washington Post* did not review *Chained Eagle*, but it did publish an article about Alvarez at the time his book was released. Sue Anne Pressley, "Catching Up With Life: The Return of Everett Alvarez," *Washington Post*, 12 November 1989, F1, F8–F9.

76. Brian Mitchell, "Jonah Speaks," 50.

77. Jeffrey Hart, "Years of the Fish," review of *In Love and War: The Story of a Family's Ordeal and Sacrifice During the Vietnam Years* by James and Sybil Stockdale, *National Review*, 3 May 1985, 52–53. The *Wall Street Journal*, another conservative publication, also gave the Stockdales' book a favorable review. The *Journal's* reviewer said *In Love and War* "should be read widely at a time when our nation is regaining an open spirit of love of country that some believed had been eclipsed forever." Edmund Fuller, "A POW's Story," review of *In Love and War* by James and Sybil Stockdale, *Wall Street Journal*, 9 October 1984, 26.

78. Kevin Buckley, review of *In Love and War* by James and Sybil Stockdale, *New York Times*, 28 April 1985, BR25.

79. Duncan Spencer, "Two Paths of Glory," review of *In Love and War* by James and Sybil Stockdale, *Washington Post*, 23 September 1984, 233. James Stockdale later ran as the running mate of Independent candidate H. Ross Perot in the 1992 presidential election.

80. Veterans Administration, *Myths and Realities*, 53.

81. Ibid., 60.

82. Ibid., 17, 21.

83. Ibid.

84. Egendorf et al., *Legacies of Vietnam*, 29.

85. *Myths and Realities*, 16, 25.

86. Ibid., 16.

87. Ibid., 25.

88. Ibid., 16.

89. Egendorf et al., *Legacies of Vietnam*, 29.

90. Ibid.

### Chapter 7: Those Who Came Before and After

1. Nathaniel Fick, *One Bullet Away: The Making of a Marine Officer* (New York: Houghton Mifflin Company, 2005), 234–35.

2. Ibid., 235.

3. Ibid., 234–37.

4. Ibid., 237–39.

5. Kovic, *Born on the Fourth of July*, 195–203.

6. Fick, *One Bullet Away*, 242.

7. Hynes, *The Soldiers' Tale*, 95–97.

8. Kieran, *Forever Vietnam*, 87.

9. Paul Fussell, *Doing Battle: The Making of a Skeptic* (New York: Little, Brown, and Company, 1996), vii.

10. Ibid., 114, 124, 175, 177.

11. Kieran, *Forever Vietnam*, 204.

12. Ibid., 219.

13. Ibid., 228.

14. Audie Murphy, *To Hell and Back* (New York: Owl Books, 2002), 4–5.

15. Fussell, *Doing Battle*, 27–28.

16. Craig M. Mullaney, *The Unforgiving Minute: A Soldier's Education* (New York: Penguin Press, 2009), 73.

17. Ibid., 111; Marcus Luttrell and Patrick Robinson, *Lone Survivor: The Eyewitness Account of Operation Redwing and the Lost Heroes of SEAL Team 10* (New York: Little, Brown, and Company, 2007), 17; and Sean Parnell and John R. Bruning, *Outlaw Platoon: Heroes, Renegades, Infidels, and the Brotherhood of War in Afghanistan* (New York: William Morrow, 2012), 89.

18. Anthony Swofford, *Jarhead* (New York: Scribner, 2003), 5–7.

19. Benjamin Busch, *Dust to Dust: A Memoir* (New York: Harper Collins, 2012), 236.

20. Fick, *One Bullet Away*, 10.

21. Thomas E. Ricks, *Making the Corps* (New York: Scribner, 1997), 168.

22. Beth Bailey, *America's Army: Making the All-Volunteer Force* (Cambridge, MA: Harvard University Press, 2007), 241–42.

23. Klay, *Redeployment*, 234.

24. Fick, *One Bullet Away*, 204.

25. Ibid., 282.

26. David Bellavia and John R. Bruning, *House to House: An Epic Memoir of War* (New York: Free Press, 2008), 144.

27. Mullaney, *The Unforgiving Minute*, 266.

28. Parnell and Bruning, *Outlaw Platoon*, 5, 91, 221.

29. Fick, *One Bullet Away*, 72.

30. Aaron B. O'Connell, *Underdogs: The Making of the Modern Marine Corps* (Cambridge, MA: Harvard University Press, 2012), 37, 54; Ricks, *Making the Corps*, 66, 71, 73, 191, 195, 213–14, 266.

31. Donovan Campbell, *Joker One: A Marine Platoon's Story of Courage, Leadership, and Brotherhood* (New York: Random House, 2009), 178.

32. Bellavia and Bruning, *House to House*, 48, 69.

33. Parnell and Bruning, *Outlaw Platoon,* 24, 27, 135, 191–94, 206, 303, 328.

34. James Brady, *The Coldest Winter: A Memoir of Korea* (New York: Orion Books, 1990), 240.

35. Kayla Williams and Michael E. Staub, *Love My Rifle More Than You: Young and Female in the U.S. Army* (New York: W.W. Norton, 2006), 276.

36. Ibid., 277.

37. Swofford, *Jarhead*, 239.

38. Murphy, *To Hell and Back*, 13–14; E. B. Sledge, *With the Old Breed: At Peleliu and Okinawa* (Novato, CA: Presidio Press, 2010), 298–99.

39. Brady, *The Coldest Winter*, 118.

40. John Muirhead, *Those Who Fall* (New York: Random House, 1986), 183.

41. Ibid., 21.

42. Williams and Staub, *Love My Rifle*, 197.

43. Ibid., 212–15.

44. Mullaney, *The Unforgiving Minute*, 335.

45. Ibid.

46. Donald R. Burgett, *Currahee!* (Boston: Houghton Mifflin Company, 1967), 140.

47. Harold L. Bond, *Return to Cassino: A Memoir of the Fight for Rome* (Garden City, NY: Doubleday, 1964), 192–94.

48. James J. Fahey, *Pacific War Diary: 1942–1945* (Boston: Houghton Mifflin Company, 1963), 56–58; E. J. Kahn Jr., *GI Jungle: An American Soldier in Australia and New Guinea* (New York: Simon and Schuster, 1943), 20, 39.

49. Brady, *The Coldest Winter*, 176–77, 180–81, 188–90.

50. Swofford, *Jarhead*, 140.

51. Williams and Staub, *Love My Rifle*, 253–54.

52. Ibid., 199.

53. Swofford, *Jarhead*, 239–40.

54. Williams and Staub, *Love My Rifle*, 247–52.

55. Sledge, *With the Old Breed*, 118, 120, 122–23, 152–53, 198–99.

56. Robert Leckie, *Helmet for My Pillow: From Parris Island to the Pacific* (New York: Bantam, 2010), 84–85, 117.

57. Fahey, *Pacific War Diary*, 231.

58. Hynes, *The Soldiers' Tale*, 186–87.

59. Murphy, *To Hell and Back*, 14, 54, 68–70, 79, 82.

60. William Manchester, *Goodbye, Darkness: A Memoir of the Pacific War* (Boston: Little, Brown, and Company, 1979), 146–57.

61. Elmer Bendiner, *The Fall of Fortresses* (New York: G.P. Putnam, 1980), 32, 56, 116–21, 145, 252–58.

62. Ibid., 145–46.

63. Kahn Jr., *GI Jungle*, 136–37.

64. Gregory Boyington, *Baa Baa Black Sheep* (New York: G.P. Putnam, 1958), 131.

65. Kahn Jr., *GI Jungle*, 102–3.

66. Ibid., 134.

67. Boyington, *Baa Baa Black Sheep*, 34.

68. Martin Russ, *The Last Parallel: A Marine's War Journal* (New York: Rhinehart and Company, 1957), 127.

69. Swofford, *Jarhead*, 92.

70. Klay, *Redeployment*, 119–28.

71. Williams and Staub, *Love My Rifle*, 18, 21.

72. Mullaney, *The Unforgiving Minute*, 339.

73. Williams and Staub, *Love My Rifle*, 13–14, 20–22, 71–72, 167–68, 172–73, 198–99, 207–8, 212.

74. Brady, *The Coldest Winter*, 123.

75. Lair, *Armed with Abundance*, 236.

76. Mullaney, *The Unforgiving Minute*, 339–40.

77. Manchester, *Goodbye, Darkness*, 140–41, 233–37.

78. Brady, *The Coldest Winter*, 125.

79. Parnell and Bruning, *Outlaw Platoon*, 294.

80. Bellavia and Bruning, *House to House*, 273–81.

81. Sledge, *With the Old Breed*, 266–67.

82. Mullaney, *The Unforgiving Minute*, 349.

83. Williams and Staub, *Love My Rifle*, 274.

84. Kayla Williams, *Plenty of Time When We Get Home: Love and Recovery in the Aftermath of War* (New York: W.W. Norton and Company, 2014), 37–38, 40, 168.

85. Murphy, *To Hell and Back*, 273.

86. Ibid., 273–74.

87. Kieran, *Forever Vietnam*, 87.

88. Ibid., 86–87.

89. Fussell, *Doing Battle*, 183.

90. Fick, *One Bullet Away*, 362–63.

91. Luttrell and Robinson, *Lone Survivor*, 240.

ᵃⁱ

166

92. Williams, *Plenty of Time*, 66–68, 76, 120, 165.

93. Russ, *The Last Parallel*, 3–6.

94. Ibid., 6.

95. Ibid., 13.

96. Boyington, *Baa Baa Black Sheep*, 123–24.

97. Kieran, *Forever Vietnam*, 68–87.

98. Sledge, *With the Old Breed*, 142–44, 277–78.

99. Manchester, *Goodbye, Darkness*, 373.

100. Ibid., 384.

101. Swofford, *Jarhead*, 44, 207.

102. Ibid., 212.

103. Parnell and Bruning, *Outlaw Platoon*, 178.

104. Campbell, *Joker One*, 57.

105. Ibid., 179.

106. Mullaney, *The Unforgiving Minute*, 304–5.

107. Manchester, *Goodbye, Darkness*, 398.

108. Ibid., 3.

109. Ibid., 7, 11, 60, 174–75, 225, 255, 369–72, 379.

110. Ibid., 11, 60, 246, 374.

111. Murphy, *To Hell and Back*, 273.

112. Kieran, *Forever Vietnam*, 87.

113. Bendiner, *The Fall of Fortresses*, 12, 16, 80, 111, 148, 153–54, 228, 238–39.

114. Swofford, *Jarhead*, 10–11, 14–17, 240–41.

115. Williams and Staub, *Love My Rifle*, 193, 282.

116. Campbell, *Joker One*, 135, 211–17, 251; Fick, *One Bullet Away*, 316–18, 334–36.

117. Campbell, *Joker One*, 7–8.

118. Philips, *War!*, 26–27.

119. Ibid., 20–25.

120. Ibid., 22, 58.

121. Ibid., 23.

122. Ibid., 28.

123. Muirhead, *Those Who Fall*, 11.

124. Russ, *The Last Parallel*, 47, 286.

125. Brady, *The Coldest Winter*, 79, 99, 106.

126. Andrew Exum, *This Man's Army: A Soldier's Story from the Front Lines of the War on Terrorism* (New York: Gotham Books, 2004), 75–76; Parnell and Bruning, *Outlaw Platoon*, 133–134.

127. Exum, *This Man's Army*, xi.

128. Campbell, *Joker One*, 51.

129. Ibid., x, 194–95, 226–27, 229–33, 307.

130. Philips, *War!*, 275–82.

131. Ibid., 14.

132. Baskir and Strauss, *Chance and Circumstance*, 9–10, 19.

133. Bailey, *America's Army*, 10.

134. Baskir and Strauss, *Chance and Circumstance*, 19–20.

135. Fussell, *Doing Battle*, 8, 12, 15.

136. Sledge, *With the Old Breed*, 167.

137. Ibid.

138. Kahn Jr., *GI Jungle*, 150.

139. Ralph Ingersoll, *The Battle Is the Pay-Off* (New York: Harcourt, Brace and Company, 1943), 1.

140. Bond, *Return to Cassino*, 15, 58, 149.

141. Bailey, *America's Army*, 259.

142. Ibid., 257–59.

143. Campbell, *Joker One*, 9.

144. Busch, *Dust to Dust*, 21.

145. Fick, *One Bullet Away*, 4.

146. Mullaney, *The Unforgiving Minute*, 13–17, 73–79, 197.

147. Fussell, *Doing Battle*, 92.

148. Parnell and Bruning, *Outlaw Platoon*, 293–305.

149. Fick, *One Bullet Away*, 361.

150. Ibid., 362.

## Conclusion

1. Linderman, *Embattled Courage*, 266–74; David W. Blight, *Race and Reunion: The Civil War in American Memory* (Cambridge, MA: Belknap/Harvard University Press, 2001), 149–50.

2. Blight, *Race and Reunion*, 170–89.

3. Ibid., 181.

4. Ibid., 182–83.

5. Linderman, *Embattled Courage*, 275–97.

6. Blight, *Race and Reunion*, 185–86.

7. Herring, "Vietnam Remembered," 163.

8. Ibid.

# Bibliography

*Primary Sources*

I. PRIMARY VETERAN NARRATIVE GROUP

Anderson, Charles R. *The Grunts*. San Rafael, CA: Presidio Press, 1976.

————. *Vietnam: The Other War*. Novato, CA: Presidio Press, 1982.

Anton, Frank, and Tommy Denton. *Why Didn't You Get Me Out? A POW's Nightmare in Vietnam*. New York: St. Martin's Press, 2000.

Alvarez, Everett, Jr., and Anthony S. Pitch. *Chained Eagle: The Heroic Story of the First American Shot Down over North Vietnam*. New York: Donald I. Fine, 1989.

Baker, Mark. *Nam: The Vietnam War in the Words of the Soldiers Who Fought There*. New York: Berkley Books, 1983.

Bradford, Alfred S. *Some Even Volunteered: The First Wolfhounds Pacify Vietnam*. Westport, CT: Praeger Publishing, 1994.

Brennan, Matthew. *Brennan's War: Vietnam 1965–69*. Novato, CA: Presidio Press, 1985.

Broyles, William, Jr. *Brothers in Arms: A Journey from War to Peace*. New York: Alfred A. Knopf, 1986.

Callaway, Joseph W., Jr. *Mekong First Light*. New York: Presidio Press/Ballantine Books, 2004.

Calley, William, and John Sack. *Lieutenant Calley: His Own Story*. New York: Viking, 1971.

Caputo, Philip. *A Rumor of War*. New York: Owl Books, 1996.

Clark, Johnnie M. *Guns Up!* New York: Ballantine Books, 2002.

Denton, Jeremiah. *When Hell Was in Session*. New York: Reader's Digest Press, 1976.

Donovan, David. *Once a Warrior King: Memories of an Officer in Vietnam*. New York: McGraw-Hill, 1985.

Downs, Frederick, Jr. *Aftermath: A Soldier's Return to America from Vietnam*. New York: W. W. Norton, 1984.

———. *The Killing Zone: My Life in the Vietnam War*. New York: W. W. Norton, 1978.

———. *No Longer Enemies, Not Yet Friends: An American Soldier Returns to Vietnam*. New York: W. W. Norton, 1991.

Duncan, Donald. *The New Legions*. New York: Random House, 1967.

Ehrhart, W. D. *Busted: A Vietnam Veteran in Nixon's America*. With a foreword by H. Bruce Franklin. Amherst: University of Massachusetts Press, 1995.

———. *Passing Time: Memoir of a Vietnam Veteran against the War*. Amherst: University of Massachusetts Press, 1995. Originally published as *Marking Time*. New York: Avon Books, 1986.

———. *Vietnam-Perkasie: A Combat Marine Memoir*. Amherst: University of Massachusetts Press, 1995.

French, Albert. *Patches of Fire: A Story of War and Redemption*. New York: Anchor Books, 1998.

Goff, Stanley, Robert Sanders, and Clark Smith, *Brothers: Black Soldiers in the Nam*. Novato, CA: Presidio Press, 1982.

Guarino, Larry. *A POW's Story: 2801 Days in Hanoi*. New York: Ivy, 1990.

Hackworth, David H., and Julie Sherman. *About Face*. New York: Simon and Schuster, 1989.

Heinemann, Larry. *Black Virgin Mountain: A Return to Vietnam*. New York: Doubleday, 2005.

Hemphill, Robert. *Platoon, Bravo Company*. Fredericksburg, VA: St. Martin's Paperbacks, 2001.

Kane, Rod. *Veteran's Day: A Combat Odyssey*. New York: Pocket Book, 1990.

Kerrey, Bob. *When I Was a Young Man: A Memoir*. New York: Harcourt, 2002.

Ketwig, John. *And a Hard Rain Fell: A G.I.'s True Story of the War in Vietnam*. New York: Macmillan, 1985.

Kidder, Tracy. *My Detachment: A Memoir*. New York: Random House, 2005.

Kovic, Ron. *Born on the Fourth of July*. New York: Akashic, 2005.

Lanning, Michael Lee. *The Only War We Had: A Platoon Leader's Journal of Vietnam*. New York: Ivy Books, 1987.

———. *Vietnam, 1969–1970: A Company Commander's Journal*. College Station: Texas A&M University Press, 2007.

Marcinko, Richard. *Rogue Warrior*. New York: Pocket Books, 1992.

Mason, Robert. *Chickenhawk*. New York: Penguin, 2005.

———. *Chickenhawk Back in the World: Life after Vietnam*. New York: Viking, 1993.

McCain, John. *Faith of My Fathers*. New York: Random House, 1999.

McDonough, James R. *Platoon Leader.* Novato, CA: Presidio, 1985.                171

Nasmyth, Spike. *2,355 Days: A POW's Story.* New York: Orion, 1991.

Norman, Michael. *These Good Men: Friendships Forged from War.* New York: Crown Publishers, 1989.

O'Brien, Tim. *If I Die in a Combat Zone, Box Me Up and Ship Me Home.* New York: Delta, 1989.

Ogden, Richard E. *Green Knight, Red Mourning.* New York: Pinnacle Books, 2002.

Parks, David. *G.I. Diary.* Washington, DC: Howard University Press, 1984.

Powell, Colin. *My American Journey.* New York: Random House, 1995.

Puller, Lewis B., Jr. *Fortunate Son.* New York: Grove Weindenfeld, 1991.

Risner, Robinson. *The Passing of the Night: My Seven Years as a Prisoner of the North Vietnamese.* Old Saybrook, CT: Konecky & Konecky, 1973.

Rowe, James N. *Five Years to Freedom.* New York: Ballantine/Presidio Press, 2005.

Santoli, Al. *Everything We Had: An Oral History of the Vietnam War by Thirty-Three American Soldiers Who Fought It.* New York: Ballantine, 1983.

Smith, Winnie. *American Daughter Gone to War: On the Frontlines with an Army Nurse in Vietnam.* New York: Pocket Books, 1994.

Stockdale, James, and Sybil Stockdale. *In Love and War: The Story of a Family's Ordeal and Sacrifice during the Vietnam Years.* New York: Harper & Row, 1984.

Terry, Wallace. *Bloods: An Oral History of the Vietnam War by Black Veterans.* New York: Ballantine, 1985.

Tripp, Nathaniel. *Father, Soldier, Son: Memoir of a Platoon Leader in Vietnam.* South Royalton, VT: Steerforth Press, 1996.

Van Devanter, Lynda, with Christopher Morgan. *Home before Morning: The Story of an Army Nurse in Vietnam.* New York: Beaufort Books, 1983.

Weigl, Bruce. *The Circle of Hahn: A Memoir.* New York: Grove Press, 2000.

Westmoreland, William C. *A Soldier Reports.* Garden City, NY: Doubleday, 1976.

Wolff, Tobias. *In Pharaoh's Army: Memories of the Lost War.* New York: Alfred A. Knopf, 1994.

Yezzo, Dominick. *A GI's Vietnam Diary.* New York: Franklin and Watts, 1974.

## II. OTHER PRIMARY SOURCES

Baughman, Ronald. "Interview with W.D. Ehrhart (6 June 1991)." In *Dictionary of Literary Biography Documentary Series.* Vol. 9, *American Writers of the Vietnam War*, edited by Ronald Baughman, 63–82. Detroit, MI: Gale Research Inc., 1991.

Bellavia, David, and John R. Bruning. *House to House: An Epic Memoir of War.* New York: Free Press, 2008.

Benavidez, Roy B., and Oscar Griffin. *The Three Wars of Roy Benavidez.* San Antonio, TX: Corona Publishing Company, 1986.

172  Bendiner, Elmer. *The Fall of Fortresses*. New York: G.P. Putnam, 1980.

Birdwell, Dwight W. *A Hundred Miles of Bad Road: An Armored Cavalryman in Vietnam, 1967–1968*. Novato, CA: Presidio Press, 2000.

Bond, Harold L. *Return to Cassino: A Memoir of the Fight for Rome*. Garden City, NY: Doubleday, 1964.

Boyington, Gregory. *Baa Baa Black Sheep*. New York: G.P. Putnam, 1958.

Brady, James. *The Coldest Winter: A Memoir of Korea*. New York: Orion Books, 1990.

Burgett, Donald R. *Currahee!* Boston: Houghton Mifflin Company, 1967.

Busch, Benjamin. *Dust to Dust: A Memoir*. New York: Harper Collins, 2012.

Campbell, Donovan. *Joker One: A Marine Platoon's Story of Courage, Leadership, and Brotherhood*. New York: Random House, 2009.

Chanoff, David, and Doan Van Toai. *Portrait of the Enemy*. New York: Random House, 1986.

Cummings, Delano. *Moon Dash Warrior: The Story of an American Indian in Vietnam, a Marine from the Land of the Lumbee*. Livermore, ME: Signal Tree Publications, 2001.

Daly, James A., and Lee Bergman. *Black Prisoner of War: A Conscientious Objector's Vietnam Memoir*. Lawrence: University Press of Kansas, 2000. Originally published as *A Hero's Welcome: The Conscience of Sergeant James Daly versus the U.S. Army*. Indianapolis, IN: Bobbs-Merrill, 1975.

*Dead Presidents*. Directed by Albert Hughes and Allen Hughes. 1995. Santa Monica, CA: Caravan Pictures, 1996. VHS.

Del Rosario, Carina A., ed. *A Different Battle: Stories of Asian Pacific American Veterans*. Seattle: Wing Luke Asian Museum, 1999.

Duncan, Donald. "The Whole Thing Was a Lie!" *Ramparts* 4, no. 10 (February 1966): 12–24.

Emanuel, Ed. *Soul Patrol*. New York: Ballantine Books, 2003.

Enthoven, Alain. "Memorandum for Secretary of Defense," 4 May 1967, *The Pentagon Papers*, 462. In John Helmer, *Bringing the War Home: The American Soldier in Vietnam and After*, 26. New York: The Free Press, 1974.

Exum, Andrew. *This Man's Army: A Soldier's Story from the Front Lines of the War on Terrorism*. New York: Gotham Books, 2004.

Fahey, James J. *Pacific War Diary: 1942–1945*. Boston: Houghton Mifflin Company, 1963.

Fick, Nathaniel. *One Bullet Away: The Making of a Marine Officer*. New York: Houghton Mifflin Company, 2005.

*First Blood*. Directed by Ted Kotcheff. 1982. United States: Anabasis N.V., 2002. DVD.

Fussell, Paul. *Doing Battle: The Making of a Skeptic.* New York: Little, Brown, and 173 Company, 1996.

Garcia, Manny. *An Accidental Soldier: Memoirs of a Mestizo in Vietnam.* Albuquerque: University of New Mexico Press, 2003.

Gillam, James T. *War in the Central Highlands of Vietnam, 1968–1970: A Historian's Experience.* Lewiston, NY: The Edwin Mellen Press, 2006.

Greene, Bob. *Homecoming: When the Soldiers Returned from Vietnam.* New York: Putnam, 1989.

*Hamburger Hill.* Directed by John Irvin. 1987. New York: RKO Pictures, 1988. VHS.

Hampton, Lynn. *Fighting Strength: Memoirs of a Combat Nurse in Vietnam.* New York: Warner Books, 1992.

Hayslip, Le Ly, and Jay Wurts. *When Heaven and Earth Changed Places.* New York: Doubleday, 1989.

Hess, Martha. *Then the Americans Came: Voices from Vietnam.* New York: Four Walls Eight Windows, 1993.

Ingersoll, Ralph. *The Battle Is the Pay-Off.* New York: Harcourt, Brace and Company, 1943.

Jackson, James E., Jr. "18 Months as a Prisoner of the Vietcong." *Ebony*, August 1968, 114–19.

Kahn, E. J., Jr. *GI Jungle: An American Soldier in Australia and New Guinea.* New York: Simon and Schuster, 1943.

Klay, Phil. *Redeployment.* New York: The Penguin Press, 2014.

Leckie, Robert. *Helmet for My Pillow: From Parris Island to the Pacific.* New York: Bantam, 2010.

Luttrell, Marcus and Patrick Robinson. *Lone Survivor: The Eyewitness Account of Operation Redwing and the Lost Heroes of SEAL Team 10.* New York: Little, Brown, and Company, 2007.

Manchester, William. *Goodbye, Darkness: A Memoir of the Pacific War.* Boston: Little, Brown, and Company, 1979.

Marshall, Kathryn. *In the Combat Zone: An Oral History of American Women in Vietnam, 1966–1975.* Boston: Little, Brown, 1987.

Muirhead, John. *Those Who Fall.* New York: Random House, 1986.

Mullaney, Craig M. *The Unforgiving Minute: A Soldier's Education.* New York: Penguin Press, 2009.

Murphy, Audie. *To Hell and Back.* New York: Owl Books, 2002.

O'Brien, Tim. "How to Tell a True War Story." In *The Things They Carried: A Work of Fiction*, 73–91. Boston: Houghton Mifflin, 1990.

Parnell, Sean, and John R. Bruning. *Outlaw Platoon: Heroes, Renegades, Infidels, and the Brotherhood of War in Afghanistan.* New York: William Morrow, 2012.

174     Powell, Mary Reynolds. *A World of Hurt: Between Innocence and Arrogance in Vietnam.* Cleveland, OH: Greenleaf Enterprises, 2000.

*Rambo: First Blood Part II.* Directed by George P. Cosmatos. 1985. United States: Anabasis N.V., 1986. VHS.

Ramirez, Juan. *A Patriot After All: The Story of a Chicano Vietnam Vet.* Albuquerque: University of New Mexico Press, 1999.

"Record Counts by Age and Time of Death or Declaration of Death." Combat Area Casualties Current File (CACCF). National Archives and Records Administration. Obtained from www.archives.gov.

Russ, Martin. *The Last Parallel: A Marine's War Journal.* New York: Rhinehart and Company, 1957.

Sledge, E. B. *With the Old Breed: At Peleliu and Okinawa.* Novato, CA: Presidio Press, 2010.

Swofford, Anthony. *Jarhead: A Marine's Chronicle of the Gulf War and Other Battles.* New York: Scribner, 2003.

TeCube, Leroy. *A Year in Nam: A Native American Soldier's Story.* Lincoln: University of Nebraska Press, 1999.

"Transcript: Kerry Testifies Before Senate Panel, 1971." From NPR.org, 25 April 2006, obtained 12 December 2008.

Trujillo, Charley. *Soldados: Chicanos in Vietnam.* San Jose, CA: Chusma House Publishers, 1990.

US Commissioner of Immigration and Naturalization. *Annual Reports, 1947–75.* In Bok-Lim Kim, "Asian Wives of U.S. Servicemen: Women in the Shadows," *Amerasia* 4, no. 1 (1977): 91–115.

Vance, Samuel. *The Courageous and the Proud.* New York: W.W. Norton and Company, 1970.

*Walking Dead, The.* Directed by Preston A. Whitmore II. 1995. Savoy Pictures, 1996. VHS.

Whitmore, Terry, and Richard P. Weber. *Memphis, Nam, Sweden: The Story of a Black Deserter.* Jackson: University Press of Mississippi, 1997.

Williams, Fenton A. *Just before the Dawn: A Doctor's Experiences in Vietnam.* New York: Exposition Press, 1971.

Williams, Kayla. *Plenty of Time When We Get Home: Love and Recovery in the Aftermath of War.* New York: W.W. Norton and Company, 2014.

Williams, Kayla, and Michael E. Staub. *Love My Rifle More Than You: Young and Female in the U.S. Army.* New York: W.W. Norton, 2006.

Ybarra, Lea, ed. *Vietnam Veteranos: Chicanos Recall the War.* Austin: University of Texas Press, 2004.

III. MAGAZINE AND NEWSPAPER ARTICLES

"4 Writers Try to Make Sense of the Vietnam-Book Boom." *New York Times,* August 4, 1987, C17.

Apple, R.W., Jr. "Negro and White Fight Side by Side." *New York Times,* January 3, 1966, 7.

———. "Lodge Worried over Behavior of G.I.'s in Saigon." *New York Times,* August 13, 1966, 3.

"Armed Forces: Democracy in the Foxhole." *Time,* May 26, 1967.

"Birdmen with Black Rifles." *Ebony,* October 1966, 37.

Biskind, Peter. "The Vietnam Oscars." *Vanity Fair,* March 2008.

"Black Power in Viet Nam." *Time,* September 19, 1969.

"Blacks Blast Movie and TV Industries' Perpetuation of Old Stereotyped Images." *Jet,* November 28, 1988, 64.

Booker, Simeon. "Negroes in Vietnam: 'We Are Americans Too.'" *Ebony,* November 1965, 98.

"Books: Viet Nam in Print." *Time,* November 17, 1967, 116.

Bryan, C. D. B. "Growing Up the Hard Way." *New York Times,* August 15, 1976.

Buckley, Kevin. Review of *In Love and War* by James and Sybil Stockdale. *New York Times,* April 28, 1985, BR25.

"Cleaning Up Saigon." *Time,* December 1, 1969.

"Disneyland East." *Time,* May 6, 1966.

"Five-Day Bonanza." *Time,* December 22, 1967.

"Fulbright Declares He Regrets Charge of U.S. 'Arrogance.'" *New York Times,* May 18, 1966, 8.

Fuller, Edmund. "A POW's Story." Review of *In Love and War* by James and Sybil Stockdale. *Wall Street Journal,* October 9, 1984, 26.

Grant, Zalin. "Vietnam as Fable." *New Republic,* March 25, 1978, 22–23.

Greenberg, David. Review of *Busted: A Vietnam Veteran in Nixon's America* by W. D. Ehrhart. *Washington Post,* December 24, 1995, X04.

Gruson, Sidney. "'R and R' Tours on Taiwan: American Servicemen Bring a Mixed Blessing to the Island." *New York Times,* February 14, 1968, 6.

"Hanoi Asks Nun to Rehabilitate Ex-prostitutes." *New York Times,* February 6, 1977, L9.

Hart, Jeffrey. "Years of the Fish." Review of *In Love and War: The Story of a Family's Ordeal and Sacrifice During the Vietnam Years* by James and Sybil Stockdale. *National Review,* May 3, 1985, 52–53.

"Huckleberry Finn in Vietnam." *New Republic,* January 6, 1968.

176   Jackson, James E., Jr. "18 Months as a Prisoner of the Vietcong." *Ebony*, August 1968, 118.

Kastor, Elizabeth. "The Combat Bachelor's War Within; Rod Kane's 'Veteran's Day,' Transcript of a 20-Year Obsession with Vietnam." *Washington Post*, April 19, 1990, E1.

Kenworthy, E. W. "Fulbright Issues a Warning to U.S." *New York Times*, May 6, 1966, 2.

Manegold, Catherine S. "Suicide of a Veteran, Amid Pain and Fame." *New York Times*, May 14, 1994, 9.

Marin, Peter. "Coming to Terms with Vietnam." *Harper's*, December 1980, 41.

McDowell, Edwin. "Publishing: Vietnam Rediscovered." *New York Times*, December 2, 1983, C25.

"Miss 'Black America' takes Soul to Vietnam." *Ebony*, May 1970, 88–94.

Mitchell, Brian. "Jonah Speaks." Review of *Chained Eagle: The Heroic Story of the First American Shot Down over North Vietnam* by Everett Alvarez and Anthony S. Pitch. *National Review*, March 19, 1990, 51.

O'Brien, Tim. "The Violent Vet." *Esquire*, December 1979, 96–104.

Pressley, Sue Anne. "Catching Up With Life: The Return of Everett Alvarez." *Washington Post*, November 12, 1989, F1, F8–F9.

"Publishers and Librarians Sign Vietnam Protest." *Publishers Weekly* 193 (January 1968): 24–25.

"Publishers Rally in Support of Vietnam Moratorium." *Publishers Weekly* 196 (October 1969): 36–37.

Randal, Jonathan. "Red-Light Limits Opposed in Saigon." *New York Times*, November 14, 1966, 13.

Samuels, Alan. "I Quit! From Solo to Chorus." Review of *The New Legions* by Donald Duncan. *Nation*, September 26, 1967, 284–85.

"South Viet Nam: Soul Alley." *Time*, December 14, 1970.

Spencer, Duncan. "Two Paths of Glory." Review of *In Love and War* by James and Sybil Stockdale. *Washington Post*, September 23, 1984, 233.

"Sydney Greets U.S. Servicemen from Vietnam." *New York Times*, October 6, 1967, 5.

Trumbull, Robert. "For R and R, It's Australia First, Last, Always." January 10, 1969, 10.

Turner, Charles H. "When Johnny Comes Marching to Hawaii on R&R." *New York Times*, March 21, 1971, XX1, 21.

Uhl, Michael. "On the Lam from Vietnam." Review of *Busted: A Vietnam Veteran in Nixon's America* by W. D. Ehrhart. *Nation*, September 18, 1995, 286.

Webb, James. "Viet Vets Didn't Kill Babies and They Aren't Suicidal." *Washington Post*, April 6, 1986, C1.

Weinraub, Bernard. "Pleiku, Open to G.I.'s, Is Problem City." *New York Times*, August 12, 1968, 3.

Williams, Roger Neville. "What Sergeant Daly Saw." Review of *A Hero's Welcome: The Conscience of Sergeant James Daly vs. The United States Army* by James A. Daly and Lee Bergman. *Nation*, December 27, 1975, 699.

IV. BOOKS AND JOURNAL ARTICLES

Anderson, Terry H. *The Movement and the Sixties.* New York: Oxford University Press, 1995.

Appy, Christian G. *Working-Class War: American Combat Soldiers and Vietnam.* Chapel Hill: The University of North Carolina Press, 1993.

Bacevich, Andrew J. *The Limits of Power: The End of American Exceptionalism.* New York: Metropolitan Books, 2008.

Bailey, Beth. *Sex in the Heartland.* Cambridge, MA: Harvard University Press, 1999.

———. *America's Army: Making the All-Volunteer Force.* Cambridge, MA: Harvard University Press, 2007.

Baritz, Loren. *Backfire: A History of How American Culture Led Us into Vietnam and Made Us Fight the Way We Did.* New York: William Morrow, 1985.

Baskir, Lawrence M., and William A. Strauss. *Chance and Circumstance: The Draft, the War and the Vietnam Generation.* New York: Vintage Books, 1978.

Beamish, Thomas D., Harvey Molotch, and Richard Flacks. "Who Supports the Troops? Vietnam, The Gulf War, and the Making of Collective Memory." *Social Problems* 42, no. 3 (August 1995): 344–60.

Beavers, Herman. "Contemporary Afro-American Studies and the Study of the Vietnam War." *Vietnam Generation* 1, no. 2 (1989): 6–13.

Beidler, Philip D. *Late Thoughts on an Old War: The Legacy of Vietnam.* Athens: University of Georgia Press, 2004.

Bilton, Michael, and Kevin Sim. *Four Hours in My Lai.* New York: Viking, 1992.

Bleakney, Julia. *Revisiting Vietnam: Memoirs, Memorials, Museums.* New York: Routledge, 2006.

Blight, David W. *Race and Reunion: The Civil War in American Memory.* Cambridge, MA: Belknap/Harvard University Press, 2001.

Boose, Lynda. "Techno-muscularity and the 'Boy Eternal': From the Quagmire to the Gulf." In *Cultures of United States Imperialism,* edited by Amy Kaplan and Donald E. Pease, 581–617. Durham, NC: Duke University Press, 1993.

Brigham, Robert K. *ARVN: Life and Death in the South Vietnamese Army.* Lawrence: University Press of Kansas, 2006.

Brownmiller, Susan. *Against Our Will: Men, Women, and Rape.* New York: Fawcett Columbine, 1975.

178    Childers, Thomas. *Soldier from the War Returning: The Greatest Generation's Troubled Homecoming from World War II*. Boston: Houghton Mifflin Harcourt, 2009.

Clifton, Merritt. *Those Who Were There: Eyewitness Accounts of the War in Southeast Asia, 1956–1975, & Aftermath*. Paradise, CA: Dustbooks, 1984.

Cortright, David. *Soldiers in Revolt: The American Military Today*. New York: Anchor Press, 1975.

Culter, John Alba. "Disappeared Men: Chicana/o Authenticity and the American War in Viet Nam." *American Literature* 81, no. 3 (September 2009): 583–611.

Dean, Eric T., Jr. *Shook over Hell: Post-traumatic Stress, Vietnam, and the Civil War*. Cambridge, MA: Harvard University Press, 1997.

D'Emilio, John, and Estelle B. Freedman. *Intimate Matters: A History of Sexuality in America*. New York: Harper and Row, 1998.

Dower, John. *Embracing Defeat: Japan in the Wake of World War II*. New York: W.W. Norton & Company, 1999.

———. *War without Mercy: Race and Power in the Pacific War*. New York: Pantheon Books, 1986.

Egendorf, Arthur, US Committee on Veterans Affairs, US Veterans Administration, US Center for Policy Research, and Vietnam Era Research Project. *Legacies of Vietnam: Comparative Adjustment of Veterans and Their Peers*. Washington: United States Government Printing Office, 1981.

Engelhardt, Tom. *The End of Victory Culture: Cold War America and the Disillusioning of a Generation*. New York: Basic Books, 1995.

Feeny, Paul, and Jim Allaway. "The Ecological Impact of the Air War." In *Vietnam and America: A Documented History*, edited by Marvin E. Gettleman, Jane Franklin, Marilyn B. Young, and H. Bruce Franklin, 461–69. New York: Grove Press, 1985.

Fitzgerald, Frances. *Fire in the Lake: The Vietnamese and the Americans in Vietnam*. Boston: Little, Brown and Company, 1972.

Franklin, H. Bruce. *Vietnam and Other American Fantasies*. Amherst: University of Massachusetts, 2000.

Fussell, Paul. *The Great War and Modern Memory*. New York: Oxford University Press, 2000.

Gabriel, Richard A., and Paul L. Savage. *Crisis in Command: Mismanagement in the Army*. New York: Hill and Wang, 1978.

Gambone, Michael D. *The Greatest Generation Comes Home: The Veteran in American Society*. College Station: Texas A&M University Press, 2005.

Gitlin, Todd. *The Whole World Is Watching: Mass Media in the Making & Unmaking of the New Left*. Berkeley: University of California Press, 2003.

Goldman, Peter. *Report from Black America*. New York: Simon and Schuster, 1970.

Graham, Don. *No Name on the Bullet: A Biography of Audie Murphy.* New York: Viking, 1989.

Graham, Herman. *The Brothers' Vietnam War: Black Power, Manhood, and the Military Experience.* Gainesville: University Press of Florida, 2003.

Guzman, Ralph. "Mexican American Casualties in Vietnam." *La Raza* 1, no. 1 (1971): 12–15.

Helmer, John. *Bringing the War Home: The American Soldier in Vietnam and After.* New York: The Free Press, 1974.

Herring, George C. *America's Longest War: The United States and Vietnam, 1950–1975.* New York: John Wiley & Sons, 1979.

———. "Vietnam Remembered." *Journal of American History* 73, no. 1 (June 1986): 152–64.

Hersh, Seymour M. *My Lai 4: A Report on the Massacre and Its Aftermath.* New York: Random House, 1970.

Herzog, Tobey C. *Vietnam War Stories: Innocence Lost.* New York: Routledge, 1992.

Holm, Tom. *Strong Hearts, Wounded Souls: Native American Veterans of the Vietnam War.* Austin: University of Texas Press, 1996.

Howes, Craig. *Voices of the Vietnam P.O.W.s: Witnesses to Their Fight.* New York: Oxford University Press, 1993.

Hynes, Samuel. *The Soldiers' Tale: Bearing Witness to Modern War.* New York: Allen Lane/The Penguin Press, 1997.

Huntington, Samuel P. *The Soldier and the State: The Theory and Politics of Civil-Military Relations.* Cambridge, MA: The Belknap Press of Harvard University Press, 1964.

Janowitz, Morris. *The Professional Soldier: A Social and Political Portrait.* Glencoe, IL: The Free Press, 1960.

Jason, Philip K., ed. *Fourteen Landing Zones: Approaches to Vietnam War Literature.* Iowa City: University of Iowa Press, 1991.

Jeffords, Susan. *The Remasculinization of America: Gender and the Vietnam War.* Indianapolis: Indiana University Press, 1989.

Joseph, Peniel E. *Waiting 'Till the Midnight Hour: A Narrative of Black Power in America.* New York: Henry Holt and Company, 2006.

Kieran, David. *Forever Vietnam: How a Divisive War Changed American Public Memory.* Boston: University of Massachusetts Press, 2014.

Kindsvatter, Peter S. *American Soldiers: Ground Combat in the World Wars, Korea, and Vietnam.* Lawrence: Kansas University Press, 2003.

Kinsey, Alfred C., Wardell B. Pomeroy, and Clyde E. Martin. *Sexual Behavior in the Human Male.* Philadelphia: W.B. Saunders Company, 1948.

180     Kitsch, Carolyn. *Pages from the Past: History and Memory in American Magazines.* Chapel Hill: The University of North Carolina Press, 2005.

Knightly, Philip. *The First Casualty: The War Correspondent as Hero and Myth-Maker from the Crimea to Iraq.* 3rd ed. Baltimore, MD: The Johns Hopkins University Press, 2004.

Kozloff, Nikolas. "Vietnam, the African American Community, and the *Pittsburgh New Courier.*" *Historian* 63 (Spring 2001): 521–38.

Krepinevich, Andrew F. *The Army and Vietnam.* Baltimore: The Johns Hopkins University Press, 1986.

Kulka, Richard A., William E. Schlenger, John A. Fairbank, Richard L. Hough, B. Kathleen Jordan, Charles R. Marmar, and Daniel S. Weiss. *Trauma and the Vietnam War Generation: Report of Findings from the National Vietnam Veterans Readjustment Study.* New York: Brunner/Mazel, 1990.

Kusmer, Kenneth L. *Down and Out, On the Road: The Homeless in American History.* New York: Oxford University Press, 2002.

Lair, Meredith H. *Armed with Abundance: Consumerism and Soldiering in the Vietnam War.* Chapel Hill: The University of North Carolina Press, 2011.

Lawson, Jacqueline. "'She's a Pretty Woman . . . for a Gook': The Misogyny of the Vietnam War." In *Fourteen Landing Zones: Approaches to Vietnam War Literature*, edited by Philip K. Jason, 17–34. Iowa City: University of Iowa Press, 1991.

Lembke, Jerry. *The Spitting Image: Myth, Memory, and the Legacy of Vietnam.* New York: New York University Press, 1998.

Linderman, Gerald F. *Embattled Courage: The Experience of Combat in the American Civil War.* New York: The Free Press, 1987.

Loeb, Jeff. "MIA: African American Autobiography of the Vietnam War." *African American Review* 31, no. 1 (Spring 1997): 105–23.

Lomperis, Timothy J. *"Reading the Wind": The Literature of the Vietnam War.* Durham, NC: Duke University Press, 1987.

Loory, Stuart H. *Defeated: Inside America's Military Machine.* New York: Random House, 1973.

Louvre, Alf, and Jefferey Walsh, eds. *Tell Me Lies about Vietnam: Cultural Battles for the Meaning of the War.* Philadelphia: Open University Press, 1988.

Luckett, Perry D. "The Black Soldier in Vietnam War Literature and Film." *War, Literature, and the Arts* 1, no.2 (1989–90): 1–27.

Martin, Andrew. *Receptions of War: Vietnam in American Culture.* Norman: University of Oklahoma Press, 1993.

McKelvey, Robert S. *The Dust of Life: America's Children Abandoned in Vietnam.* Seattle: University of Washington Press, 1999.

McNamara, Robert S., and Brian VandeMark. *In Retrospect: The Tragedy and Lessons of Vietnam*. New York: Times Books, 1995. 181

Melling, Philip H. *Vietnam in American Literature*. Boston: Twayne Publishers, 1990.

Milam, Ron. *Not a Gentleman's War: An Inside View of Junior Officers in the Vietnam War*. Chapel Hill: The University of North Carolina Press, 2009.

Moskos, Charles C., Jr. *The American Enlisted Man: The Rank and File in Today's Military*. New York: Russell Sage Foundation, 1970.

Myers, Thomas. *Walking Point: American Narratives of Vietnam*. New York: Oxford University Press, 1988.

Nelson, Deborah. *The War Behind Me: Vietnam Veterans Confront the Truth about U.S. War Crimes*. New York: Basic Books, 2008.

O'Connell, Aaron B. *Underdogs: The Making of the Modern Marine Corps*. Cambridge, MA: Harvard University Press, 2012.

Philips, Kimberly L. *War! What Is It Good For? Black Freedom Struggles and the U.S. Military from World War II to Iraq*. Chapel Hill: The University of North Carolina Press, 2012.

Polner, Murray. *No Victory Parades: The Return of the Vietnam Veteran*. New York: Holt, Rinehart and Winston, 1971.

Reeves, Michael E., and Michael J. Maxwell. "The Evolution of a Therapy Group for Vietnam Veterans on a General Psychiatry Unit." *Journal of Contemporary Psychotherapy* 17, no. 1 (Spring 1987): 22–33.

Ricks, Thomas E. *Making the Corps*. New York: Scribner, 1997.

Robertson, Marjorie J. "Homeless Veterans: An Emerging Problem?" In *The Homeless in Contemporary Society*, edited by Richard D. Bingham, Roy E. Green, and Sammis B. White, 64–81. Newbury Park, CA: Sage Publications, 1987.

Severo, Richard, and Lewis Milford. *The Wages of War: When America's Soldiers Came Home from Valley Forge to Vietnam*. New York: Simon and Schuster, 1989.

Shay, Jonathan. *Achilles in Vietnam: Combat Trauma and the Undoing of Character*. New York: Atheneum, 1994.

———. *Odysseus in America: Combat Trauma and the Trials of Homecoming*. New York: Scribner, 2002.

Sheehan, Neil. *A Bright Shining Lie: John Paul Vann and America in Vietnam*. New York: Random House, 1988.

Sherwood, John Darrell. *Black Sailor, White Navy: Racial Unrest in the Fleet during the Vietnam War Era*. New York: New York University Press, 2007.

Slocock, Caroline. "Winning Hearts and Minds: The 1st Casualty Press." *Journal of American Studies* 16, no. 1, (1982): 107–17.

Slotkin, Richard. *Gunfighter Nation: The Myth of the Frontier in Twentieth-Century America*. New York: Atheneum, 1992.

Stouffer, Samuel A., Arthur A. Lumsdaine, Marion Harper Lumsdaine, Robin M. Williams Jr., M. Brewster Smith, Irving L. Janis, Shirley A. Star, and Leonard S. Cottrell Jr., eds. *The American Soldier*. Vol. 2, *Combat and Its Aftermath*. Princeton: Princeton University Press, 1949.

Stuhldreher, Karen. "State Rape: Representations of Rape in Vietnam." *Vietnam Generation* 5, no. 1–4 (1994): 155–58.

Stur, Heather Marie. *Beyond Combat: Women and Gender in the Vietnam War Era.* New York: Cambridge University Press, 2011.

Tal, Kali. "The Mind at War: Images of Women in Vietnam Novels by Combat Veterans." *Contemporary Literature* 31, no. 1 (Spring 1990): 76–96.

Taylor, Sandra C. *Vietnamese Women at War: Fighting for Ho Chi Minh and the Revolution.* Lawrence: University Press of Kansas, 1999.

Terry II, Wallace. "Bringing the War Home." *Black Scholar* 2 (November 1970): 6–18.

Thelen, David. "Memory and American History." *Journal of American History* 75, no. 4 (March 1989): 1117–29.

Tran, Nu-Anh. "South Vietnamese Identity, American Intervention, and the Newspaper Chinh Luan." *Journal of Vietnamese Studies* 1, no. 1–2 (February 2006): 169–209.

Turner, Karen Gottschang, with Phan Thanh Hao. *Even the Women Must Fight: Memories of War from North Vietnam.* New York: John Wiley and Sons Inc., 1998.

Van Deburg, William L. *New Day in Babylon: The Black Power Movement and American Culture, 1965–1975.* Chicago: University of Chicago Press, 1992.

Veterans Administration. *Myths and Realities: A Study of Attitudes Toward Vietnam Era Veterans.* Washington, DC: US Government Printing Office, 1980.

Vuic, Karen Dixon. *Officer, Nurse, Woman: The Army Nurse Corps in the Vietnam War.* Baltimore: Johns Hopkins University Press, 2010.

Walsh, Jeffrey. *American War Literature, 1914 to Vietnam.* New York: St. Martin's Press, 1982.

Wecter, Dixon. *When Johnny Comes Marching Home.* Cambridge, MA: Houghton Mifflin, 1944.

Westheider, James. *Fighting on Two Fronts: African Americans and the Vietnam War.* New York: New York University Press, 1997.

White, Theodore H. *The Making of the President, 1968.* New York: Atheneum, 1969.

Wiest, Andrew. *Vietnam's Forgotten Army: Heroism and Betrayal in the ARVN.* New York: New York University Press, 2008.

Wilcox, Fred A. *Waiting for an Army to Die: The Tragedy of Agent Orange.* New York: 183
Random House, 1983.

Willbanks, James H. *Abandoning Vietnam: How America Left and South Vietnam Lost Its War.* Lawrence: University Press of Kansas, 2004.

Wilson, James C. *Vietnam in Prose and Film.* Jefferson, NC: McFarland & Company, 1982.

Winick, Charles, and Paul M. Kinsie. *The Lively Commerce: Prostitution in the United States.* Chicago: Quadrangle Books, 1971.

Ybarra, Lea. "Perceptions of Race and Class among Chicano Vietnam Veterans." *Viet Nam Generation* 1, no. 2 (1989): 69–93.

Young, Marilyn B. *The Vietnam Wars, 1945–1990.* New York: HarperCollins, 1991.

# Index

9 780821 422236